NO SPEED LIMIT

ST. MARTIN'S PRESS ✼ NEW YORK

NO SPEED LIMIT

THE HIGHS AND LOWS OF METH

FRANK OWEN

The names and identifying characteristics of some individuals depicted
in this book have been changed.

www.stmartins.com

Book design by Gretchen Achilles

Library of Congress Cataloging-in-Publication Data

Owen, Frank (Frank X.)
  No speed limit : the highs and lows of meth / Frank Owen.—1st ed.
    p. cm.
  ISBN-13: 978-0-312-35616-3
  ISBN-10: 0-312-35616-1
  1. Methamphetamine abuse—United States. 2. Methamphetamine abuse—United
States—Prevention. 3. Gays—Drug use—United States.

HV5822.A5 O94 2007
362.29/9—dc22   2007012957

First Edition: July 2007

10   9   8   7   6   5   4   3   2   1

TO BEAVER AND DIANA

CONTENTS

ACKNOWLEDGMENTS

Many thanks to Joey Sekula and Charlie Tahan, Tom DeKay at *The New York Times,* Tricia Romano at *The Village Voice,* my agent, Todd Shuster, at the Zachary, Shuster, Harmsworth Agency, and Chene.

And last but not least, Rebecca Heller, formerly of St. Martin's Press, who suggested the idea for the book.

MAKE ME A MACHINE

The tap-tap-tapping of the razor blade on the mirror was starting to get on my nerves. Here I was, sitting in a shoebox apartment in a rat-infested tenement on New York's Lower East Side, growing increasingly impatient as my host, a well-known fixture on the downtown art scene, meticulously cut up lines of crystal meth. The year was 1988, the last days of the wild, wild East Village, before the area turned into a yuppie dormitory, a bedroom community for Wall Street. A few months earlier, I'd arrived in the United States from Britain, a country where since the 1960s amphetamine had been the unseen dynamo that powered a wide array of working-class music and fashion movements, the common chemical thread that linked mod to skinhead to punk to rave. I'd tried Billy Whiz—the slang name by which we used to refer to amphetamine sulfate—a few times when I was a teenager growing up in Manchester, more out of subcultural curiosity than anything else. I tried it again after college, when I lived with a woman who sold small amounts of the drug out of her council flat in London. But it never seemed to have much of an effect on me beyond what I could get by drinking a couple of cups of strong coffee.

"This is not like that crap you Brits do," my American friend warned, as he continued to tap away. "This stuff is rocket fuel. You need to be very careful not to take too much."

Yeah, right. Yanks were always boasting about how everything in America was bigger and better. Methamphetamine was just amphetamine with an extra set of methyl molecules. How different could it be? Even back then, the effects of amphetamine on the human brain were well known by scientists. The drug stimulates the release of the pleasure chemicals norepinephrine, which is said to boost alertness, and dopamine, the same substance discharged during a good meal or while making love or smoking a cigarette. Finally, after what seemed like an eternity, the tapping stopped and the art critic offered me the mirror, which displayed two skinny lines of powder.

"That's it?" I laughed. "That's enough to get you high?"

"Trust me. That's more than enough," he assured me.

I bent over and inhaled one of the lines through a straw, and right away I could tell this was going to be a much more intense experience than the one I'd bargained for. My eyes immediately began to water. The pain in my right nostril was excruciating. My sinuses felt like a kitchen drain down which somebody had just poured a pint of bleach.

Thankfully, after a couple of minutes, the pain subsided to be replaced by a sensation I can only describe as utter clarity, pure lucidity. Like an electricity generator had been turned on in my head. Like my IQ had just jumped twenty points. Like reality had been revealed in all its high-definition big-screen detail. I remember thinking that this is what a child with bad eyesight must feel like when he gets his first pair of glasses: the joy of having the world rendered anew.

The odd thing about methamphetamine is that it doesn't get you that stoned, at least not in the conventional sense of the word. My fingers went numb; my face flushed, and my body seemed to vibrate like a plucked string, but I actually felt more sober after taking the drug than I did before, as if I had awoken from a long slumber. Unlike other drugs that I had tried before, meth didn't blur the senses but sharpened them to a machinelike focus. There was none of the perceptual drift I normally associated with the act of getting high. This wasn't one of those contemplative drugs that provided another excuse for inertia—attention-dispersing, ego-dissolving substances like pot or LSD, which inevitably led to an evening vegetating on the couch in front of the television or engaging in flabby musings about the meaning of life. Meth was a call to action. Most drugs are about losing control or escaping to some distant region of the mind. Meth was exactly the opposite: I felt ultrasharp. Edgy and exhilarated. Ready to roll. Equal to any task. Possessed by boundless amounts of energy. A wave of grandiosity washed over me. Give me enough meth, and I was ready to conquer the world. That night, I hurried home with a little plastic bag in my back pocket and spent the next twelve hours speed-reading *Milles Plateaux* (*A Thousand Plateaus*), a notoriously dense work of postmodern theory by Gilles Deleuze and Felix Guattari, as I furiously scribbled notes in the margins, after which I fell into a fitful sleep.

For a writer, meth seemed like manna from heaven. I'd been searching for some time for a chemical assistant to help with the writing process. Cocaine didn't work. The drug's roller-coaster ride—engendered by the compulsive need to do a line every twenty minutes—thwarted any attempt at sustained concentration. Forget alcohol. Booze just fogged my brain. Pot helped somewhat, especially at the start, when I was conceptualizing an article, but didn't really help with the hard slog of actually writing the story. But meth was the perfect solution to all the job's pesky little problems. Writer's block? No big deal. Just take a little line and it will go away. An impossible deadline to meet? Easy as pie. The drug banished any thought of sleep. Piles of boring research material to plow through? Bring it on. Meth made the most mundane press release seem enormously fascinating. Meth, I managed to convince myself, was a valuable vocational aid, a tool of the trade like a good thesaurus or a supply of freshly sharpened pencils.

Ideas flowed freely under the influence of meth. Not the trite, hippy-dippy concepts engendered by LSD or Ecstasy. These were usually practical moneymaking propositions. Meth turned me into a writing machine. All I cared about was work. Reviews, cover stories, columns, think pieces—all came easily. The one problem I found with writing on meth was the tendency to go overboard on the research. I sometimes found myself in a kind of informational loop, accumulating ever more details and going around and around in circles, as the ultimate goal of the exercise—to finish the damn piece and hand it in so I could get paid—receded ever farther into the distance. I remember a *Spin* cover story I cowrote with fellow *Melody Maker* alum Simon Reynolds entitled "Why Hendrix Still Matters," where I must have speed-read every book ever written about Jimi Hendrix, which wasn't really necessary for a four-thousand-word piece.

This compulsive propensity to accumulate material without regard to its relevancy would reach its zenith with yet another collaborative effort. A friend and I received a commission from *The Village Voice*'s now defunct supplement, *The Rock and Roll Quarterly*, to write a story about what we termed "consumer mysticism"—the idea that the seemingly banal products of pop culture were being used by ordinary consumers for spiritual uplift. This was an opportune moment to write such a piece. Utopian thinking was fashionable at the time. The coming together of technology, drugs, and music as exemplified in the rave scene seemed to offer a glimpse into a brave new world—a man-machine mash-up that some of the woollier theorists predicted was the future of human evolution. Made-up words such as "sampladelic" and "techno-pagan" summed up the zeitgeist. Since conventional linear journalism couldn't possibly encompass the profound insights we were about to lay on the reading public, we decided the best way to present our ideas was to create a large diagram, really a map of our thoughts on the five-thousand-year history of human intoxication and the various techniques used to achieve that state. So we took a big piece of paper—about four feet by two feet—and began to scrawl on it. For my part, I embarked on weeks of feverish meth-fueled activity. The final result was a gigantic jumble—a Sisyphean jigsaw puzzle with half the pieces missing—that included snippets of dialogue from David Cronenberg's *Videodrome*; observations about the cult of the DJ; quotes from George Bataille on religion; scribbled paragraphs about what we called "hallucinatory technology"; references to the early days of Jamaican dub music; musings about body modification; a brief history of acid rock; ideas about contemporary shamanism; a consideration of gymnasiums as latter-day Orgasmatrons; reflections on the use of repetition to achieve spiritual ecstasy; and more drug references than a William Burroughs novel, all linked by an intricate web of connecting lines and arrows that to anyone who wasn't on meth must have seemed like the work of bionic spiders. I seem to remember that even Carlos Castaneda and the late, great artist David Wojnarovicz made brief guest appearances. Joe Levy, the poor editor at the *Voice* who commissioned the piece, must have thought we were crazy when we handed in the finished project. With Levy's help, we eventually managed to trim the thing down into something approaching a publishable piece.

After a few months of snorting meth on a semiregular basis, the honeymoon phase of my relationship with the drug came to a close. Meth's negative effects started to become all too apparent. As the drug tightened its grip, I began to notice I was losing a lot of weight. I was skinny enough to begin with, but now I was turning practically spectral. Clothes that fit me when I had bought them now hung off me like funeral shrouds. Worse than that, I found myself increasingly irritated at the world and everyone in it, especially after the drug started to wear off. The comedown from crystal meth is famously wicked. Everything aches. Your body feels parched, like a desert that hasn't seen a rain cloud in years. Your head hurts. You can't sleep. You can't eat. Your tongue swells up to twice its normal size. All you can do is drink pint after pint of water and pray for blessed release. I've always been a bit of a cocky son of a bitch, but, under the influence of meth, I was insufferable. I would scream on the phone at publicists. I would get into shoving matches with strangers in nightclubs. If someone got in my way while I was walking down the street, I would push them roughly aside. "I wanna destroy the passerby," the Sex Pistols once sang, which pretty much summed up my attitude to the rest of humanity.

And then there were the knockdown fights I had with my then-wife. Ours was always a tempestuous relationship, not unlike one of those quarrelsome couples in a 1950s Italian neorealist movie. Blood had been spilt before. But there was always a well-defined line across which I had never crossed during our epic tussles, which on more than one occasion drew the attention of police and neighbors. Meth seemed to erase that safety barrier. It was the only drug I ever took where I felt like I could literally kill somebody. Twitching and cursing ("Motherfuckercocksuckerassholecuntpussybitchfaggot"), as if suffering from a bad case of Tourette's syndrome, I found myself turning into a meth monster.

Just as bad as the homicidal impulses were the vivid hallucinations I experienced, the result of days and days spent without sleep. One time, coming home from work late at night, I was stopped dead in my tracks by a wholly unexpected phantasmagoria—a twenty-foot-long cockroach was scuttling down the middle of Second Avenue as yellow cabs swerved to avoid the giant insect and pedestrians ran away in terror. "Hello, Frank. How was your day?" the cockroach greeted me in a heavy Mancunian accent. "Err, not too bad, actually," I replied. "Thanks for asking." On another occasion, I watched as my pet cat walked into the room and then split, amoebalike, into a hundred little kitties who each emitted ear-piercing squeals and then proceeded to swarm all over me as I was lying in bed. Another time, I witnessed a group of Mexican laborers bicycling past the window waving at me, which might not sound too bizarre, except I was sitting in a twelfth-floor office at the time. What was most striking about these delusions was how prosaic and true-to-life they appeared. This wasn't like LSD, where you knew the visual fireworks were induced by the drug. Meth hallucinations seemed like they were really happening.

But maybe the worst aspect of my dalliance with the drug was the paranoid episodes that accompanied extended use. The mere sound of police sirens in the distance spooked me. Imaginary undercover detectives followed me in the street. Sitting in my apartment, I'd hear a key in the lock and see the doorknob turning, but nobody would enter. I'd hear childlike voices whispering my name in the hallway, but when I went out to investigate, the hallway was empty. I'd peer out the window and catch brief glimpses of shadowy figures wearing fedora hats and raincoats snapping photographs from the fire escape across the street. I felt like an extra in a bad horror movie. If I didn't stop this craziness, I was headed for a nervous breakdown.

Then, just as quickly as it had begun, it ended. Fearing for his health, the art critic had decided to quit meth for good, and so my source dried up. I guess I could have made the effort to find a new supply. But meth was hard to come by in New York at that time. You couldn't just walk down to the corner bodega and buy a packet, as you could with cocaine. Anyway, I was glad to be finally done with the drug.

Twenty years later, meth is all over the news, the most talked about illegal substance since crack cocaine. The devil drug of the new millennium. The scourge of a nation. Nearly always missing from these accounts is why people do meth in the first place. Meth is the most utilitarian of all illegal substances. A potent powder that boosts energy, focuses concentration, and helps you step up at night. What's not to like? In this respect, meth is more like a machine than a drug. But just as in a dystopian sci-fi novel, the machines eventually take over the world.

My story is mild compared to some of the tales you'll read in the coming pages. I never injected the drug, and I never smoked meth, modes of intake that dramatically boost both the pleasures and the dangers. I never experienced the full-fledged, almost mystical euphoria that very-high-dose usage brings: "So much better than poems music sky sunsets family friends oh! much better than anything that ever was or ever could be amen amen amen," as Frankie Hucklenbroich describes the rush in her novel *Crystal Diary*, which details the San Francisco meth scene in the 1970s. Other than the realization that there are no chemical shortcuts to good writing, the most important thing I came away with from the experience was that crystal meth is not a substance to be taken lightly. In the beginning, meth always seems like the greatest drug in the world. And then it doesn't.

CHAPTER ONE

THE RISE OF NAZI DOPE

SPRINGFIELD, MISSOURI

S tanley Harris trundles up to meet me in an oily old truck that spits out a trail of exhaust fumes. I'm staying at a local "meth motel," one of a string of fifty-dollar-a-night establishments arranged along a neon corridor on Glenstone Avenue, on the northern edge of town. The motels are often frequented by methamphetamine manufacturers, so-called cooks, who sign in under false names and pay in cash, then go up to their rooms where they cover the door cracks with wet towels to mask the smell and then they start making the drug. Harris is here to show me some of the sights and give me a tour of some of the local meth landmarks.

"I used to sell meth out of that motel across the street." He points to another hostelry on the other side of the highway, one slightly swankier than the threadbare place where I'm staying.

Harris is a walking meth history lesson, living proof that sometimes speed doesn't kill. A roofer by trade, he's only forty-six, but he's been shooting up methamphetamine for thirty-five-years, ever since at the age of eleven he eased a spike into his arm in the school playground while trying to impress an older crowd of boys.

"I was real scared at first," he says in a raspy country accent, sounding as if his vocal chords have been rubbed raw by sandpaper. "But after I did it I felt like I was on top of the world."

In the following three and a half decades, Harris shot up meth when he was happy and he shot up meth when he was sad. He shot up even when yellow puss was oozing from gangrenous holes in his arms and his doctors told him if he didn't stop injecting himself they might have to amputate them. He continued to shoot up after twice flatlining during heart attacks. He spent half a lifetime pumping gram after gram of methamphetamine into his veins, in the process creating chaos in the lives of everybody he loved. But six months before I met him in early December 2005, Stanley Harris quit.

Harris is a stocky man with graying hair and big black circles ringing his eyes that give him the appearance of a demented panda bear. His big, hairy, tattooed arms resemble gnarled and rotted-out tree trunks. A hyperactive chatterbox, when he speaks the words come flooding out of his mouth accompanied by a barrage of facial ticks and herky-jerky hand gestures. When he does pause for a moment, he doesn't so much take a breath as wheeze like a puff of wind.

Even though at the time I spoke to him he had just pled guilty to drug manufacturing and distribution charges and was facing life in state prison as a persistent offender, Harris was a happy man.

"I'm real happy because thanks to Jesus I'm not a servant to meth anymore." He smiles, revealing a dental disaster zone. Harris doesn't have bad teeth, he has practically no teeth; some of them he lost in bar fights and motorcycle accidents, he says, but most of them fell out because of his meth habit.

As world-class dope habits go, Stanley's was a monster. At the height of his addiction, he was shooting an eight ball (an eighth of an ounce) of meth a day. But in early 2005, Harris finally hit rock bottom. He'd tried to kick the drug a number of times, but within hours of completing a treatment program he'd shoot up again. He was on parole and had already given two dirty urine samples. He was sure he was headed back to jail. It was then he decided that he was going to go on one last binge and either kill himself or let the police do the job. On his fourteenth day without sleep, Harris collapsed and was admitted to Sigma House, a local treatment center. After detoxing for a couple of days, an Alcoholics Anonymous counselor came to see him and they had a conversation about God that awoke long-dormant religious feelings in Harris.

"I used to hate Jesus Christ," says Harris, who as an impressionable teenager was so influenced by the movie *The Exorcist* that he used to get down on his knees and pray to Satan. "I thought he was a pussy. What had he ever done for Stanley? But by this point I was ready for something to work in my life because if it don't work, I might as well blow my head off."

M issourians have been mainlining methamphetamine since the 1950s. In a 1959 article, *Time* magazine reported about a new drug craze among some Kansas City, Missouri, high school students who had learned how to extract and then inject the methamphetamine contained in Valo inhalers, which could be bought at the time in local drug stores for seventy-five cents apiece. The magazine highlighted the case of Gary A. Hamilton, aged twenty-two, who was arrested after ordering tea at a lunch counter, pouring the hot water into an inhaler, and then taking pictures of himself in an automatic photo booth injecting the liquid into his arm.

A Kansas City narcotics detective was quoted as saying: "There are at least two hundred known users in the city, and at least twice as many that we don't know about."

Meth in Missouri isn't a new phenomenon, then, but a persistent and entrenched problem that has been around for decades. But something happened in the Ozarks in the early 1990s, something that dramatically changed the local meth landscape and turned a manageable problem into a genuine crisis, something that by the end of the decade had transformed the southwest corner of the state into a meth-manufacturing Mecca.

To call Missouri the meth lab capital of America is a little misleading. The phrase "meth laboratory" summons up images of foaming beakers, flaming Bunsen burners, and bubbling three-necked flasks, the sort of elaborate glassware and equipment found commonly at so-called superlab sites in California and Mexico. While it's true that Missouri has reported more "meth lab incidents"—a catchall phrase that includes not just working labs but also abandoned labs, stockpiles of ingredients, and chemical dump sites—than any other state for four years in a row (2002–2005), most of the labs seized are what the Drug Enforcement Administration calls STLs (small toxic labs): do-it-yourself operations that employ everyday household items like coffee filters, plastic bottles, Pyrex dishes, and liquid blenders to produce small amounts of the drug. To an outsider who stumbles across one, these so-called mom-and-pop labs would seem like little more than a messy garage or an untidy garden shed.

A better way to describe Missouri would be to call it the kitchen chemistry capital of the United States, a place that in the mid-1990s saw an extraordinary fivefold increase in the number of hobbyists churning out homemade meth, a phenomenon comparable to the heyday of moonshining during Prohibition and an illicit drug manufacturing boom that is only now beginning to subside. In 1992, local authorities raided nineteen meth labs in the Ozarks and the DEA raided only two in the entire state. By 2004, there were more than 2,800 meth lab incidents—that's roughly one meth lab for every two thousand Missourians. While the State Highway Patrol reported a 44 percent decrease in meth lab busts in the last six months of 2005, a drop largely credited to a new state law making it harder for local cooks to acquire the supplies of pseudoephedrine-containing cold medicines they need to make the drug, it wasn't enough of a decrease to prevent Missouri once again leading the nation in meth lab incidents.

Bathed in a late autumn glow, Springfield doesn't seem like a community ravaged by meth despite its reputation as a paradise for tweakers (chronic users). The Battlefield Mall—named in memory of Wilson's Creek, a famous Civil War battle—is packed with shoppers buying jeans at the Gap and eating hamburgers at

Ruby Tuesday. Students from Missouri State University throng the coffee bars in the newly revitalized downtown area, tapping on their laptop computers and sipping cappuccinos. Minor-league baseball fans catch a game at the new $32 million Hammons Field. Springfield is a medium-sized city with the feel of a small town, the sort of place that pandering politicians have in mind when they talk about "the heartland" and "middle America."

If meth has spurred a serious crime wave across rural America, as is often claimed in newspaper editorials, it hasn't hit Springfield. Crime is low here, astonishingly so given the city's standing as a major center for meth manufacturing. On average, about a half dozen murders are committed each year within the city limits, which is about half the national average for a place its size. Armed robbery is about a third of what it is in the rest of the country. The only crime categories in which Springfield exceeds the national average are burglary and property crimes, which local police blame on meth addicts looking to feed their habit.

The Ozarks has long had the reputation as an economically depressed region—a backwards and backwoods place. Like something from the movie *Deliverance*. But the Springfield I encountered seemed like a flourishing city with a diverse economy, low unemployment, and steady job growth. Any simplistic theories I had about poverty being the root cause of methamphetamine abuse in the Ozarks dissipated after a few days in Springfield, a city that seems to have successfully shed its roughneck past—the drinking, whoring, and gambling cowboy town of yore, the place where in 1865 Wild Bill Hickok shot to death David Tutt over a pocket watch—to become a thriving community, a great place to live and raise a family.

The other feature of Springfield life impossible not to notice is the overwhelming atmosphere of hellfire-and-brimstone religiosity that permeates the city. An apocryphal story has H. L. Mencken calling Springfield "the buckle of the Bible Belt," though he might as well have. Welcome to Jesusville, U.S.A., where the American genius for down-home, cornpone religion is on full display and where even the waitress serving you a cocktail quotes scripture. The city features dozens of different fundamentalist and evangelical denominations. Outside of Detroit, Springfield is probably the churchiest place I've ever visited in America. And we're not talking roadside tabernacles here. Shiny new houses of worship are everywhere. These are not august edifices sanctioned by time and tradition, but buildings that look like shopping malls or technical college campuses more than anything else. Springfield is the main base of the Assemblies of God, the church that spawned both Jimmy Swaggart and Jim Bakker, and the world's largest Pentecostal Protestant denomination, with more than fifty million members worldwide. The organization's headquarters over on Boonville Avenue occupies ten city blocks and includes a publishing plant that pumps out sixteen tons of gospel literature every day.

Engage ordinary people in conversation here, and you'll find many of them hold strange beliefs that sound more like political conspiracy theories than articles of faith: *Star Wars* is satanic; for instance, or Hillary Clinton, if not exactly the Antichrist, is at least his handmaiden. In the week I spent in Springfield, I got used to fielding questions from the locals like "Have you accepted Jesus as your personal lord and savior?" and "Do they believe in Jesus where you come from?" At a bible study class, a preacher asked me in what religion I was raised. I told him I was brought up Irish Catholic. "Ah, C.I.A.," he smirked. "Catholic, Irish, Alcoholic." As opposed to P.A.T., I suppose: Protestant American Tweaker. And that's another thing: don't call them Protestants. It seems that "Protestant" is a term invented by Papists.

Springfield looks serene and content enough. But scratch below the surface a little—peer behind the image of industrious piety— and you see another side to the city. Driving in from the airport, the taxi driver, wearing a trucker cap and sporting a ponytail, wanted to know what this English-sounding dude was doing in the back of his cab. I told him I was here researching a book on crystal meth.

"Sheeet," he laughed. "You've come to the right place. In this city, it's easier to get meth than a woman."

According to Nick Console, who in December 2005 was days away from retiring as the head of the Drug Enforcement Administration's Springfield office, the blame for the dramatic increase in amateur meth manufacturing in the Ozarks can be traced back to a single individual: Bob Paillet, a local meth cook who in the early '90s began casting around for a new, cheaper, less bothersome way to make the drug.

When the DEA raided Paillet's Springfield home in 1994, agents were initially baffled. They'd received a tip from an informant about the stockpiles of cold medicines, so they figured Paillet must be operating some sort of meth lab. But the presence of other chemicals puzzled them. Anhydrous ammonia? Sodium metal?

"We found things we didn't think could be used to make methamphetamine," says Console, a colorful Jesse Ventura–type character right down to the shaved head, black turtleneck, and cowboy boots. "We sent the recipe and the ingredients up to the DEA lab in Chicago and they told us: 'We've never seen anything like this before but we'll try it.' They tried the recipe, and bingo, they produced methamphetamine."

John Cornille, the DEA agent who arrested Paillet, says: "I remember the chemist's exact words: 'There is a basis in the scientific literature for such a formula, but it hasn't been seen in the United States before.' "

Though he never received any formal education in the subject, Paillet knew a lot about chemistry and spent many hours researching in the library at Missouri State University, even though he wasn't a student there. After his arrest, Paillet told Cornille that during the course of this research he came across a copy of a document stamped with a swastika that revealed how the Nazis made the methamphetamine they supplied to their battlefront troops during World War II. Unlike the other ways of manufacturing meth, the Nazi method didn't require an open heat source. Instead, the cooking process was started by dissolving the ephedrine into a solvent and then adding a mixture of the common farm fertilizer anhydrous ammonia and a reactive metal such as lithium or sodium. This new recipe had the advantage of reducing the number of stages in the process and was therefore easier to make, although the method yielded smaller amounts of the drug than usual. You could now produce a little supply of the drug in a couple of hours instead of the twenty-four hours normally needed.

Whether Hitler's chemists really used this way of manufacturing methamphetamine remains unclear. DEA chemists looked into the matter and could find no connection to the Nazis. Some scientists believe that what Paillet actually dug up was the Birch reduction method, named after the Australian scientist Arthur Birch. Whatever the truth of the matter, the "Nazi" moniker stuck. Paillet gave five of his friends fishing tackle boxes containing materials and detailed instructions on how to make meth using this method, and from there, the recipe spread, and Nazi dope labs began sprouting up all across the Ozarks like toxic mushrooms.

"I knew we were in a lot of trouble," says John Cornille, "when the first sample of Nazi meth we sent to the lab turned out to be 92 percent pure methamphetamine, which meant it was quality dope."

The DEA worried that what Paillet had discovered was potentially a Pandora's box. If the recipe got out, hundreds, maybe thousands, of people in southwest Missouri would start making their own drugs. Every user could become his own mini drug kingpin. And it wouldn't stop there. The recipe was so simple and the ingredients so readily available, it was bound to spread to the rest of the state and then into adjoining states, as it eventually did.

"We tried to alert Washington," says Console, "but the reaction we got was that 'It's a hillbilly problem; it's not a problem throughout the rest of the United States.' "

Before Bob Paillet came along, meth consumption was confined largely to a few truckers, farmhands, and factory workers, as well as members of the Ozarks criminal underworld. Outlaw motorcycle gangs, both the Hells Angels and a local variant called the Galloping Goose, dominated the meth trade in those days. The supply came directly from California, carried by bikers who stored the drug in the crankshafts of their choppers, hence the nickname "crank" for meth. Or it was manufactured locally in a small number of clandestine labs. Southwest Missouri developed a reputation as home to some of the best meth cooks in the country. So-called 417 dope—meth made in the 417 area code—was a commodity sought after as far away as California.

"There's a number of reasons why southwest Missouri became a major center for manufacturing meth in the nineteen nineties, but one of them is that there already was a history of meth manufacturing in the region traced to these outlaw motorcycle gangs," says assistant U.S. attorney Dave Rush, who has spent the last fifteen years prosecuting federal drug cases in the Ozarks.

The first biker meth labs in the Ozarks were probably set up some time in the mid-1970s in the Mark Twain National Forest, a one-and-a-half-million-acre spread that spans twenty-nine counties at the southern end of Missouri and is to this day still a popular hideout for meth cooks. More meth labs are discovered here than all the other national forests in the country combined. Ed Houston, a Christian motorcyclist, remembers visiting a Hells Angels encampment in the middle of the Mark Twain Forest in 1975. The Angels had transported an irrigation system in a U-Haul all the way from California and had set up a marijuana-growing operation hidden among the trees.

"There were men, women, and children living in tents," he recalls. "The outer perimeter was guarded by Doberman pinschers. The inner perimeter was guarded by pit bulls."

The Angels had also hooked up an electricity generator and jerry-rigged a working laboratory that churned out hash oil, PCP, and meth. They lived on the barter system, trading drugs with some of the locals in exchange for food and other essentials, before they were eventually chased out of the forest by the police. Nevertheless, other biker meth labs followed and by the '80s meth production had started to creep out of the forest and into the surrounding countryside. In 1989, the *St. Louis Post-Dispatch* reported that a number of Californians and Texans with wads of cash in hand were buying or leasing out-the-way farms on the Missouri-Arkansas border to convert into meth labs.

The biker meth produced back then differs from the ephedrine-based drug we know today. It was less potent, more difficult to make, and required bulky laboratory equipment to produce. Instead of ephedrine or pseudoephedrine as the main ingredient, bikers used phenyl acetone, better known as P2P, a dark brown, syrupy chemical employed as an industrial cleaner or in photographic processing. "It was a complicated process," says John Cornille. "It took a person with legitimate chemical knowledge to manufacture the drug. It had difficult-to-obtain items like triple neck flasks and condenser coils." Further adding to the difficulties of manufacturing meth this way, the P2P method produced a telltale nauseating smell, which meant the labs needed to be located away from population centers to prevent detection by the police.

The Ozarks' wooded terrain provided ideal cover for the biker meth labs, just as it had in the past for illegal whiskey stills. Labs were built in pig farms and behind chicken coops to mask the smell. One of the reasons meth manufacturing took root so easily in the Ozarks is that unlike cocaine and heroin, meth was considered a rural drug, one that didn't carry big-city associations and wasn't imported from a foreign country. In those days, there was a strong racial and class association with the drug. Not for nothing was meth christened "redneck cocaine."

Also, meth making tapped into a rich seam of antigovernment

sentiment common in the area, a kind of right-wing anarchism that went back to the days of Jesse James and the bushwhackers, an attitude that could be summed up as: "Keep your nose out of my backyard. Or else." In terms of a threat to the community, meth didn't appear that big of a deal. Unaware of the horrors to come when the drug broke first statewide and then throughout the Midwest, locals who prided themselves on their independence and rugged individualism tended to regard manufacturing crystal meth as little more than latter-day moonshining. The Ozarks boasted a long tradition of illicit home distilling that stretched back decades.

"The people here are very self-sufficient," says the DEA's Nick Console. "And they don't like government interference in the way they live and the way they do business."

The beginning of the end for the biker meth labs in Missouri came in 1987 when Glennon Paul Sweet, a member of the Galloping Goose heavily involved in the local drug trade, shot to death Trooper Russell Harper during a routine traffic stop on U.S. 60, just outside of Springfield. Sweet was on the way to deliver some methamphetamine when Harper pulled over his red pickup truck. Sweet leaped from the vehicle with an assault rifle and fired nearly thirty shots at the trooper, one of which hit Harper in the head, killing him. The subsequent investigation of the murder led to the discovery of half a dozen clandestine labs operated by the Galloping Goose and then a general crackdown on meth manufacturing by bikers across the region.

Bob Paillet's Nazi recipe sounded the final death knell for biker meth in Missouri. Paillet's method effectively decentralized the local meth trade, which was never that structured to begin with, broadening the appeal of the drug. "Once meth users realized that they didn't have to depend on the bikers, that they could make it themselves, and not only have enough to supply their own habit but have some left over to sell, that's when the problem really started to spiral out of control," says assistant U.S. attorney David Rush.

Meth cooks now moved from the country into the suburbs and the towns. You could make meth almost anywhere using the Nazi method. People started manufacturing the drug in motel rooms, apartments, and in the flatbeds of pickup trucks. Meth recipes, once jealously guarded secrets, became common currency. With a small outlay and only a modicum of chemical savvy, every addict could now become a cook, who in turn taught others how to cook, who in turn went on to educate even more people.

"Once the method was simplified, it became like a giant pyramid scheme," says Rush. "Pretty soon you could trace the lineage of a lot of these cooks back to two or three people."

The results proved predictable. Meth production boomed in the Ozarks. Poorly trained and understaffed local sheriff's departments couldn't keep up with all the portable meth labs springing up across the landscape. In 1996, authorities seized 24 meth labs in the Ozarks. Two years later, the number had risen over sevenfold to 174, and those were just the ones law enforcement knew about. Thanks to Bob Paillet, the strongly conservative, deeply religious city of Springfield—the queen city of the Ozarks—had turned into ground zero for the Midwest's growing crystal meth problem.

While Bob Paillet was revolutionizing the meth trade in the Ozarks, elsewhere in Missouri, a number of Californian meth cooks had relocated to the Show Me State, where they showed some of the locals how to make the drug using yet another recipe, the so-called Red P method. Instead of anhydrous ammonia, the Californians used red phosphorous, a substance commonly found in fireworks and road flares, which was heated along with pseudoephedrine and iodine to produce methamphetamine.

California used to be the state that Missourians fled to in search of a better life. Wave after wave of them moved there, from the frontier days through the Great Depression and on through the post–Word War II era, when many Missourians departed for high-paying jobs in California's booming aerospace industry. But beginning in the early 1990s the westward migration reversed itself, as Missouri saw an influx of Californians, many of them fleeing that state's high taxes and crime rates, not to mention the soaring property prices. According to the Office of Social, Economic, and Data Analysis, an estimated eighty thousand Californians moved to Missouri during the decade.

Some of these newcomers were returnees—the sons and daughters of Missourians who had previously left the state. Most of them were just ordinary middle-class people on limited budgets looking for a better life, people who were tired of just barely scraping by. For the money it cost to buy a small house in California, you could purchase a place twice the size in Missouri, one that occupied a substantial piece of land, and still have money left over. Missouri also proved attractive to conservative Christian families who wanted to raise their children in a traditional rural setting, not the secular liberal cesspool they believed California was becoming.

Hidden among the ranks of the newcomers were a small number of bikers and truckers who also had been driven out of the state but for different reasons. Because America's current methamphetamine problem largely originated there, California was the first state in the country to impose restrictions on the purchase of chemicals used to manufacture meth. This, combined with stepped-up law enforcement raids on meth labs, persuaded many Californian cooks to relocate to other parts of the country where they could practice their craft undisturbed. Police in Franklin and Jefferson counties in the eastern part of Missouri say meth became a major problem in their area after a Californian cook named John Bushdiecker moved there and set up a laboratory, where he taught a number of locals how to make the drug using the Red P method. Another Californian cook nicknamed the Wizard is credited with bringing home-style meth manufacturing to Joplin, Missouri. Chris Haycraft moved to Joplin after being injured working on a construction site in Southern California and started to make meth to support himself and his family. "I didn't go [to Joplin] looking to start a drug culture or anything," he told *The Joplin Globe* in January 2006. Though, ultimately, that was the effect.

Another one of the Californians who showed up in Missouri in the 1990s was sickly Willi Olsen, a decorated Vietnam War vet from Riverside, who had lost most of his stomach on the battlefield. He brought two young San Bernardino meth cooks, Kenny Marsh, also none too healthy, and Marsh's assistant, Hugh Escobar, to live in Independence, a suburb of Kansas City and the location of the original Garden of Eden, according to Mormon belief.

If Independence wasn't the Garden of Eden to Olsen, it sure was the land of milk and honey. Olsen got rich shipping pounds of meth from California to Independence, which he sometimes flew in personally on airlines, the packages of drugs taped to his body or hidden in false-bottomed suitcases. He owned a number of properties in the area and cruised around Independence in a sixty-foot mobile home that he'd bought locally with a suitcase full of cash. Not wanting to risk transporting the drugs anymore, Olsen brought Marsh and Escobar to Independence to help him set up a major meth-manufacturing operation there.

Olsen first discovered meth after he returned from Vietnam. Even though he was barely able to walk, he managed to get a job as a truck driver. He started to take the drug to stay awake on long hauls. Eventually, he began selling the drug to other truckers and realized that he could buy a pound of meth for $4,000 in California, add a pound of filler, and sell it for five times the price in Missouri.

Olsen already had an established market there when he decided to bring Marsh and Escobar to Independence. Soon after they arrived, however, Marsh fell ill and returned to California, where the twenty-five-year-old died of congestive heart failure, the result of his heavy meth use. In the wake of Marsh's death, Escobar split with Olsen and then taught a handful of locals how to cook the drug using Marsh's method. Just as in the Ozarks, the dissemination of this one recipe would have consequences that its creators could not have foreseen. The method spread quickly and soon Jackson County had one of the worst meth-lab problems in the country.

It grew geometrically from there. "It just went explosive. It went berserk," Independence detective Mike Skaggs, who investigated the case, told a newspaper.

Olsen and Escobar were eventually convicted and imprisoned on meth manufacturing and distribution charges, but not before they'd shared their recipe with a new generation of meth cooks in the area.

What distinguishes meth from other illegal drugs is the ability to make the substance quickly and cheaply at home. Sure, you can grow your own marijuana. But you have to spend thousands of dollars on lamps and other equipment, and then you have to wait months for the plants to grow. With meth, a hundred dollars' worth of materials can yield a thousand dollars' worth of dope within a couple of hours. So the financial incentive is obvious. But more than a cheap high, meth is attractive because of the outlaw lifestyle that surrounds the manufacturing of the drug. Talk to practically any meth cook in the Ozarks and they'll tell you pretty much the same thing: The ritual of gathering the ingredients and cooking the drug gets them just as excited as the drug itself. "I got higher off the cooking than I did off the dope," says Stanley Harris.

Harris started making meth after his drug habit bankrupted his roofing business. Why continue giving money to drug dealers, he reasoned, when you could make the stuff yourself? Harris bought five thousand pseudoephedrine pills and a hundred lithium batteries in North Dakota and came back to Springfield with the supplies. That night, he went out into the countryside to steal some anhydrous ammonia and the next day made his first batch of meth—a quarter of a pound.

While economic necessity was the reason Harris first started to manufacture the drug, his increasing fascination with the chemistry behind the cooking process was why he continued in the business. Harris learned the basics from a friend, but he perfected his craft by reading Uncle Fester's *Secrets of Methamphetamine Manufacture*, an underground how-to book widely read in Missouri meth circles. "I knew how to make dope before I read Uncle Fester, but he taught me the chemistry behind what I was doing," he says. Soon Harris gained the reputation as being one of the best cooks in town, producing pounds of high-quality product from which he earned as much as $2,000 a day. "I'll tell you how powerful the dope I made was," he says. "I could give it to a girl and she'd come in her pants. Men, too."

Cops like to portray meth cooks as Beavis and Butthead types, dumb stoners who wouldn't know one end of a sep funnel from another. But many of the meth cooks I talked to not only took pride in their work but were often quite knowledgeable about the science that underpinned the manufacturing process. They have to be. Different from regular drug dealers who express their status through ostentatious displays of guns, cars, and jewelry, a meth cook's standing is determined solely by his ability to produce Grade A dope. Like a chef in a four-star restaurant, meth cooks often employ helpers who, in exchange for meth, do the menial preparatory work. One person's job might be to buy the cold pills. Another is sent out to get the batteries. Yet others rub their fingers raw punching pills from blister packs. Manufacturing the drug begins with the cook grinding up pseudoephedrine pills and soaking them in a solvent, and goes on to involve the pouring, stirring, and filtering of various chemicals, a process so laborious that it's enough to send most people to sleep. But to meth cooks and their followers who watch in awe and admiration, it's a magical procedure, a ritual that verges on the religious, a form of latter-day alchemy that transforms a base product—Sudafed—into something equivalent to gold.

Stanley Harris heads down Glenstone Avenue and takes a right on Kearney Street. At the corner of National Avenue and Kearney, he points to a Walgreens. "Before they changed the law, I used to go in there and buy every packet of Sudafed on the shelf," he says. When the state rationed the number of packets of cold medicines to two per person per month, Harris got around the law by smurfing—that is, he and a colleague would start at the Dollar General store near his west Springfield home and buy two packets each there. Then they would drive to another store and then another store, often ending up at the Fast and Friendly in Kansas City nearly two hundred miles away.

"If you figure two boxes contains a hundred pills, after you extract them that's about six grams of pseudoephedrine, which makes about four and a half to five grams of pure dope," he explains. "Multiply that by how many stores you go to and how many people you take with you, then that's a lot of meth."

Just around the corner from Walgreens sits another landmark and yet another source of chemicals, the Hiland Dairy bottling plant. Harris gestures toward the anhydrous ammonia tanks lying on the ground that are used to run the plant's cooling system. Before the milk company beefed up security, Hiland used to be a major target for meth cooks in the area looking to steal the anhydrous ammonia to make Nazi dope. Armed with bolt cutters, Harris and his associates would sneak under the fence in the middle of the night and tiptoe up to the tank, pop open the valve, and then drain off some of the supply into an empty fire extinguisher or a propane tank.

"What screwed it up was that one of my friends shot the pipeline with a gun and they had a big anhydrous leak right there," he says.

Why did he do that?

"Because he's an idiot," Harris laughs.

Of all the chemicals in the methamphetamine cookbook, anhydrous ammonia is the one that local police fear the most. And for good reason. The chemical has an extremely low boiling point of −28 degrees, which means that if it is exposed to air, the liquid immediately turns into a cloud of noxious gas that can sear lungs and damage eyes. If the chemical touches human skin, all the moisture is sucked out, peeling back the flesh and causing gruesome and sometimes fatal burns, a hideous fate that meth cooks call "being frosted." In 1999, two meth cooks, who had just stolen some ammonia from a farm, were traveling along Interstate 55 when the fire extinguisher containing the chemical ruptured, filling the vehicle with a suffocating cloud of smoke that killed one of the occupants and severely burned the other.

Because anhydrous ammonia is the lone ingredient that meth cooks can't buy at a supermarket or in a hardware store, a thriving black market has grown up in which the liquid, which sells commercially for about one to two dollars a gallon, can fetch as much as four hundred dollars for the same amount. So-called gas men have appeared on the scene—people whose only job is to steal anhydrous ammonia and sell it to the highest bidder. After the police clamped down on anhydrous ammonia thieves in Springfield, the gas men started stealing the chemical outside the city limits. Anhydrous ammonia tanks are dotted all over the Missouri countryside, especially in the spring growing season. Farmers use it as a fertilizer to add nitrogen to the soil and often leave the tanks out in their fields overnight.

Harris heads down National and swings right onto Commercial Street, and immediately the cityscape changes. Here, weeds grow between the cracks in the sidewalk. Ramshackle wooden bungalows slump in the murky darkness. Soup kitchens, secondhand clothing stores, and homeless shelters line the strip.

"Is this a working-class neighborhood?" I ask.

"More like a dope-class neighborhood," says Harris. "A lot of meth addicts live around here."

As its name suggests, Commercial Street used to be a major shopping hub. The Atlantic-Pacific railway arrived here in 1870, and in the coming decades a vibrant small-business district grew up around the rail yards. The area started to decline in the early 1960s when train travel fell in popularity. By the early 1970s, when Harris's father opened a small hole-in-the-wall café on the strip, Commercial Street was a hangout for thieves, gamblers, fences, bikers, drug dealers, and dopers.

Surprisingly, given all the meth he has consumed, Harris has vivid memories of those days as a young boy not yet in his teens— the Nine Ball Pool Hall, where players would wage $1,000 on a single game; fighting for money with other boys in the back alley, while older men bet on the outcome; waiting at the bottom of the Jefferson Street Footbridge, now a historic monument, looking to rob unsuspecting pedestrians of their money; the gunshots that rang out in the Cave Bar strip club one night when a couple of Jesse James types pulled up in a Cadillac, took two shotguns from the trunk, walked inside, and let loose with all four barrels. He also remembers the drugs, especially methamphetamine, which you could easily purchase at any of the dive bars along Commercial Street.

"It was the good stuff, the old P2P dope, not the anhydrous crap," says Harris. "Hells Angels shipped it in from California to Kansas City, and then it trickled down from there."

The meth scene in Springfield started to change for the worse in the early 1990s, according to Harris, after Nazi dope started to become all the rage. "We called it 'chicken scratch meth' because it made you cluck around like a chicken," says Harris. "It was different from the P2P dope. The anhydrous dope made people crazy. People became scandalous. That's when all the domestic violence started. On the P2P dope you wouldn't see people out at four in the morning mowing their lawns. On the anhydrous dope you did."

Harris turns off the strip and steers down a narrow side road, then makes a left onto Brower Street and stops in the middle of the block. Until the police cleaned the place up a couple of years back, this area was known as Meth Alley, the spot to come to if you wanted to buy some home-brewed stimulants. At the height of the mom-and-pop-lab craze, half the houses on this one block sold the drug. "That was a dope house," says Harris. "That house right there with the porch light on, that was a dope house. This house right over here with the fenced-in yard, there was a dope house. That empty lot, they tore it down, that was a dope house. Everybody had dope. It was everywhere. People would be driving around cooking dope in their cars."

Politicians love to portray methamphetamine as the crack co-caine of the new millennium. But the meth trade in Springfield hasn't created anything like the kind of violent social disruption that the crack business did in many inner-city neighborhoods during the 1980s. Rival drug gangs don't battle each other in the street over drug turf. Because anybody can make the drug, there's no turf to protect. Ordinary citizens aren't scared to walk the streets. You don't see dealers hawking their wares on street corners. You don't see drug addicts stumbling along the sidewalks. Most of the meth activity here takes place behind closed doors and blacked-out windows. The biggest fear civilians have to worry about is a meth lab exploding on their block.

Still, one particularly brutal meth-related incident did shock Springfield to its core. In 1999, a pregnant Erin Vanderhoef and her three children were all killed in their Springfield home in what became known as the most heinous mass murder in the history of southwest Missouri. One of the killers, Richard DeLong, the father of Vanderhoef's unborn child, was a meth addict who at the urging of his girlfriend, Stacie Leffingwell, also addicted to the drug, killed the mother and her children. Leffingwell was jealous of Vanderhoef, who was trying to reestablish her relationship with DeLong. Leffingwell was dying of AIDS, which she contracted from sharing dirty needles. She was also peeved that DeLong was paying child support to Vanderhoef, which meant there was less money to spend on their drug habits. "The meth bitch from hell," is how one local prosecutor described her.

On the evening of January 19, DeLong, Leffingwell, and Bobby Lingle, who had been promised an eight ball of methamphetamine to participate in the killings, appeared on the doorstep of Vanderhoef's home. While Lingle accompanied Vanderhoef to the local super-market to buy coffee and donuts, DeLong and Leffingwell took the three children into separate bedrooms and strangled eight-year-old Darlene, ten-year-old Chris, and eleven-year-old Jimmy, using a cord from a Nintendo computer game. When Vanderhoef got back from the supermarket, DeLong and Leffingwell told her that the children had been acting up and they had put them to bed. Vander-hoef, who was days away from giving birth, sat down on a couch to rest, at which point DeLong crept up behind her and wrapped a cord around her neck. While Leffingwell held down Vanderhoef's arms, DeLong stuffed a rag into the mother's mouth to prevent her from screaming and hogtied her, roping her neck to her feet so that the struggling Vanderhoef eventually suffocated herself.

The three killers were soon arrested. DeLong and Lingle even-tually received multiple life sentences, not just for the slaying of Vanderhoef and her children but also for the murder of the unborn baby. Leffingwell died of AIDS before she could face justice.

"The crime had meth written all over it," says Greene County prosecutor Cynthia Rushefksy.

The Vanderhoef killings were stunning in their depravity, all the more so because four of the five victims were children. But the crimes were also exceptional. That one incident alone doubled Springfield's murder rate that year.

The meth trade in the Ozarks poses a difficult challenge for local law enforcement. Unlike other drugs, where a big bust can cause a significant disruption to the business, leading to a drop in supply and a spike in the price, dismantling small-scale meth labs is a bit like a game of Whac-A-Mole. Each time you take down one, an-other one pops up in a different location. A significant amount of cocaine and marijuana is seized in transit. The bigger the distance from the manufacturer to the consumer, the more chances drug agents have to intercept the product. With meth, however, the drug is often consumed by a small group of people within the same tight geographical area in which it's manufactured. As University of California, Los Angeles, professor Mark Kleiman has written on the realitybasedcommunity.netblog: "Meth is simply not a good enforcement target because it has no obvious 'choke point.' In particular, the hand-to-hand, acquaintance-to-acquaintance, low-frequency style of retail meth dealing makes it pretty close to invulnerable to enforcement, especially in rural areas where undercover work is hard."

In his office on the fifth floor of Hammons Tower, a massive T-shaped monolith on the edge of downtown that looks like it was designed by Darth Vader, Assistant U.S. Attorney Dave Rush sits back in his leather chair and says, "I'm a little offended that the national media has suddenly discovered methamphetamine. We've been dealing with this problem since the early nineteen nineties. But it wasn't regarded as a real problem because it affected only blue-collar whites in rural America."

Rush has been fighting meth for well over a decade. But it's only in the last few years that law enforcement has started to get a handle on the situation. One of the most frustrating aspects of battling the mom-and-pop meth labs is that when these facilities are raided, the quantity of drugs seized is often very small, an ounce or less. In the past, this meant that meth cooks received little more than a slap on the wrist for their crimes. But that changed after Rush and his colleagues started arresting meth manufacturers under federal drug conspiracy laws, which allows prosecutors to charge them with all the drugs produced in the lifetime of the conspiracy, not just the amount found when one of their labs is busted. Cooks, who were used to being sentenced to parole or short stints in state prison, now faced the possibility of spending the rest of their lives in the federal system, where there is no possibility of parole.

"Once we started locking up the cooks for long periods of time, we saw a dramatic decrease in meth labs," says Rush.

As well as going after the cooks, law enforcement also targeted the suppliers of meth-making ingredients, particularly pseudoephedrine.

In 2002, a joint federal, state, and local investigation was launched called Operation Ice Palace, which targeted The Castle, a head shop housed in a cavernous corrugated metal warehouse shaped like a medieval fort complete with a moat and a drawbridge. Located on Highway 76, about eight miles outside of the country music resort of Branson, The Castle sold millions of pseudoephedrine pills to customers who, one can safely assume, weren't using all those cold medicines to unblock their sinuses. This was where Stanley Harris used to buy five-thousand-pill consignments to fuel his meth-making operation.

"It was the KMart of head shops," says Branson's nattily dressed police chief, Steve Dalton, while standing outside the abandoned metal structure. At the time The Castle was in business, Dalton headed the Combined Ozarks Multi-jurisdictional Enforcement Team (COMET), which played a key role in the eventual takedown of the notorious establishment. "Meth cooks came from all over southwest Missouri and northern Arkansas to buy pseudoephedrine here."

Under federal law, it is illegal to distribute pseudoephedrine knowing it will be used to manufacture meth. Penalties for selling what under normal circumstances is a perfectly legal product—the main ingredient in dozens of common cold preparations—when you know, or should reasonably know, that it's being used to make methamphetamine can be extremely harsh, as The Castle's owner, David Deputy, was about to find out.

Undercover agents staked out Deputy's place and began conducting controlled buys. They soon discovered that the Castle's employees, including the owner's daughter, Melissa, routinely sold up to twenty boxes of Actifed and Dove pseudoephedrine products to the same customers several times a month, clearly far more pills than were necessary to treat colds. They also found out that The Castle didn't just sell directly to meth cooks, but supplied mini-marts and other small businesses that used the legitimate sales of over-the-counter products as a smoke screen to hide a large-scale illegal pseudoephedrine distribution network, of which The Castle was the regional hub. Two small Jonesboro novelty shops alone ordered more than four hundred thousand pills—enough to make thirty-five pounds of methamphetamine—from The Castle over a nineteen-month period.

Throughout 2003, undercover detectives made numerous purchases at stores all across the region. An employee of a Laundromat in Joplin sold 1,152 pills to undercover operatives. A Springfield discount liquor store sold 3,288 pills. At a convenience store in Shell Knob, a worker sold 936 thirty-milligram and sixty-milligram tablets to undercover detectives from the Missouri State Highway patrol. The fifty-five-year-old owner of Sims General Store in McDonald County even admitted to manufacturing up to five kilograms of meth on the premises using pseudoephedrine he'd obtained for the shop.

The investigation also uncovered a sales agent for The Castle's distribution arm, D and D, whose job was to supply hundreds of boxes of pseudoephedrine every month to video stores, bars, and other nonconventional businesses he regularly visited. He provided the outlets with multiple fake invoices for each transaction so as to appear to comply with federal regulations. All in all, the feds estimated he sold roughly three kilograms of pseudoephedrine illegally.

In April 2004, after a two-year investigation, thirty-eight people were indicted. Fifteen more were arrested in subsequent indictments. Among those arrested was The Castle's owner, David Deputy, and four of his employees, including his daughter. Deputy—who had been licensed by the DEA to sell pseudoephedrine since 1999—was accused of purchasing close to 140,000 boxes of pseudoephedrine tablets from several wholesale suppliers, which amounted to nearly seven million pills. Between the pseudoephedrine he sold directly to customers and the pseudoephedrine he distributed to other outlets, the feds estimated he made close to a million dollars in profit from these illegal sales. In the summer of 2005, he was convicted and sentenced to twenty years in federal prison without parole and ordered to forfeit the Castle property.

The punishments handed out were tough, maybe even draconian. One Ozark County convenience store owner got fourteen years in federal prison after admitting to selling what amounted to less than three hundred grams of pseudoephedrine. But Operation Ice Palace was meant to send a clear message, a signal to manufacturers and their suppliers that law enforcement was now serious about cleaning up this meth mess. Even if you weren't directly involved in making the drug, by supplying the chemicals you were just as guilty as the cooks in the government's eyes.

In July 2005, Missouri enacted one of the toughest laws in the country restricting the sales of medicines containing pseudoephedrine. Under the new law, only pharmacists can sell pseudoephedrine products like Sudafed and they are forced to keep them behind the counter, not on the shelves. Sales are limited to adults ages eighteen and older. The law also requires customers to show ID and sign a log that the police can inspect at any time. (A previous law that came into effect two years before, limiting pseudoephedrine sales to two packets per person, was widely flouted by meth cooks.) Since then, a new federal law has come into effect, the Combat Meth Act, which was passed in March 2006 as an add-on bill to the renewed PATRIOT Act. Cosponsored by Missouri senator Jim Talent, the federal statute duplicates many of the provisions of the state law, but because it applies on the national level it has the additional benefit of preventing meth cooks from traveling out of state to purchase their pseudoephedrine.

By limiting pseudoephedrine purchases, Missouri seems to be winning the war on meth as far as the small-time operators are concerned. Meth labs have been shutting down all across the state. Pseudoephedrine pills have become so difficult to procure in bulk that they can fetch as much as a dollar a pill on the black market in Springfield. Yet little has changed when it comes to the demand side of the equation. Far from disappearing, the meth trade in Missouri has simply taken a new direction. People still want the drug, so instead of making it themselves, they buy imported "ice," a crystalline form of meth made in massive labs in Mexico, which is transported across the border into Texas and then shipped to Missouri along Interstate 44, a notorious drug pipeline. When everybody and their cousin was making meth and selling it cheaply, organized criminals mostly stayed away because there was no real money to be made. Now, sophisticated international drug-smuggling syndicates are moving in and taking over, and the meth trade today more closely resembles the cocaine business. In early 2006, seven Mexican nationals pled guilty to federal charges of conspiring to distribute more than ten pounds of meth in the Ozarks. It seems that home-cooked Missouri dope is becoming yet another casualty of globalization.

"The good news is that we're seeing a lot less of these mom-and-pop labs," says Chief Dalton. "The bad news is that we've seen a big escalation in burglaries and thefts because meth addicts have to pay for it now, whereas before they could make it themselves. The demand is still there. Unless there's something worked out to curb that, I don't know if it's going to get much better anytime soon."

CHAPTER TWO

THE DEVIL'S DRUG

THE OZARKS

On a moonlit night deep in the heart of the Missouri countryside, the world is coming to an end. And not a moment too soon for the approximately three hundred Jesus enthusiasts who have gathered to hear local author and former methamphetamine addict Steve Box speak at the Hurley Baptist Church, a brick chapel with a white steeple surrounded by a shadowy tapestry of patchwork fields. Faith runs deep in this region. So does the drug culture. Hurley (population 161) is located in Stone County, a place where meth cooks are as common as preachers, and small-scale meth laboratories have replaced the illegal whiskey stills that used to dot these hills.

During my stay in the Ozarks, I kept hearing the name Steve Box repeated over and over. Box, it was said, had the power of healing. He had supposedly cured hundreds of addicts at his antimeth rallies simply by laying his hands on their heads and casting out the demons within. It seems that Box is to tweakers what Jesus was to lepers. This I had to see with my own eyes.

"Are you rapture ready?" the white-haired old lady stationed at the doorway of the church asks with a beatific smile as she hands me a copy of Box's slim volume, *Meth=Sorcery*, the cover of which depicts Satan mixing up a batch of methamphetamine in a giant cauldron.

The people here tonight believe wholeheartedly in the rapture—

the prediction that Jesus Christ is coming back to earth sometime soon, whereupon a battle will commence, a final struggle between good and evil, a bloody Armageddon after which the faithful will be raised up ("raptured") into heaven, while the rest of us heathens will be cast into some deep, dark pit somewhere. The death of millions of people and the destruction of all civilization is blissfully welcomed as the fulfillment of biblical prophecy.

And it gets stranger. Omens portending the coming apocalypse are said to be everywhere—war, terrorism, famine, pestilence, hurricanes, and so forth. The online Rapture Index, the self-proclaimed "Dow Jones Industrial Average of end-time activity," adds up all the different signs and assigns a number—the higher the number the faster the world is speeding toward apocalypse. The latest indication that the end is nigh: methamphetamine. The God-fearing folks assembled at the Hurley Baptist Church see the dramatic increase in meth activity in their community over the last ten years not as a simple scourge caused by human weakness and folly nor as a public health problem, but rather as a demonic conspiracy organized by Satan himself.

Steve Box sounds like he is describing a scene from a Hollywood horror movie—*The Omen* as directed by zombiemeister George A. Romero, perhaps—when he writes in another one of his self-published books, *Leviathan: the Nation Testifies*, "There will be millions who will not worship the Beast. These people will most likely be hunted day and night by an army or militia that is on methamphetamine: their only objective, to hunt and kill Christians."

Inside the church, the atmosphere is upbeat and informal. Some of the congregants packed into the polished pews wouldn't look out of place at a Black Sabbath concert. "You don't have to look holy to be holy," one heavily tattooed fellow says. Other churchgoers carry well-thumbed Bibles and sport the local uniform of dungarees, checkered shirts, and work boots. One of the faithful wears a T-shirt that reads: THERE IS NO HIGH LIKE THE MOST HIGH. Nearly everybody in the crowd—mothers, fathers, wives, husbands, sons, and daughters—has either been addicted to methamphetamine or is close to somebody who has.

While waiting for Box to appear, the crowd is entertained by a quintet banging out some old-time hillbilly banjo music, soon to be joined by a member of the Christian Motorcycle Association, a gray-haired old biker named Ed Houston, decked out in denim and leather decorated with hog patches. Ed grabs the mike and proceeds to perform a self-penned ditty, a lachrymose antiabortion song called "Cry for the Children."

"Their blood runs like a river in the name of women's rights," he croons with a passion, draining every last drop of emotion out of the lyrics in that overwrought manner familiar to viewers of *American Idol*. And then he begs. "Get back on your knees and pray for the children."

The audience applauds and hoots as Ed exits the stage whooping: "Yeeee-haw. Ain't God good?"

With the musical acts over, the pastor of the church makes an announcement: "Please welcome Steve Box." The man everybody has come to see bounds onto the altar dressed casually in a light brown shirt and olive green pants, while behind him a projection screen displays the message: "For he will reveal through the word of Christ, the truth about methamphetamine." The crowd rises to its feet to greet him. Box is a heavyset guy in his late thirties, tanned and broad-shouldered, with swept back dark hair and a neatly trimmed goatee. He looks like a former athlete. Box actually threw away a promising college football career because of his meth addiction. Puffing up his chest, he launches into his sermon. "Tonight, I stand here and proclaim liberty to the captives," he says, styling himself as a kind of Meth Moses looking to lead the drug-addicted Israelites out of chemical bondage.

Box peppers his preaching not only with references to the Bible but to numerous scientific studies he claims to have read. One such study, he says, shows that "methamphetamine creates an acid that eats a hole into your brain." Another one supposedly revealed that "in lab rats they feed methamphetamine to, they abandon their children." The alarmist oratory escalates when Box says, "I wish every meth lab in the world would blow up in Jesus' name." Then, realizing that might not jibe with the image of Christ as a man of peace, he modifies his comment: "That doesn't mean I want to see anybody killed, of course."

The most compelling part of the sermon comes when Box describes his own experience with the drug, which led on one occasion to an attempted murder arrest in Las Vegas, charges that were later dropped. "Let me tell what life was like for me when I was on methamphetamine," he tells the spellbound audience. "I visited the county jail on a regular basis for domestic violence. I wiretapped my own phone to spy on my wife. I held my best friend at gunpoint all night long. I ripped off my own family. I believed there was a plot to kill me and everybody was in on it, including my own parents. I'd be driving down the road and I'd hear my kids yelling out of a strangers' house. So I'd get my gun out and break in and I'd be standing in one of your living rooms with a twelve-gauge. I used to have a Rolex, new trucks, a big brick home, a welding business, and I lost it all because of methamphetamine."

Tears start to roll down his cheeks. "I've got friends who still believe to this day they have flies and bugs that live inside their head," he sobs.

Box kicked methamphetamine seven years ago with the aid of his pastor, Billy Ray Harvill, after which he began poring over the Bible looking for messages that would help him make sense of the experience he'd just gone through. Box was struck by a number of passages in the Book of Revelations that mention sorcery ("For by thy sorceries were all nations deceived"). Divining a hidden meaning in these verses that heretofore had remained obscure, he came to believe that the sorcery talked about in the Bible was actually a prediction of today's methamphetamine problem.

Now it all made sense. The hallucinations he suffered under the influence of meth weren't the result of sleep deprivation but communications from the demonic realm. The shadow people he saw lurking in the ditches weren't tricks of the mind but satanic emissaries. And the ritual of cooking the drug, the gathering of the ingredients, and the mixing of various chemicals and potions to produce a substance that controls people's minds—what else was that but pure, unadulterated sorcery, the same witchcraft that the Bible says is a sure sign that the world as we know it is about to expire?

Back at the church, Box keeps the brimstone boiling when he brings up a controversial topic. "A lot of preachers are teaching against the rapture," he says. The audience is aghast. It seems some religious leaders have been backing away from all the *Left Behind* hysteria, possibly fearful that this mock-apocalyptic rhetoric makes Christians look like a bunch of crazy people. A theological schism has developed between those who take the Book of Revelations with a grain of salt, regard the prophecies contained within as more allegorical than actual, and those who believe it's the God's honest truth.

Box is having none of this. "I believe there is a time coming on the earth like there never has been and never will be again," he proclaims. "These are the end times. And methamphetamine is the end-time drug. Jesus Christ is coming back and methamphetamine is probably the biggest indicator that the end time is near."

The congregation responds with the joyful cry, "Praise the Lord."

During a momentary lull in the proceedings, a gently plucked guitar starts up in the background. The audience grows hushed. Something dramatic is about to happen. Box lowers his voice to a whisper: "Is there anybody out there who has a love for methamphetamine right now? Raise your hand and come forward."

A frail hand gingerly goes up at the back of the church.

"C'mon down here and make a public confession. Jesus is watching," says Box, his voice now hoarse from all the preaching.

A young woman with pierced eyebrows staggers to the front of

the congregation. Her head is bowed and her long, straggly hair partially hides a forlorn face. Dressed in black from head to toe, she
looks like someone attending their own funeral. A pathetic figure,
she moans and clutches her stomach, as if she's about to throw up on
the plush green carpet at any moment. I'm told that the woman I'll
call Betty is a twofer—not only a meth addict but a Satanist to boot.

"It's okay, when I was set free, I puked," Box tries to comfort her.
"I know you been into witchcraft. That's all right. I know you been
into methamphetamine. That's all right, too. We're gonna cast that
devil right out of you. The Holy Ghost is more powerful than any
demon."

On cue, a dozen church ladies, a mixture of young and old, sur-
round Betty and place their hands on the crown of her head and on
her back. One of them anoints her forehead with holy oil in preparation for the healing.

"Say this prayer," Box instructs Betty. "Lord Jesus."

"Lord Jesus," she weakly mumbles.

"Forgive me for all my witchcraft sins."

"Forgive me for all my witchcraft sins."

"Forgive me for all my sins of methamphetamine."

"Forgive me for all my sins of methamphetamine."

"I command every demon of witchcraft, I command every demon of methamphetamine, to leave this woman tonight and at this
hour in Jesus' name."

At which point, as if out of nowhere, one of the church ladies lets
out a yell and starts to wail: "ULU-ULU-ULU-ULU-ULU-ULU . . ."

Box begins to babble in some unintelligible dialect: "KALEM-
SHIM-SHOLOW-SHA-SHALAY-SHALOO-KALOO . . ."

It takes me a few moments to realize what this din is meant to
signify. Box has supposedly been seized by the Holy Ghost and is
now speaking in tongues—a commonplace religious ritual in these
parts. With the fervor at a fever pitch, Betty emits a loud grunt and
collapses onto the floor, after which the church ladies gently pick
her up and guide her back into the pews.

Afterward, standing outside in the church parking lot smoking a cigarette and chatting with the excited congregants, I find out that Betty isn't really a devil worshiper. All she had done was cast a couple of innocuous spells and light a few candles.

"There's no difference," says a Rob Zombie look-alike, who is clutching a Bible. The nasty-looking chemical burns up and down the lengths of his arms give away his former pastime as a meth cook. "The Bible says it's all witchcraft," he says. "You'd be surprised how many people worship Satan in this area."

This wasn't the first time Betty attended a methamphetamine exorcism. Three days earlier, she had gone through the same ritual at another Christian meth recovery meeting, this one at a Salvation Army center in Springfield, about twenty miles from here, and she had been rewarded for her performance with a turkey and a Wal-Mart gift card for her kids.

It's easy to make fun of these people, especially in the wake of the Ted Haggard scandal, when the president of the politically powerful National Association of Evangelicals was forced to resign after being accused of paying for sex and buying methamphetamine from a male escort (charges he denied), but to dismiss Box and his followers as Holy Roller fanatics is to ignore something important happening in the country at the moment. Not just in the Ozarks, but in church basements all across America, methamphetamine ministries are springing up, part of a wider Christian rehab movement, a genuine grass-roots revolution that challenges basic liberal secular assumptions about how best to treat drug addiction. Especially in rural areas where meth addicts can wait for months for a bed to open up in an inpatient treatment facility, small groups of believers, many of them former tweakers themselves, are banding together to attack the meth problem at the local level, taking up the slack and filling in the gaps, providing support and counseling to anyone who seeks it. It's a phenomenon encouraged by President George W. Bush's

Access to Recovery program, which allows public tax dollars to be spent on private faith-based drug treatment. Many of these groups take their inspiration from the Alabama pediatrician Mary Holley and her Mothers Against Methamphetamine organization. Holley started the group after her meth-addicted brother committed suicide. Even though she's a doctor, and presumably a woman of science, Holley promotes Christian rehab as a more effective way of treating meth addicts than secular treatment programs, on the basis that drug addiction is as much a disease of the spirit as it is of the mind or the body.

There is nothing new about faith-based drug treatment, of course. Reaching back to the temperance movements and evangelical crusades of the eighteenth and nineteenth centuries, when, as with today's recovering meth addicts, former alcoholics would stand up at revival meetings to testify to the role religion played in curing them, faith in America has always played a key part in reforming the inebriated. Many believe, and studies have shown, that a spiritual awakening often accompanies the personal transformation necessary to defeat a tough addiction. And using religious conversion as a way of kicking drugs is not just confined to Protestant sects. A century later, the former street hustler Malcolm X famously gave up his drug habit under the influence of the Nation of Islam. More bizarrely, Ashley Smith (the woman held hostage by an accused rapist who killed four people as he made his escape from an Atlanta courthouse in March 2005) became a Christian heroine when she secured her release by reading her captor passages from Rick Warren's best-selling spiritual guide *The Purpose Driven Life*. Her squeaky-clean image was somewhat tarnished, though, when it was also revealed that she had given the convict crystal meth from her personal stash. Appearing on *The Oprah Winfrey Show* with Smith, Warren said the incident illustrated that "you don't have to be perfect to be used by God." Smith, whose child had been taken away from her because of her meth habit, claims she hasn't used the drug since the incident, though whether that's due to the shock of being held hostage or the intervention of God remains unclear.

The Christian rehab phenomenon is not without controversy. Critics worry on constitutional grounds about the erosion of the separation between church and state. In addition, they charge that what addicts need isn't Bible study but professional help. There's also the suspicion that what these programs are really about is not curing drug addiction but winning converts to the fundamentalist Christian cause. In December 2005, a Detroit man, with the assistance of the American Civil Liberties Union, filed a lawsuit to have a marijuana possession conviction squashed, claiming he was punished for not completing a court-mandated drug treatment program run by a Pentecostal church, when he objected to being told he had to renounce his Catholic faith and convert to Pentecostalism or otherwise risk being sent to prison. What is more, some see a political agenda at work here—an ideological attempt to further roll back the welfare state (the so-called culture of dependency) and place preachers in charge of delivering important social services as they were in a previous era.

It's tempting to interpret the methamphetamine ministries as the latest battle in the war of ideas between science and religion currently raging across America, much like the heated debate over evolution. But the Christian approach and the secular approach are surprisingly similar in some respects. Both employ the same vaguely New Agey therapeutic jargon about "healing" and "emotional growth." Both play on irrational fears about meth while demonizing the drug. Drug treatment experts call meth an epidemic, and the Christians call it a plague—while statistical evidence suggests that neither is true. Both camps see meth users as victims—victims of Satan on the one hand, victims of neurochemistry on the other—and unquestionably regard drug use as a disease, an alien outside force that robs addicts of the ability to control their own actions; the upshot of both views is to let junkies off the hook for their bad behavior. Satan made me do it. Or the drug made me do it. Both are essentially lame excuses that don't stand up in the court of common sense. The more levelheaded outlook that addiction is at least partially a choice—the product of willful desire and human volition—is anathema to both points of view. And both seem to share the belief that addiction is a form of possession. The Christians use more flowery language to describe the state, but the underlying idea is the same. Scientists believe meth hijacks the brain. The Christians believe it hijacks the soul. Meth is said to overwhelm us like a terrorist attack. Nowhere is the possibility considered that meth doesn't hijack anything, but simply inserts itself into the circumstances of a person's life, and it's up to that person to determine what the outcome, either negative or positive, will be. There's nothing magical about meth that automatically turns people into addicts. As John Booth Davies writes in *The Myth of Addiction*: "[P]eople take drugs because they want to and because it makes sense for them to do so given the choices available, rather than because they are compelled to by the pharmacology of the drugs they take." Character is destiny. And never is that more true than when it comes to meth. Still, the Christians may be on to something when they say the key to beating a serious meth dependency is to achieve some sort of spiritual awakening, what might be called a transcendence of self.

Bill McLemore looks like a bouncer at a biker bar: a big, barrel-chested man with a shiny, shaved dome, a gray beard, and a complex web of tattoos depicting skulls, bullets, and daggers that snake up his chunky arms. The last thing you would mistake McLemore for is a minister of God. But every Monday night, McLemore holds meetings at Springfield's Salvation Army Community Center that attract a regular crowd of thirty to forty recovering meth addicts, who sit on folding chairs in a nondescript, fluorescent-lit space and listen to McLemore preach while he stands next to a cardboard cutout of Jesus.

A few minutes before the meeting is scheduled to begin, I'm sitting with McLemore in a side room, when he rolls up his sleeve to show me a tattoo he himself had inked. McLemore learned the art of tattooing during a lengthy stay in prison. "See that eagle?" He points to a remarkably vivid image of the regal bird with its wings outstretched on the inside of his left arm. "See the lines on the wings? That's the veins I used to shoot dope. If I was high, I would just look for the line and I'd know where to hit the vein."

I compliment him on the intricacy of the design. He thanks me and says: "I used to have a big following in the tattoo world back when it was mainly drunken sailors and bikers."

McLemore's life story sounds like something from a Johnny Cash song. Even as a young boy growing up in Dodge City, Kansas, McLemore had a reputation for violence. Other kids' parents wouldn't let their children play with him after he savagely beat a playmate with a hammer. "I hurt him real bad," he recalls. "I was a crazy little kid."

Horrible things happened to McLemore in his early teens. He claims he was sometimes forced to sleep in a chicken house during the winter and nearly froze to death. He also says he was sexually abused after he was put in foster care. At the age of seventeen he joined the Marines but was discharged after he attempted to hang himself with a sock. Back home in Kansas, he began selling drugs, mainly meth, pot, and acid. "I liked selling drugs because of the control it gave me over other people," he says. An attempt to collect a drug debt earned him a one-year sentence for robbery. The one-year sentence turned into five and half years after he broke out of state prison twice, the first time only to turn himself in a few days later, the second time when he had only eleven days left on his sentence.

McLemore continued to sell drugs while in prison. He would cajole women he knew to swallow small balloons of drugs and then get them to retrieve the balloons in the visitor's bathroom. While inside, he put his time to good use by earning a college degree in horticulture, not because of any innate love of nature but because he wanted to grow marijuana when he was released.

After prison, McLemore ended up going into the tattoo business. "I found out that the tattoo world and the drug world went hand in hand," he says. He owned a string of ink parlors that stretched from California to Kansas, which he used as fronts for a sizeable meth-distribution operation. He would buy the drug in San Diego or in Tijuana and transport it back to Kansas hidden in his motorcycle. One time, he and a rival band of dealers got into a gun battle in the parking lot of a Dallas hotel over a large consignment of meth both groups wanted to purchase. "I've had guns stuck to my head," he says. "I've had bullets fly past my ear. But I never killed anybody, thank the Lord."

McLemore, by now a full-fledged meth addict, came to Springfield in 1996, just as the Nazi dope craze was taking off, and learned how to cook meth using anhydrous ammonia. "I moved to Springfield to get away from meth," he laughs.

Probably the worst thing he ever did was expose his stepchildren to the drug. "I used to tell people what sort of father would I be if I gave my kids bad dope?" he says. "That's how Satan uses meth to take hold of your mind. Instead of feeding my kids, I gave them dope to shut them up."

McLemore credits Steve Box with inspiring him to finally conquer his meth addiction. Three years ago, he attended one of Box's *Meth=Sorcery* rallies. McLemore had gone to the rally to humor his wife, who was also addicted to meth. As soon as the event was over, he planned to meet with a friend to pick up a quarter of an ounce of dope. But that plan was permanently put on hold, says McLemore, when he opened the church door, felt a strong breeze brush past his face, and heard a voice in his ear saying, "It's time."

"I immediately began to cry," he says. "I looked in the room and there was all these people I sold drugs to, people I did drugs with, people that I ran around with. I remember thinking, 'Man, I can't let these guys see my crying,' but I couldn't stop. I cried through the whole service and for weeks afterwards."

McLemore claims he hasn't touched meth since.

Most of the people—both the fresh-faced youngsters and the grizzled old-timers—who come to McLemore's Salvation Army meetings have done time in prison because of meth. Nearly all of them have undergone various court-mandated treatment programs and none of them worked. The state of Missouri has expended much time and money trying to get these people to clean up, but nothing seems to stick; not the one-on-one counseling, not the self-esteem seminars, not the 12-step programs. "I've been twelve-stepped to death," one of the attendees says. Typically, they complete a program, and within hours of leaving are getting high again. For many of the folks here tonight, Jesus is their last resort.

"Medical science says they can't get you off meth," McLemore tells the audience. "Guess what? They're right. They can't. God is the only one that can heal you."

Methamphetamine has a reputation as an easy drug to get addicted to and a hard drug to quit. "Nobody uses meth just once" is a commonly heard antimeth slogan. "Meth Is Death," a Web site aimed at teenagers sponsored by the Tennessee District Attorneys General Conference, claimed "99 percent of first-time meth users are hooked after the first try," a statement so obviously ludicrous that the Web site was recently forced to take it down. Counterintuitive as it may seem, doctors say nicotine is the most habit-forming substance, since cigarettes are the only drug where the majority of users become dependent. We're asked to believe that meth possesses magical powers so seductive, so irresistible, that hardly anybody can escape its embrace.

Federal statistics tell a different story. Every year, the Substance Abuse and Mental Health Services Administration interviews seventy thousand people aged twelve and over about their drug, alcohol, and tobacco intake for the National Survey on Drug Use and Health. That information is then extrapolated to come up with "prevalence estimates" for particular drugs across the whole nation. Despite the obvious flaw that consumers of illegal substances have a natural incentive to lie about their habits, the NSDUH is the most comprehensive set of data available about drug use in America and is widely cited by both academics and journalists. While the 2005 survey estimates that about 10.4 million Americans aged twelve and older (4.2 percent of the population) have tried methamphetamine sometime in their lives, only 512,000 (about 0.2 percent of the population) can be classified as regular users, generally defined as people who have taken the drug at least once in the previous month. That means less than 6 percent of those who have tried meth continue to use the drug. The wide disparity between lifetime use and past-month use strongly suggests that not only is meth not instantly addictive but the average meth consumer is someone who uses the drug sporadically or tries it a few times and then stops. Hardly the stereotypical "speak freak" who is hooked for life. Daily meth users represent not just a small minority of American society but also a small minority of people who have ever tried the drug.

An associated fallacy is that once you've acquired a habit, a meth addiction is almost unbeatable. There's a common myth perpetuated by journalists and members of law enforcement that compared to other drugs, meth addiction is close to being untreatable. Meth is portrayed as a kind of superdrug—more potent and more addictive, and therefore more dangerous than any other drug. DEA head Karen Tandy echoed this sentiment when she told the International Conference on Tackling Drug Abuse in February 2005: "The success rate for treating methamphetamine abuse and addiction is shockingly low, a one-digit success rate."

In reality, if you look at the figures, methamphetamine is no harder to kick than heroin or cocaine, which still means it's very difficult—a long, grueling, and often unrewarding slog. People do quit meth all the time under the auspices of professional counselors, but at nowhere near the rate drug-treatment professionals would have you believe. Relapse rates are high for all forms of treatment, no matter what the approach and what the drug. The dirty little secret of the drug-treatment industry is that for the majority of people recovery programs don't work, at least if the goal of treatment is long-term and complete abstinence. It's estimated that well over half of all meth addicts, even after going through numerous programs, will continue to use. According to the CSAT Methamphetamine Treatment Project, the highly touted Matrix Model—an intensive and expensive sixteen-week behavioral therapy program originally invented in the 1980s to treat cocaine addiction—shows a 60 percent drop-out rate, and of those who complete the program slightly more than half remain meth free twelve months later. Imagine a cure for tuberculosis that healed only a quarter of those afflicted with the disease; that wouldn't be regarded as much of a medical breakthrough. And the Matrix Model is one of the more successful programs for treating meth addiction. (Where formal treatment programs do show success is in reducing, though not completely eliminating, problem drug use. The government-funded Drug Abuse Treatment Outcome Survey [DATOS] found that the overall drop in the use of any illegal drug following treatment was often quite dramatic. It's also true that the longer you stay in a program, the more likely you are to give up drugs for good.)

You don't have to go as far as the controversial psychiatrist Thomas Szasz (*The Myth of Mental Illness*)—who once quipped to journalist and author Will Self, "Putting drug addicts in treatment centers is somewhat like confining people with tuberculosis together and then getting them to cough over one another"—to realize that there's a large population of addicts out there that mainstream medicine has failed to reach.

Enter the Jesus folks. For many years now, so-called faith-based drug treatment has been a favorite cause among right-wing politicians, one of the centerpieces of George W. Bush's "compassionate conservatism" campaign. (Bush credits religion with helping him quit alcohol.) The Jesus approach is said to have a proven track record of success in getting addicts to stop using drugs. God, not government, is the answer to addiction, according to supporters. They claim that faith-based programs not only work better than secular programs but do so at a fraction of the cost. But in a 2001 article in the *American Prospect*, journalist Eyal Press debunked some of these claims. According to Press, in 2000, then U.S. Representative Jim Talent (D-MO) contended on his Web site that faith-based programs "have a 60–80 percent cure rate," next to the "6–13 percent success rate" for conventional treatment programs and they cost "only $25–$35 a day," compared with "$600 a day for conventional treatment programs." Talent claimed he got his figures from the National Institute on Drug Abuse, but the organization denied he got the data from them, saying that the role faith plays in drug treatment was still inconclusive. Teen Challenge, one of the most well known and controversial of the Christian rehab organizations, routinely boasts that it has the largest success rate of any existing drug program—more than 80 percent of the people who complete the program stay off drugs. But Press pointed out that the 80 percent figure is based only on the people who complete the program. According to the article, less than 20 percent of those who start the program go on to finish.

The fact of the matter is that beyond anecdotal evidence, nobody really knows just how effective faith-based treatment is compared to its secular counterpart, which is somewhat surprising given the millions of federal tax dollars being pumped into these groups. No reliable studies as yet exist on how successful religious groups are in helping alcoholics and drug addicts stay clean and sober. Studies do exist showing that regular churchgoers have lower incidences of drug and alcohol abuse than in nonchurchgoers. But whether once someone is addicted, religion makes any difference, is still a moot point. In the realm of drug treatment, where failure is the norm, it makes sense to allow the Christians to take a stab at the issue. But in the end, the Christian approach is no more likely to solve America's meth problem than the temperance movement cured America of alcoholism. The riddle of addiction—why some people become addicted to drugs, while others can get just as high yet walk away relatively unscathed—is wrapped up in the mystery of human desire. Until someone finds out how to untangle that knot, all forms of treatment, whether religious or otherwise, are likely to remain at best partial solutions.

"No nation has succeeded in treating its way out of a major cocaine or heroin problem," write University of Maryland's Peter Reuter and University of Chicago's Harold Pollack in their paper "How Much Can Treatment Reduce National Drug Problems?" And the same is probably true of methamphetamine.

"Treatment is bullshit," says the brash young DEA agent as he steers the car down U.S. 65 out of Springfield to the nearby country music resort of Branson, a town that sells itself as "America's Family Destination." It's a kind of Las Vegas without the sin and where, according to my federal escort, half the restaurant workers are on crystal meth. Outside the window, the rolling green hills of the Ozarks extend as far as the eye can see, an undulating blanket of verdant loveliness whose forested folds hide many a meth lab. "You know why treatment is bullshit?" he continues. "Because that's where they go to learn to be better cooks. It's like finishing school for them." That's the kind of tough talk you'd expect from a DEA field agent, the sort of cynical take you often hear from cops on the liberal mantra that professional medical help is the solution to America's drug problem. Except the cooks I talked to said exactly the same thing. "I liked going to treatment," one of them said, "because I could catch up with the latest meth recipes."

"It's weak-minded people, that's all it is," says the agent. "Weak-minded people," he repeats.

One of the most common ways that people quit drugs is through the exercise of their own free will; this is called "spontaneous recovery." Treatment specialists don't like to admit it ("Relying on spontaneous recovery to cure a meth addiction is like relying on winning the lottery to pay your rent," one psychiatrist told me), but every year thousands of addicts quietly and successfully overcome their addiction on their own without the help of professional counselors or self-help groups, and then they move on with their lives. People reach a point where they decide the costs of their drug taking outweigh the benefits and decide to stop. And then, without fanfare or public attention, they do so. These people, according to Robert Granfield and William A. Cloud in their fascinating book *Coming Clean: Overcoming Addiction Without Treatment*, are "our next door neighbors, our colleagues at work, and our relatives. They are our teachers, our doctors, our lawyers, and our social workers. They build our houses and they figure our taxes. . . . In effect, they are the proverbial elephants in the room that nobody sees." What they are not are former addicts who have made a career out of their recovery.

Though there are no statistics that I am aware of, if meth addiction is like other addictions, it's probable that just as many people have quit the drug through self-recovery as all the treatment programs combined. (Some researchers estimate that as many as 80 percent of alcoholics quit booze on their own.) If you can quit on your own, say the 12-steppers, you didn't have the disease in the first place. But that's the point. People who self-recover reject the idea—which is really a metaphor—that addiction is a disease and refuse to let themselves be defined for the rest of their lives solely by one aspect of their personality. To them, addiction is not some incurable disease but a bad habit that they've outgrown, something that they did in the past but have now chosen to leave behind.

Equally clear, however, is the fact that there are those who do need some sort of help, whether it be vaguely religious like 12-step programs or more secular in tone like behavioral therapy. The problem is that sometimes the so-called cure can make the so-called disease even worse. Time and again, in interview after interview with meth addicts, I was surprised just how many of them complained that the major drawback of conventional treatment programs, including the 12-step approach, was that too much time was spent talking about the drug, which served only to further whet their appetites. "By the end of a meeting, I'd be sweating bullets," one said. "I couldn't wait for the meeting to end so I could rush home and cook some dope." It's not hard to see why a bunch of fiending tweakers sitting around in a circle swapping war stories might actually enflame, not dampen, their desire to do the drug.

At first I thought this was the result of coerced therapy. Many of the meth addicts I met had been forced into treatment by judges in drug courts who gave them the option of going into a program or going to prison. And who wouldn't choose the former over the latter? But if you look at the figures, people who enter treatment of their own volition and people who enter treatment because they're forced to will succeed or fail at pretty much the same rate. No, the real problem was the content of these programs. "You constantly reminisce the drug," said another former meth addict. "You sit there and talk all the time about meth—remember when me and her used to go out and steal Sudafed from Wal-Mart, remember when we shot that big dose in our arm. You freak out, constantly thinking about it."

The other thing that came up frequently was how the meth addicts spent much of their time in treatment learning new techniques to manufacture the drug. Proponents of self-help groups and 12-step programs often cite the sense of comradeship that such programs engender among drug users; instead of feeling isolated and alone, addicts can find strength in each other's struggles. But community isn't necessarily a good thing when it comes to kicking meth. Self-help groups can easily turn into chemistry classes. "I learned how to make red phosphorus and turn it into white phosphorus and just how dangerous it was when I was in treatment," was a typical comment.

Talking to the Jesus folks in Springfield, three points soon became clear. First, the Bible reading is really a kind of distraction. It serves a useful purpose by stopping them from fixating on methamphetamine. Jesus helps them take their minds off the drug. Second, it fills an existential void and gives them a sense of purpose beyond their own selfish desire to get high. And third, their newfound faith imbues their up-to-now chaotic lives with a narrative structure. Ruin followed by redemption—an old storyline, perhaps, but one that still plays well in the Ozarks.

Age, as much as anything, is a factor in why junkies retire their habits. After so many years, users simply get tired; they "mature out," as sociologists say. While the forty-seven-year-old Bill McLemore credits Jesus with his miraculous recovery, he seems like he was ready to quit anyway. Jesus just provided him with the plotline.

Bible thumping and casting out demons might seem like a poor substitute for professional counseling, but the Jesus approach does appear to have a beneficial effect among some of the chronically addicted. Obviously, it's not going to work for everybody. But as I traveled across the American Bible Belt doing research for my book, Steve Box's tome *Meth=Sorcery* came up again and again in conversation among former addicts, especially the veteran needle junkies, the ones who had been addicted five, ten, fifteen years or more, the ones whose habits had proven resistant to conventional treatment but who had read the book and finally found the motivation to quit. McLemore claims that he and Box have helped thousands of meth addicts "quit" the drug. I doubt that figure is accurate.

But as one woman in Tennessee said: "I went through a dozen different treatment programs and all they did was make me want to do more meth. It wasn't until I read *Meth=Sorcery* in prison that I finally summoned up the courage to stop using for good."

Sitting in Ruby Tuesday sucking on a plate of ribs, Stanley Harris effuses about his newfound love of Jesus, but it's the 12-step program that he credits with saving his life. "Are you hip to the Big

Book?" he asks me. At first, I thought he was talking about the Bible, but then he explained that he was referring to the other Big Book, the founding text of the Alcoholics Anonymous movement that has been adapted to treat other forms of addiction and which Harris was introduced to during a stay at Sigma House, a local treatment center. Detractors often lambaste 12-step as a cult. But I suspect that it's precisely its cultlike properties—the intense focus on a single goal, the rigid, almost paramilitary discipline, the oft-repeated mantras—that make it so popular.

When I met Stanley he was six months into the program. He had completed the first step—he admitted he was powerless in the face of his addiction. Then he went on to the second step—he embraced the idea that a power greater than him could cure his illness. And then the third step—he surrendered his life to that higher power, which in his case meant Jesus. Recently, he had just completed the eighth step—he'd made an inventory of all the people he'd hurt, including his wife and children, and he had apologized to them all.

Unlike the other recovering Christian meth addicts I met in Springfield, Harris didn't undergo some sort of blinding religious epiphany, a Paul-on-the-road-to-Damascus moment, a cathartic turning point. His is a slow and grueling journey to sobriety that is still in its early stages. No one method works for everybody, he says. Sometimes a combination of methods is best.

Studying the Bible helps, but the practical advice contained in the Big Book helps more. Harris admits he often has cravings, frequently feels RID (restless, irritable, and discontented), as they say in AA meetings. "For those times when you really want to get high, just studying the Bible isn't enough," says Harris. "That's where the Big Book comes in."

Who knows if Stanley will permanently kick his addiction? But he's optimistic. "If you combine the practical side of this thing with the spiritual side of this thing, I believe it's possible to beat this drug," he says, and then smiles a toothless grin.

CHAPTER THREE

COOKING CRANK WITH UNCLE FESTER

GREEN BAY, WISCONSIN

was expecting some kind of Goth ghoul, a Dr. Frankenstein type ("More power, Igor!") or a mad scientist bent on world destruction. After all, the man I was about to meet is a veritable legend among kitchen chemists the world over. The very sound of his name causes DEA agents, some of his most avid readers, to become prickly. "The most dangerous man in America," the now-defunct *George* magazine once dubbed him, albeit half-jokingly.

So imagine my surprise when a mud-splattered white Jeep Cherokee—one adorned with bumper stickers that read BRING OUR TROOPS HOME AND PUT THEM ON THE MEXICAN BORDER and POLITICIANS PREFER UNARMED PEASANTS—pulled up to the curb at the Austin Straubel International Airport and out popped Archie Bunker.

"Hi, I'm Steve Preisler. Welcome to Green Bay."

A balding, middle-aged man with brown, leathery skin who sports a ginger walrus moustache, Steve Preisler is a regular working stiff. During the week, he toils nine to five as an industrial chemist at an electroplating factory in a blackened building down by the rail yard. He lives modestly in a two-story wood-frame house in a quiet blue-collar neighborhood. When he gets home in the evening, he enjoys playing with his kids, eleven-year-old Casey and eight-year-old Alyssa—that is, when they're not staying with their mother.

For relaxation, he enjoys quaffing a cold brew while watching a Green Bay Packers game or catching a wrestling match at his local sports bar. "Wrestling isn't fake, people are," he likes to say. Every year, he quits smoking for a month to train for the Green Bay marathon, and then starts up again after he runs the race.

He admires Pat Buchanan, doesn't much care for liberals, and writes letters to the local newspaper complaining about multiculturalism, which he claims is leading America to ruin. He thinks the government should get serious about cracking down on illegal immigrants, who he blames for stealing jobs from real Americans. (When he farts, he doesn't try to disguise the act but lifts up his leg like a dog about to urinate and announces to the world: "There you go, cutting some cheese again.")

Steve Preisler could be any guy in any blue-collar town in any state in America. Except, late at night, once the kids are asleep and the house is quiet, he sits down at a battered old computer and taps out word after incendiary word, producing a string of controversial books published under the nom-de-plume Uncle Fester, among them *Silent Death*, a how-to guide for budding terrorists and assassins that teaches the ins and outs of making such deadly substances as botulinum, ricin, and sarin gas ("the poor man's atom bomb"), the same book used by the Japanese cult Aum Shinrikyo when it staged the 1995 gas attack on the Tokyo subway; *Vest Busters*, a step-by-step manual on how to create Teflon-coated bullets (so-called cop-killers) intended to pierce Kevlar vests, a slim but notorious volume that angered police organizations nationwide when it was first released in 2000; and his most famous tome, now in its seventh edition and with over a hundred thousand copies sold, *Secrets of Methamphetamine Manufacture*, a do-it-yourself handbook to making crystal meth covering in great detail "the many and varied synthetic routes" to cooking the drug, from methods that yield stash amounts to full-scale industrial production.

It's not technically illegal to publish such information in this country, even if that information seems to aid and abet criminal activity. Though Congress did consider passing a law in the 1990s that would have outlawed instructional drug books like Fester's, *Secrets of Methamphetamine Manufacture* is "for information purposes only. Neither the author nor the publisher intends for any of the information in this book to be used for criminal purposes," as the disclaimer at the beginning of the book says. This legal fig leaf is rather contradicted by passages like the following, in which Uncle Fester advises would-be meth cooks on how to avoid DEA surveillance when buying chemicals:

A very common and quite stale trick is for the narco swine to place a radio tracking device in the packing materials surrounding jugs of chemicals purchased by suspected drug manufacturers. If such a device is found it is cause for clear thinking action, rather than panic. It is best not to smash such a transmitter, but rather keep it in hand, and toss it into the back of another pickup truck at a stoplight.

Also included in *Secrets of Methamphetamine Manufacture* are other handy tips to deter drug agents. "A nice addition to any underground laboratory is a self-destruct device," he writes, sounding like Martha Stewart—if Stewart were a bomb-throwing anarchist. "This consists of a few sticks of dynamite with a blasting cap, held inside an easily opened metal can. If Johnny Law pays an uninvited visit to his lab, the underground chemist lights the fuse and dives out the window."

Secrets of Methamphetamine Manufacture—along with it's companion volume, *Advanced Techniques of Clandestine Psychedelic and Amphetamine Manufacture*—are generally regarded as the holy books of modern-day clandestine meth manufacturing, so much so that mere possession of these volumes has been used as evidence in numerous drug cases. One such case attracted nationwide attention and became a cause celebre in March 2000, when agents from a local drug task force raided a meth lab in a trailer park on the outskirts of

Denver. Inside the trailer, agents found Uncle Fester's *Advanced Techniques,* while outside in the trash, they discovered a receipt from the Tattered Cover Bookstore, an independent bookseller that is something of a venerable institution in Denver. Seeking to prove that the owner of the trailer had bought Fester's book from Tattered Cover, the police tried to force the bookstore to release the sales records, but the owner refused. Eventually, in what was seen as a major victory for the First Amendment and privacy rights, the Colorado Supreme Court sided with the bookstore. (Even if the cops had won, it would have done little to help their case, as it was later revealed that the meth lab operator had actually purchased a volume about Japanese calligraphy.)

"I'm proud to say that Uncle Fester has done more than anybody else to turn cooking meth into what it is today—a national pastime," Preisler boasts.

Except for a few entertaining passages like the ones quoted above, *Secrets* is mostly page after page of chemical formulas and jargon. If you don't know the difference between a tube furnace and a vacuum adaptor, Fester's book will make little sense. The author recommends at least two semesters of college-level chemistry to fully grasp the contents. And this may be why Fester is still free to write what he does: How could you get a jury to even understand Fester's work, let alone convict him for his writings?

Preiesler says he hasn't manufactured any product in years. Despite the rumors that he keeps a secret lab hidden away somewhere to try out new recipes, he claims he's a law-abiding, upstanding member of his community. It's a perverse tribute to American liberty that Fester can get away with writing this stuff, even in the wake of 9/11. In most other countries in the world his books would have been banned or he would have been locked up long ago.

"There's not much we can do about him," one cop told the *Green Bay Press-Gazette.* "As far as we know he's not breaking any law."

Maybe it's something in the soil, but Wisconsin is a state that has provided a fertile breeding ground for a bounteous crop of misfits and oddballs. Liberace was born here and so was cannibal killer Jeffrey Dahmer. Wisconsin is known as the home of a number of important outsider artists, including Fred Smith, who constructed over two hundred life-size figurines out of concrete and beer bottles and displayed them in his Wisconsin Concrete Park near Phillips; and Dr. Evermore and his science-fiction sculpture park just outside Baraboo made out of scrap metal and discarded bits of machinery. But none were stranger than Ed Gein (the model for Norman Bates from *Psycho* and later Leatherface from *The Texas Chainsaw Massacre* and Buffalo Bill from *The Silence of the Lambs*), who lived in the farming community of Plainfield, thirty miles west of where Steve Preisler was born, and famously tailored a whole wardrobe made out of human skin donated by his victims.

Preisler was always a little peculiar. He grew up on the family farm in the quiet country town of Dale, about fifty miles outside of Green Bay, and when as a kid adults asked him what he wanted to be when he grew up, he replied: "I want to be a gladiator." He was disappointed when he found out that the gladiatorial arenas were no longer in operation. During high school, he earned the nickname "Psycho," when as the captain of the wrestling team he bit an opponent in the chest. Preisler proudly shows me his red varsity jacket festooned with wrestling medals, with the moniker neatly stitched on the left breast.

"That's a great wrasslin' name," he says. "Almost as good as the Undertaker, but not quite."

It's tempting to link the strange turn that Preisler took in later life to the very ordinariness of his early surroundings. Dale was a small corner of rural America settled by the descendents of German, Irish, and Dutch immigrants, where the cows outnumbered the people and where one day was pretty much the same as the next. There was a feed mill, a couple of taverns, a small grocery store, and not much else. One of five siblings, he was up at five thirty every morning to milk the cows, after which it was time for school, followed by more chores when he got home in the evening. "Being a farmer is a seventy-hour workweek," he says. "I worked as hard on that damn farm as I do at my miserable day job." A smart and inquisitive kid who developed an early interest in science, he spent what little free time he had devouring his father's *Encyclopedia Britannica*, one volume after another.

Preisler's eccentric ways followed him to college in Milwaukee, where he studied chemistry and biology at Marquette University, a well-regarded Jesuit college with a reputation for rigorous courses and teachers who worked the student body hard. Preisler conducted his first-ever clandestine chemistry experiment when he began making fifteen-milliliter batches of nitroglycerine in his dormitory room. "It's quite entertaining stuff," he recalls. "Stick a bit of toilet paper into the nitroglycerine and put on a pair of goggles, grab a hammer and whack: 'Boom.' " The loud explosions and the plumes of red gas coming from his room earned Preisler another nickname, "Uncle Fester," after the character in the *Addams Family* television show who liked to blow things up.

Preisler soon grew bored with making explosives. He wanted a bigger challenge, something more difficult to manufacture. Preisler wasn't a big druggie. He sometimes smoked pot and took the occasional tab of LSD, but beer was his favorite intoxicant. Nevertheless, the idea of making methamphetamine intrigued him ever since he had started to visit a local head shop about a mile from campus called Pipe Dreams, where he would buy issues of the underground comic *Dr. Atomic*, in which the eponymous mad scientist would embark on drug-addled science-fiction adventures with his pot-smoking hippie sidekick, Billy Kropotkin.

As well as marijuana bongs and chemicals for freebasing cocaine, the store also sold a number of early clandestine chemistry primers, which Preisler purchased and read. He was sorely disappointed with the guides. For one thing, they contained no references to the scientific literature, so he was unable to do additional research in the college library to verify if these recipes would even work. He vowed that one day he would write his own book, complete with legitimate scientific sources for the formulas, just like in a regular chemistry textbook.

Throwing away the shoddily written tomes, Preisler embarked on his own research, scouring chemical abstracts and patent literature, and eventually he came up with a recipe for making meth he thought would work. "You could obtain chemicals pretty easily in those days, and the ones I couldn't buy I could pilfer from the college lab," he says. "I already had a collection of glassware and equipment. It seemed like a fun project and I was curious to see if I could manufacture it."

Preisler brought together a bunch of his friends to gather the necessary ingredients, and once he had everything he needed, he began: After reacting phenylacetic acid with acetic anhydride and sodium acetate to produce phenyl acetone (a.k.a. P2P), he vacuum-distilled the precursor, then used the Leuckardt-Wallach reaction to react methylamine with formic acid, and two days later, voilà— a quarter-pound batch of 98 percent pure methamphetamine. Preisler and his buddies kept some for themselves and sold the rest on campus. And so began a five-year-long bender, with Preisler using the drug nearly every day and manufacturing it every few weeks.

After graduating from Marquette in 1982, Preisler took a job at a company making polymers for roof coating. After six months on the job, one day a couple of plainclothes detectives appeared at his workplace. When Preisler was leaving the plant, the detectives pounced just as he got in his car. He was arrested after the police found an ounce of meth in a Gerber baby food jar hidden beneath the front seat of the car. Next, they swarmed down on the meth laboratory that he had set up in nearby Menesha and carried off all the glassware—round-bottomed flasks, distilling columns, and crystallization equipment, some of which bore traces of the drug.

"One of the people who was part of our little crank social club got busted, and rather than take his penny-ante bust he ratted out everybody," explains Preisler.

After two hung juries, Preisler eventually accepted a plea deal— five years in the big house for conspiracy to manufacture and distribute a controlled substance. In those days, drug laws were less harsh. Given the size of Preisler's operation, anybody convicted of such a crime today would likely receive ten to twenty years.

He was housed at the Waupun Correctional Institution with murderers and rapists. Prison embittered Preisler, souring him against authority in all its forms. "I met some interesting characters there but mostly they were a really dense bunch; most couldn't even write their own names," he says. He spent his days alternately being bored with his surroundings and pissed off that his freedom had been taken away from him for what he saw as little more than an interesting chemistry experiment. He became determined to exact some measure of revenge but was stumped as to how.

Then, one night, he was watching Barbara Walters on television when, just like in the comic books, a lightbulb lit up over his head, "Barbara had her panties in a twist about what she kept calling 'terrorist publishers,'" says Preisler. The now-defunct underground publisher Paladin Press had just put out the notorious book *Hit Man: A Technical Manual for Independent Contractors*, by Rex Feral—a guide on how to become a killer for hire and fulfill murder contracts. Nearly a decade later, in 1993, the book was allegedly used by one James Perry to carry out a triple murder in Maryland. The families of the murder victims sued and demanded millions of dollars in compensation, claiming that the book "aided and abetted" Perry's crimes. Eventually Paladin settled out of court and agreed to stop publishing *Hit Man*. But at the time of the Walters segment, books on how to commit murder and mayhem were freely available.

"I looked at Barbara and thought, 'I know how to piss you off,'" says Preisler. "I yelled down the cell block and asked a guy if I could borrow his typewriter."

It took Preisler three and a half months to write the first draft.

When he finished, he mailed the typo-ridden manuscript—complete with cover page listing the author as Uncle Fester—to Paladin's main rivals, Loompanics, the Port Townsend publishers best known at that time for Eddie the Wire's *Complete Guide to Lock Picking*. Eighteen months later, in 1987, Uncle Fester's *Secrets of Methamphetamine Manufacture* was published and proved an immediate success, soon becoming Loompanics's best-selling book.

Up until Uncle Fester's book came along, methamphetamine recipes were jealously guarded secrets—esoteric knowledge known only to a few initiates, mainly outlaw bikers and few assorted lowlifes. "The book helped create a new market for meth," says Preisler, who served three and a half years in prison before being released. "It was the first published material that told you how to make meth that actually worked."

I ask him if he was surprised that meth manufacturing had become such a popular pasttime, in part because of his book. "Not at all," he replied in his rusticated Wisconsin accent. "That was my intention from the very start. I was hoping, 'Oh, you didn't like me cooking crank? Well, how would you like to deal with ten thousand just like me?' Right from the beginning, it was intended as a big 'fuck you' to the authorities that put me in prison."

You could say that the history of clandestine chemistry—defined here as regular chemistry twisted for means both nefarious and otherwise—began with whoever first came up with the idea of distilling a poison to surreptitiously dispatch a rival. Other early examples of clandestine chemistry might include alchemy, witchcraft, and fermenting alcohol. Indeed, you could argue that clandestine chemistry foreshadowed legitimate chemistry.

But all this is mere speculation. The roots of modern-day clandestine chemistry, however, are certain. This phenomenon began in early 1960s California, when it became increasingly difficult to simply turn up at a doctor's office claiming to be afflicted by some mystery ailment and score a supply of methamphetamine. In response, a number of speed labs began springing up in the San Francisco area and in the hills around San Diego to meet the needs of this new black market. This pattern repeated again a couple of years later when Sandoz Laboratory withdrew LSD and the first illicit LSD labs then popped up, and yet again in 1965 when Parke-Davis withdrew the powerful dissociative phencyclidine and the first PCP labs surfaced.

Prior to the 1960s the major drug clandestinely prepared was heroin. But illicit drug labs really took off in this country with the speed-lab phenomenon. By 1968, one study estimated that there were five to ten large-scale labs operating in the Bay Area alone, supplemented by an unknown number of smaller mom-and-pop operations.

"A speed laboratory," Dr. Roger C. Smith wrote in his seminal 1968 study, "The Marketplace of Speed: Violence and Compulsive Methamphetamine Behavior," "may range from a well-organized, highly efficient operation, capable of producing five to twenty-five pounds of speed per week consistently, to a kitchen or bathroom in a small apartment, producing less than an ounce per week, to a college chemistry laboratory where a student produces speed only occasionally, when he needs money or feels the chances of detection are slight."

The large labs had skilled chemists to prepare the product— unlike today, when meth recipes have been so simplified that practically anybody can learn to be a meth cook. Back then, you didn't need to be Einstein, but you did need to know how to read a chemistry textbook and operate a professional laboratory to successfully manufacture the drug.

A 1970 paper by J. W. Gunn et al in the *Journal of Forensic Science* commented: "It appears that the illicit production of dangerous drugs has become an intellectual and professional challenge to many individuals associated with their misuse. Some of the more knowledgeable and experienced chemists have achieved clandestine production which approaches commercial scale."

The article added, "Many of these clandestine manufacturers are as well aware as any graduate student of chemistry how to use scientific literature as a resource."

Before Uncle Fester, the first clandestine chemist to receive any public notoriety was Owsley Stanley, a Kentucky blueblood and the man of whom it was said he "did for LSD what Henry Ford did for the motor car."

"God's secret agent," hippie guru Timothy Leary once called him.

Stanley and his associates became famous for churning out hundreds of thousands, if not millions of tabs of high-quality acid with color-coded names like Orange Sunshine, Purple Pie, Yellow Smash, Blue Cheer, and White Lightning. But Stanley actually got his start in the clandestine lab business after the scientific whiz kid was introduced to methamphetamine while studying at the University of California, Berkeley. He liked the drug so much he decided to manufacture it for himself.

According to *The Brotherhood of Eternal Love*, a book by Stewart Tendler and David May,

> [Owsley] persuaded his girlfriend . . . a chemistry student . . . to use her term practical project to make a hundred grams. The project was a great success, persuading Owsley . . . to open the Marine Methedrine Factory in a shop on Virginia Street, close to the campus. However, Methedrine [the brand name for methamphetamine] was proscribed; early in 1965, the police swooped to close up the laboratory in the shop's bathroom, and seized all of Owsley's equipment and chemical stores. They took away jars of what they thought were the finished product, only to discover on analysis that the chemicals were not Methedrine and were in fact quite legal. They had captured drugs that were on their way to becoming

Methedrine, while the finished product was actually locked away
in the boot of Owsley's car which they did not search.

Rattled, but undeterred, Owsley escaped to Los Angeles and used the profits from his meth business to set up his famous LSD lab. Just how much LSD he produced is unknown. But powerful "Owsley acid" flooded the Bay Area, and practically overnight he became a hippie folk hero.

Owsley was the man who first introduced the Hells Angels to the world of clandestine labs, a move that would end up changing the very nature of the business. After he met the group through the author Ken Kesey at one of Kesey's trippy parties, Owsley employed the Angels to distribute and sell his products throughout the Bay Area. Pre-Altamont, some hippies had formed an unlikely alliance with the Hells Angels. Blame it on a bad case of radical chic, but some saw the Angels as a kind of community police force. Owsley gave the Angels raw LSD crystals and they turned them into LSD tablets that sold on the street for anywhere from three to five dollars a pop. On a good week, they could make $70,000 and up.

"The move was quite propitious," writes Yogi Shan in his paper "Clandestine Chemistry Primer," "for the previously aimless socio-pathic group, motorcycle gangs being hierarchically, sociologically, and logistically ideal for the purpose of large-scale drug trafficking."

Some Angels earned so much money dealing Owsley acid that they traded in their Harleys for Jaguars and Cadillacs. Owsley's introduction opened the door for the Hells Angels and other motorcy-cle gangs to eventually dominate with violence and intimidation not just the trade in acid but also in methamphetamine.

While methamphetamine isn't the only drug produced in clandestine labs, it's far and away the most popular because, compared to MDMA, PCP, and LSD, the stimulant is relatively easy to make and even easier to sell. For a three-year period in the mid-1970s, at the height of the angel dust craze, PCP labs outnumbered meth labs, but by the end of the 1970s over half the clandestine labs seized by the DEA were producing meth. Federal drug agents as early as 1968 had created a watch list of materials used in clandestine chemistry, but by the late 1970s the DEA had become so alarmed by the rising number of illicit labs being seized that they started to set up storefront operations—government-owned chemical supply houses—to keep tabs on clandestine lab operators. In 1983, in testimony before the U.S. House of Representatives Select Committee on Crime, a former lab operator revealed that with a paltry investment of only $200 and overhead of only $1,800 per month, he earned a profit of $360,000 a year. The operator had never taken a chemistry course in his life; instead, he had learned how to make meth from his cellmate while serving time in prison.

With the advent of the Internet, clandestine chemistry came out from the shadows and into the full glare of the media spotlight. What was once forbidden knowledge, a field of endeavor shrouded in myth and legend, became the subject of much discussion on Web sites and in Internet chat rooms. Any motivated user with a modem and a computer could now download recipes for making a wide variety of synthetic drugs. As a result, meth manufacturing went from being a minority pastime to a popular craze.

There were a number of Web sites devoted to kitchen chemistry, many of them now closed, but the most famous was The Hive. The Hive was set up in 1997 as an information exchange mainly for chemists interested in manufacturing Ecstasy, but it also featured a separate forum on methamphetamine called "Stimlants." (The two drugs are not that dissimilar chemically.) The Hive was a genuine cultural phenomenon, attracting thousands of chemists, from amateurs just starting out in the field to experienced practitioners, who flocked to the Web site to engage in often heated discussions about such topics as how best to extract the pseudoephedrine from pills and which was better—P2P meth or ephedrine-based meth. The Hive even spawned its own unique lingo. "Bees" were clandestine chemists, "dreaming" was the process of making drugs, and "honey" was the final product of their efforts. The acronym SWIM (Some-body Who Isn't Me) is said to have originated with The Hive and was widely used by those who posted as a way to try and avoid any legal ramifications. UTFSE (Use The Fucking Search Engine) was another common acronym employed against newbies who had stumbled onto the site and were asking stupid questions that had already been answered in previous posts.

The Hive was the brainchild of Hobart Huson, a Texan better known in the drug world as Strike, the author of three books on clan-destine chemistry—*Total Synthesis, Total Synthesis II,* and *Sources*—which give detailed instructions on not only how to make Ecstasy and methamphetamine but where to buy the chemicals. In 2001, NBC's *Dateline* ran a segment on The Hive, revealing for the first time publicly Huson's name and that he was also the proprietor of Science Alliance, a chemical company that law enforcement suspected was providing glassware and chemicals to drug manufacturers. Not long after the *Dateline* segment aired, Huson was arrested after one of the largest Ecstasy labs ever discovered in this country was raided in an industrial park in Escondido, California. The lab, which the DEA es-timated was capable of producing up to eight million dollars' worth of Ecstasy a month, was hidden in a forty-foot shipping container outfitted with a ventilation system, the only access to which was through a false bookcase in an adjoining Internet pornography busi-ness. Authorities claimed that the lab operators bought the materials to make Ecstasy from Science Alliance and learned how to make the drug by reading Huson's books. Huson cooperated with authorities in return for a reduced sentence and supplied information about his customers to the authorities. This led to several other arrests, includ-ing the indictment of two Duke University students who were trying to set up an Ecstasy lab in their dorm room. Fearing that the DEA was now running the operation, the bees abandoned The Hive in droves, and the Web site shut down for good soon afterward.

C landestine chemistry isn't just synthesizing drugs, though. The kid making fireworks in the garden shed is a clandestine chemist. The backwoods hillbilly brewing moonshine in the forest is a clandestine chemist. The witch cutting herbs to cast a spell is a clandestine chemist. Members of Al Qaeda are clandestine chemists, too. And that's the real reason for the current stink about methamphetamine, according to Uncle Fester.

"This is why meth cooks scare the living hell out of the authorities," says Steve Preisler. "The same skills used to make crank could just as easily be put to use making explosives. It's all kitchen chemistry. The skill base is the same."

What happens when such knowledge falls into the hands of dangerous fanatics was well illustrated by an incident that happened in the summer of 1994, when an unknown group staged a nerve gas attack in the city of Matsumoto, Japan, killing seven people and injuring 144. The Japanese authorities were perplexed not just about who carried out the attack but the exact nature of the nerve agent employed. A source in the Japanese military tipped off TV Asahi about an American expert on such matters who lived in Green Bay, Wisconsin, and a camera crew and reporter were dispatched to Uncle Fester's humble home. Preisler ended up appearing on Japanese TV dressed in an orange hazmat suit, demonstrating how to manufacture nerve gas in his messy kitchen. "I didn't actually make the gas; I just pretended to," he assures me.

The television reporter showed Preisler copies of the lab reports concerning the incident, which he studied for hours. It soon became obvious to him that the agent used was sarin—a colorless, odorless liquid discovered by the Nazis and said to be five hundred times more toxic than cyanide gas. Becoming equally clear was the realization that whoever carried out this attack was familiar with Uncle Fester's *Silent Death*. The production method utilized was almost exactly the same as the one detailed in his book.

As would later be revealed, the Aum Shinrikyo doomsday cult was behind the Matsumoto attack. Nine months later cult members released sarin in the Tokyo subway system, killing twelve people and hospitalizing more than five thousand others, though Preisler thinks the Japanese were lucky: The casualty count could have been higher.

"They should have made it in an aerosol," he told one journalist at the time, "but that wasn't covered in the edition they had."

The cultists had been stockpiling large amounts of the deadly substance in preparation for a coming war with the West and had used Uncle Fester's book to manufacture the chemical. After the trouble in Tokyo, Uncle Fester's name came up during senate hearings in Washington, when John Sopko, a member of the U.S. Senate Permanent Subcommittee on Investigations, highlighted the role that *Silent Death* had played in the attack. "Uncle Fester is the dark side of Yankee ingenuity," he told *George* magazine. "The man is a menace to society."

I asked Priesler if it bothered him that *Silent Death* was used as a blueprint to launch an attack that killed and injured so many innocent people. "It wasn't my intention when writing the book to have some crazy foreign cult blow up the subway, if that's what you mean," says the proudly provincial Preisler, who has never flown on a plane or left the country and who has lived his whole life in the same state. "But it didn't disturb me. It happened over in Tokyo, and Tokyo always gets destroyed in the Godzilla movies."

Preisler likes being Uncle Fester. He gets pleasure from the fans that show up unannounced on his door step and ask to snap pictures of him with their cell phones. When they urge him, "Fester, do your cackle again," he always obliges: "Ha-ha-ha-ha-ha-ha." He loves seeing his name in the paper and he likes receiving e-mails from readers: "Uncle Fester, can you help me fix my batch?" or "Uncle Fester, you're my hero." Some of the electronic missives he gets are obviously from amateurs. One of them writes: "Is 0.6 ounces the same as 6 grams? I can't seem to get the answer from anyone." Others are well tutored. Preisler shows me another e-mail, this one from Pedro in Brazil, a self-described "disgruntled medical student," who wanted to corner the Brazilian market by making tons of meth. He had already bought a fermentation vessel from a winery and had a good source for P2P in Argentina, but he was having trouble getting hold of enough Raney nickel, a metal sometimes used as a catalyst in meth production, and wanted Fester's advice on an alternative route. Preisler claims he's just an ordinary working-class guy, but if that were really true, one suspects he would go out of his mind with boredom. Clearly, he enjoys his cult status, but he admits it has a downside.

Preisler's reputation among his neighbors, one of whom had already started a petition to have his kids taken away and have him removed from the neighborhood, plunged to an all-time low when he appeared on the cover of the *Green Bay Press-Gazette* six weeks after 9/11 accompanying a story headlined: "Uncle Fester: Menace or Genius?" In the story, Fester was quoted saying not to worry about the anthrax scare that was happening at the time: "Anthrax in the hands of the bin Laden crew is just a little more dangerous than the boogeyman. The bin Laden crew has proved incapable of effectively using this tool."

"They were trying to turn me into Osama bin Preisler," he complains.

When he goes out to jog, Preisler claims the local cops take the opportunity to rummage through his trash looking for incriminating evidence. "They think I'm still cooking meth," he says. The police obviously haven't read *Secrets of Methamphetamine Manufacture,* which features a section entitled "The Telltale Trashcan" that warns meth cooks not to put any empty ephedrine bottles, Sudafed packets, or disassembled lithium batteries in their garbage.

One incident particularly infuriated Preisler. In 2003, one of his brothers was getting married when police crashed the wedding reception. "I never found out which branch of the gendarmes it was, but they were trying to make a murder case," Preisler explains. "My brother's former wife was poisoned at her workplace and she died. Someone spiked her water with paint-thinning solvent. They'd already caught and convicted the perp. But they thought Fester might be involved somehow.

"Classless bunch of fucks," he mutters.

Since the incident, his relationship with his three brothers Richard, Frank, and Fred, which was always somewhat strained, has gotten even thornier. "My brothers, jealous fucks as they are, disapprove strongly," he says. "They think what I do is unpatriotic and contrary to the interests of the government. Dumb fucks. They couldn't string two words together and have it make sense."

"I always assume my phones are tapped," he says. "I always presume my e-mails are read. I'm not doing anything so there's nothing to know."

Preisler's house is a mess. Kiddie junk—balled-up tissues, candy wrappers, abandoned crayons, a pair of children's socks, some underwear, fast-food detritus, and chewed-up toys—litters the floor. Next door in the kitchen Fuzzums the Great Dane and Jersey the Labrador are busy ripping apart the Venetian blinds, while the sink is left to overflow with dirty dishes and empty beer bottles. On a side table lays a pamphlet from the National Alliance, which Fester when quizzed describes as "a civil rights organization for white people," though others prefer the term "hate group." Uncle Fester's books have a fervent following among militiamen and neo-Nazi types. *Silent Death* is a favorite at survivalist expos. Indeed, in 1993, a fifty-four-year-old white supremacist named Thomas Lavy from Arkansas was detained by custom agents at the Canadian border with 20,000 rounds of ammunition, 130 grams of ricin, and a well-thumbed copy of *Silent Death*.

Preisler describes his own political position as libertarian. "I pretty much hate all governments," he says. "They all need a good thumb in the eye. Especially since the media is so manipulated by them."

I'm interested in knowing what he thinks about the Combat Meth Act, Washington's late-in-the-game attempt to stamp out small-time meth cooks, Uncle Fester's fan base. The act requires that retail outlets move all pseudoephedrine products behind the counter. The law also places tight limits on how many pills can be bought per person and demands that customers show ID and sign a log book. Critics charge that limiting pseudoephedrine purchases may close down a number of the small mom-and-pop labs, but they doubt it will do anything to stem the flow of meth from the Mexican superlabs, which already supply most of the meth consumed in this country. The legislation, they say, may end up actually increasing the Mexican cartels' market share.

"I call it the Mexican Mafia Meth Monopoly Act," says Preisler. "I'm not sure what consequences are going to flow out of this Sudafed ban, other than making people go back to brewing P2P meth or giving the Mexican Mafia a virtual monopoly on the meth trade. It's a prime example of beating up on the little guy while ignoring the heavyweights who dominate meth manufacturing."

Preisler puts in a videotape, *Cooking Crank with Uncle Fester*. He slumps on a black leather couch in front of the TV, and his face lights up when he sees himself on the screen. *Cooking Crank* is a low-budget effort, consisting mainly of long, grainy shots of Uncle Fester sitting at a kitchen table and demonstrating a simple method to make methamphetamine. "This is the safe way to make crank," he says on the video. "We don't have explosive hazards and there are no toxic by-products. It doesn't produce plumes of aroma, so the person in the next room will have no idea what is going on." With little more equipment than a beaker, a flask, a sep funnel, some coffee filters, a vacuum pump, and an old Grölsch beer bottle, he shows how to convert 120 cold pills into two grams of the drug.

Step by step, he takes the viewer through a laborious process that begins with Fester grinding up Wal-Mart pseudoephedrine pills in a blender and then soaking them in alcohol to filter out the impurities, and goes on to involve a lot of pouring, stirring, and straining of various chemicals that to the uninitiated looks about as exciting as downtown Green Bay on a Saturday night. Basically, the process consists of two stages. The first phase involves the extraction of the pseudoephedrine from the pills. In the second phase, the pure pseudoephedrine is converted into methamphetamine by mixing it with iodine and hypophosphorous acid in a reaction flask that is then boiled on a kitchen stove, after which the mixture is poured into a beaker. Another flask is filled with hydrochloric acid and connected to the beaker via a tube through which hydrogen bubbles pass into the solution, a process known as "gassing." After the mixture is gassed, it's then evaporated using a vacuum pump, leaving a gooey white mud, which is allowed to air-dry into methamphetamine crystals.

One thing I learned from *Cooking Crank with Uncle Fester* is that it takes twice as long to complete the initial stage of the process as it does to actually cook the drug. The exciting part—the end stage, when heat is applied and the chemicals react and the liquids start to bubble, and the crank starts to appear out of a milky mist—doesn't last very long. The boring part—the initial stage of extracting the pseudoephedrine from the pills—seems to go on forever.

Separating the gunk that accompanies the pure pseudoephedrine is a tiresome chore, made deliberately so by chemists working for the big pharmaceutical companies who have spent years, as well as expended much money and brainpower, coming up with ever more novel pill formulations that are meant to prevent cooks from turning a legitimate product into an illegal drug. What used to be straightforward chemistry—dissolving the tablets in water and then separating the active ingredient from the filler—has become increasingly complex. The various harmless additives that the pharmaceutical companies have added can turn the subsequent reaction into a gooey mess. But every time a new variation of the pills appears on the store shelves, within days Uncle Fester has usually figured out a way to get around the latest chemical barrier thrown up by the big drug companies.

"The end-stage reaction hasn't changed much in ten years," Preisler tells me. "But the pill formulations change every six months. Extracting pills can be quite challenging. But no matter how they formulate it, it can be cracked. These people making crank, they're the most ingenious bunch. Nothing can stop them. Roadblock after roadblock is tossed in their way and they just blow right on though. We've been described as cockroaches; you just can't get rid of us. It's not like a bunch of people sitting around smoking pot; they get wired up and start thinking."

What to Preisler is an intellectual challenge is a toxic nightmare to anyone who lives near a meth lab. What about the hazards of explosions? What about the noxious gases generated during the cooking process? What about the risk of death or serious injury, not just to the cook but to anyone in the immediate vicinity? What about the poisonous sludge left over from the cooking process? It's estimated that for every pound of meth produced five pounds of hazardous by-products are left behind. Preisler believes the warnings about the toxic dangers associated with manufacturing meth are greatly exaggerated. "A typical meth lab is no more dangerous than an auto body shop," he says.

It's not just Preisler who thinks that there's an element of chemophobia—the irrational fear of chemicals—in the media coverage of meth. We've all seen the dramatic television footage of policemen wearing hazmat suits gingerly removing jars of colored liquids from home meth labs as if they were radioactive waste. The impression given is that these labs are mini-Chernobyls waiting to explode and the chemicals contained inside are extremely deadly, "some of the most explosive and carcinogenic substances known to science," as one newspaper report said. But some experts wonder whether the elaborate precautions that police and first responders take when entering a meth lab are more about show than science. "The hazmat suits are bullshit," says Dr. John P. Morgan, a professor of pharmacology at the City University of New York Medical School. "There is some danger, and maybe I'll have to apologize to a lot of EMT workers who have pulmonary damage or terrible skin problems because of exposure to meth labs. But where's the evidence that meth labs are so toxic? At the moment it doesn't exist."

Jeffrey Boles, a chemistry professor at Tennessee Technological University who is doing pioneering work on fingerprinting meth labs, adopts a more moderate tone. "I wouldn't be surprised if seventy percent of the time or more the hazmat suits weren't necessary," he says. "The problem is we don't know. Right now, the level of danger when a policeman or first responder enters a meth lab is unknown. The amount of meth on surfaces or in the air in the residences can vary five-thousand-fold from place to place and from technique to technique and depending on what chemicals you use."

Just how dangerous the cooking process is depends a lot on the method used. While the recipe Preisler demonstrates on the video doesn't seem that hazardous, other methods—especially ones involving anhydrous ammonia or the highly flammable liquid ethyl ether—up the risk factor considerably. Phosphine gas, an unwanted by-product of making meth using the Red P method, is another hazard. A small number of cooks have died from accidentally inhaling the poisonous fumes. But it's not so much the chemicals that are so dangerous as the people handling them, only an estimated 10 percent of whom are trained chemists. The vast majority of meth cooks aren't skilled scientists like Uncle Fester. The less experienced the manufacturer, the more likely an accident will occur.

"The number one reason meth labs explode is careless use of solvents," says Preisler. "To minimize the risk, you should have good ventilation and avoid large spills. Some of the acids can be dangerous to work with, so you should also wear eyeglasses. And be careful with iodine; it can attack your thyroid gland."

As the night winds down and the beer runs low, I ask Preisler about his own experiences taking the drug. While Preisler downplays the pitfalls of making the drug, he's under no illusion about the dangers of chronic, long-term use. Fester has never injected meth, nor has he ever smoked the drug. "Too hard on the lungs," he says. He always took it through the nostrils. The man who did more than any other person alive to popularize meth manufacturing as a hobby, Priesler is now the voice of moderation.

"Meth is a good drug for short-term use, but it makes a lousy long-term companion," he says. "Prolonged use, day after day after day, will wear a person out. It's the type of drug you can do for a couple of days in a row. After that you have to take a prolonged break."

He points to a photograph of a scantily clad female on his computer screen. "See the girls who likes to send me naughty pictures over the Internet? She likes to inject it, and you can see the damage it does to her. She looks beaten. She looks like she's been run through a wringer."

Fester has a message for his fans: "Too much meth is bad for you. There's no arguing about that. It will turn your head into a messed-up puddle of goo."

CHAPTER FOUR

A WONDER DRUG IS BORN

Writers and reporters often correctly characterize methamphetamine as a totally artificial substance, but delve into the earliest history of amphetamine and you'll find that this synthetic drug owes its very existence to the ma huang plant, a yellowish green desert shrub with stalks that resemble the bristles of a broom. Better known to Westerners as *ephedra vulgaris,* or simply "ephedra," the Chinese had for more than five thousand years used the stems of this unprepossessing plant as an herbal remedy to treat a variety of ailments including coughs, colds, and breathing problems. Zen monks consumed ephedra to promote concentration during meditation. Sentries guarding the Great Wall of China ate the plant to stay awake at night. In America, settlers in colonial times used ephedra to treat kidney complaints and venereal disease. Mormon pioneers drank ephedra tea (which they called Jerusalem tea) because their religion forbad coffee.

A big breakthrough came in 1887, when Japanese chemist Nagayoshi Nagai managed to extract the plant's active ingredient, ephedrine, a chemical similar to the adrenaline found in human bodies. This led German scientist L. Edeleano in the same year to synthesize a new compound using ephedrine as a base. He called the volatile liquid phenylisopropylamine, today better known as amphetamine. Since Edeleano had no idea that what he had discovered had any legitimate medical use, or that the compound possessed untapped psychoactive properties, the substance lay largely forgotten for more than thirty years.

During the early 1920s, the pioneering work of K. K. Chen and C. F. Schmidt popularized ephedrine in Western medical circles as a potential treatment for asthma attacks. But there was a problem. The relative scarcity of the ephedra plant meant there was a shortage of ephedrine. This sent chemists scrambling for a synthetic copy. In 1919, a Japanese scientist A. Ogata, who was trying to make a synthetic alternative to ephedrine, had invented a new way of making amphetamine. He tweaked Edeleano's original formula by adding an extra set of methyl molecules and came up with a more potent variant that he called d-phenylisopropylmethylamine, later rechristened methamphetamine. The scientific literature records that Ogata was the first chemist to synthesize methamphetamine using phenyl acetone; the Hells Angels used the same method to manufacture "biker meth," or "prope dope," in the 1960s and 1970s.

"Studies of ephedrine were critical to the development of Western pharmacology," says Dr. John P. Morgan of the City University of New York. "In the search for ephedrine, we ended up making amphetamine."

Amphetamine probably would have remained an obscure substance if it weren't for the efforts of one man. Eight years after Ogata's discovery, Gordon Alles, a young British research chemist working at the University of California, Los Angeles, also was looking for an inexpensive and effective ephedrine substitute when he too resynthesized Edeleano's amphetamine recipe. After testing it on animals, he then decided to try out the substance on himself, and found that when he swallowed the chemical it made him feel less tired, increased his level of alertness and, if taken in a big enough dose, created a sense of euphoria. Alles touted the newly rediscovered chemical—which he called Alpha-Phenyl-Ethyimine, later shortened to amphetamine—as a bronchodilator, a drug that would, like ephedrine, ease breathing by enlarging bronchial and nasal passages. But Alles was also well aware that amphetamine had the potential to serve many other purposes.

Alles didn't invent amphetamine, as he sometimes inaccurately claimed, but he was the scientist who made the chemical ready for the medical market. He sold his formula to the big pharmaceutical company Smith, Kline and French, and they introduced the first ever commercially available form of the drug in America in 1932 as Benzedrine, an amphetamine inhaler, available as an over-the-counter product to treat asthma and congestion.

Within a short time, doctors discovered more and more medical uses for the drug. In 1935, researchers found out that it was an effective treatment for narcolepsy. The next year, Prof. Abraham Myerson of Tufts University School of Medicine advised his colleagues at a meeting of the American Psychological Association to prescribe amphetamine to severely depressed and suicidal patients. Two years later, a Rhode Island doctor named Charles Bradley noticed that Benzedrine had the contradictory effect of calming hyperactive children and in some of them led to "remarkably improved school performance," a finding that would eventually lead to the development of Ritalin. In the same year, the American Medical Association, which raved about "the feeling of exhilaration and sense of well-being" that amphetamine produced, was so impressed with Benzedrine's potential that the organization approved the drug for sale in tablet form via prescription, saying the drug showed promise in the treatment of Parkinson's disease.

There seemed no end to Benzedrine's therapeutic value, no limit to the drug's multipurpose utility—before long, amphetamine was used to treat obesity, epilepsy, schizophrenia, cerebral palsy, hypertension, "irritable colon," "caffeine mania," and even hiccups. The drug was also promoted as a potential remedy for alcoholism, as well as heroin and cocaine addiction, just as heroin when it was first introduced in 1898 was promoted as a cure for opium and morphine addiction. According to Patricia Case's presentation at a national methamphetamine conference held in Salt Lake City in August 2005, one newspaper in the 1940s ran a story headlined "Drug Held Cure for Alcoholism"; a Dr. W. Bloomberg was quoted as saying, "Benzedrine gives a lift like alcohol, but is less harmful." In 1946, a

Long Island toxicologist named Dr. Abraham Freireich reportedly found yet another use for the drug when he revived nineteen people who had attempted to commit suicide with barbiturate sleeping pills by injecting them with massive doses of Benzedrine. In the same year, medical researcher W. R. Bett catalogued thirty-nine different "clinical uses" for Benzedrine. Smith, Kline and French had managed to convince the medical community that Benzedrine was a wonder drug, one with few serious side effects and many possible applications that went far beyond simply being a decongestant.

Yet, as early as 1936, Benzedrine's potential for abuse was starting to become apparent. A study was being conducted at the University of Minnesota on the psychological effects of amphetamine and student subjects spread the word to their friends on campus that this new drug could help them stay up all night to cram for exams. Not long after, some students started to collapse from the effects of the drug. Similar incidents were reported the next year at the universities of Wisconsin and Chicago. *Time* magazine reported in 1937 that "the use . . . of a new, powerful but poisonous brain stimulant called Benzedrine . . . kept college directors of health in dithers of worry."

The first published report of amphetamine addiction appeared a year later, and the phrase "amphetamine psychosis" started popping up in the medical journals. However in 1940, an article in the prestigious *Journal of the American Medical Association* assured physicians that amphetamine showed little or no potential to create addiction in users.

"Amphetamines were unique," wrote Lester Grinspoon and Peter Hedblom in their classic 1975 study, *The Speed Culture: Amphetamine Use and Abuse in America.* "Never before had a powerful psychoactive drug been introduced in such quantities in so short a period of time, and never before had a drug with such a high addictive potential and capable of causing long-term or irreversible physical and psychological damage been so enthusiastically embraced by the medical profession as a panacea or so extravagantly promoted by the drug industry."

One of the great untold stories of World War II is the role amphetamine and methamphetamine played in the conflict. Every side routinely supplied various forms of the drug to their troops in order to decrease tiredness and hunger and to bolster aggression. American GIs consumed an estimated 200 million pills. Amphetamine factories were set up at the naval base in San Diego to supply troops heading out to the South Pacific. Benzedrine tablets even became a standard issue item in field kits alongside soap and bandages.

Across the Atlantic, the Royal Air Force started issuing pills to pilots to keep them awake on bombing missions after a German flyer was shot down and was found to be carrying methamphetamine tablets. The army followed suit, and by the end of the conflict British troops had consumed, according to some estimates, as many as 72 million tablets. A newspaper report from just after the war claimed that RAF pilots fought the Battle of Britain dosed on methamphetamine.

Back in America, Smith, Kline and French ran advertisements in medical magazines trumpeting Benzedrine's contribution to the war effort. One such commercial depicting a group of battle-weary GIs was headlined: "For Men in Combat When the Going Gets Tough." Another advert was addressed to "physicians in the Armed Forces" offering them free Benzedrine inhalers "for his personal use." Yet another one boasted, "Benzedrine inhaler is now an official item of issue in the Army Air Forces."

The Air Surgeons Office called Benzedrine the most effective available drug "for temporarily postponing sleep when desire for sleep endangers the security of the mission."

The Allies consumed mostly regular amphetamine in the form of Benzedrine. But the Japanese and the Germans pumped up their forces an extra couple of notches with the most powerful drug in this category, methamphetamine. The energy that powered the Nazi war machine was supplied by Pervitin, the brand name for the meth tablets that were produced by the Temmler pharmaceutical company in Berlin. After military doctors tested the drug on university students in 1939, the drug was then quickly distributed to soldiers. Between April and July of 1940 alone, the Wehrmacht shipped more than 35 million tablets of Pervitin and another brand, Isophan, to frontline troops in Poland and France. (As far back as 1883, another stimulant, cocaine, had been surreptitiously issued to members of the Bavarian army to test the drug's battle effectiveness.) One military observer noted: "Troops who have been given Pervitin are very useful in modern battle conditions when used in mass attacks."

While a soldier stationed in Poland, the author Heinrich Böll wrote his parents to complain about the living conditions and to ask for a favor: "It's tough out here and I hope you'll understand if I only write to you once every two to four days. . . . Today I'm writing you mainly to ask for some Pervitin." In a follow-up letter, he asked his parents once again to secure him some pills: "Perhaps, you can get me some more Pervitin so I can have a backup supply."

By the end of the war, Nazi chemists were working on a new pill to supply to troops. They code named it D-IX—a dangerous cocktail of cocaine, methamphetamine, and morphine, a mixture that would today be called a speedball, the same type of uptown/downtown combo that killed comedian John Belushi. Knowing the effects of the drug on the human mind and body, it's reasonable to presume that the ferocity of the Nazi Blitzkrieg was fueled not just by a murderous ideology but also by copious amounts of methamphetamine.

Japan also went to war wired on meth. Kamikaze pilots took large doses of the drug before suicide missions. The Japanese government also gave meth tablets to munitions workers to help increase output. Veterans of the war in the South Pacific wondered if the protracted and bloody nature of the battles had something to do with the fact that both sides were high on amphetamines.

In postwar Japan, pharmaceutical companies sold large stockpiles—hundreds of thousands of pounds—of military-made liquid meth left over from the conflict to the public without prescriptions. An advertising campaign targeted the demoralized population, promising them "enhanced vitality" if they took "wake-a-mine," as the ampoules of injectable methamphetamine were known. Oddly, while you needed a prescription to get methamphetamine tablets, the ampoules could be obtained easily at the local store. The result was the world's first major methamphetamine crisis. An estimated 5 percent of the population between the ages of eighteen and twenty-five abused the drug, many of them becoming intravenous meth addicts.

Back in the States, the immediate postwar period saw amphetamine rise to new heights of popularity, just as an unknown number of war veterans returned home with Benzedrine habits. According to Grinspoon and Hedblom, "World War II probably gave the greatest impetus to date to legal medically authorized as well as illegal black market abuse of these pills on a worldwide scale."

Benzedrine would become most widely used not as a treatment for serious illness, but as America's first mass-marketed lifestyle drug. By now, Benzedrine's ability to curb appetites and elevate energy levels was well known among the general public. It was perfectly normal for housewives to use Benzedrine as a diet aid or for fatigued doctors and overworked businessmen to take a pill in order to combat tiredness, as there was little or no stigma attached to doing so. Beginning in 1940, reports began to surface about athletes taking amphetamine to enhance their performance. As early as 1943, more than half the prescriptions written for Benzedrine went to people looking to lose some weight, obtain a bit of a boost, or stay awake for long periods of time.

The Hollywood set loved Benzedrine; the phrase "Hollywood gin" referred to the trendy combination of Benzedrine and alcohol.

The megalomaniacal producer David O. Selznick binged on Benzedrine throughout the making of *Gone with the Wind* to get him through the grueling shooting schedule. One actress on the set later recalled seeing Selznick gobble amphetamine pills "like popcorn . . . crushing up Benzedrine and licking the pieces from his hand, a grain at a time"—which gives a new meaning to Scarlett O'Hara's famous line in the movie: "As God is my witness, I'll never be hungry again."

Theatrical types took the new drug, too. On Broadway, "bolts and jolts" referred to taking Benzedrine ("the popular stay-awake drug," as it was referred to in the press) along with barbiturate sleeping pills. The idea was that one drug knocked you out, while the other jerked you back to life.

The drug was so prevalent that even horses were dosed; in 1945, Cosey, the filly that won the Fairmont Steeplechase, was disqualified after the animal tested positive for amphetamine. Farmers fed the drug to chickens to keep them awake so they could lay more eggs. Not only was amphetamine not a cause for public concern, but it could even be a source of amusement. Witness the popularity of the 1946 boogie-woogie novelty song "Who Put the Benzedrine in Mrs. Murphy's Ovaltine?" by Harry "the Hipster" Gibson.

Yet, the year before that, the *New England Journal of Medicine* had highlighted the case of a forty-nine-year-old alcoholic lawyer who was prescribed Benzedrine and quit drinking only to become an amphetamine addict. He was hospitalized for amphetamine psychosis after suffering delusions that his soldier son—who was serving overseas at the time—was hovering overhead in a helicopter.

Then, in 1947, the first documented abuse of Benzedrine inhalers in the medical literature was reported by R. R. Monroe and H. J. Drell, who conducted an important study at Fort Harrison military prison in Indiana. They found that a quarter of the roughly thousand prisoners surveyed admitted to abusing the inhalers behind bars. By this time, a variety of groups, not just soldiers but also jazz musicians and juvenile delinquents, had discovered that they could catch a major buzz by breaking open the inhalers and dunking the amphetamine-soaked strips found inside into coffee; or by swallowing or chewing the bits of cotton whole. Each inhaler contained 250 mg of amphetamine, enough of a wallop to keep someone high for a day or two. "We used to share the inhalers, sitting in a cafeteria with a cup of hot coffee," recalled writer Herbert Huncke, one of the original Beats. "By the time you got up and walked out you would be a new man. They were delightful, just euphoric. The world was beautiful."

The medical establishment dismissed reports of Benzedrine's addictive potential as atypical, affecting only a tiny minority of people who took the drug. Most doctors continued to believe that Benzedrine was perfectly safe when taken under medical supervision, and they largely ignored the small but growing body of evidence in the medical literature detailing the downside of amphetamine use.

During this period, a modest illicit trade in Benzedrine tablets began to grow alongside the legitimate commercial market, about the same time the word "bennies" (Benzedrine pills) became part of the pop-culture lexicon. Unlike the inhalers, you needed a doctor's prescription to secure a supply of the amphetamine tablets, at least in theory. But for those who didn't have the time or inclination to pay a visit to a physician, a black market was created. One major source of nonprescription pills was the army surplus supplies that were advertised in the back pages of newspapers. People purchased the field kits just for the Benzedrine contained inside. Another source was crooked pharmacists, who for the right price would sell the drug to customers under the counter.

One of the most famous crimes of the early 1950s—the kidnapping and murder of six-year-old Bobby Greenlease—was blamed on Benzedrine after one of the murderers, Carl Austin Hall, admitted he was high on alcohol and bennies when he committed the ghastly deed. Hall explained to investigators how he purchased the drug without a prescription. He would hand the pharmacist a $20 bill and say, "This is my prescription." He added: "For twenty dollars most anyone can buy bennies."

By 1951, federal law required a prescription for all products containing amphetamine, but that did little to halt amphetamine abuse. The newspapers began to notice the growing problem. "Benzedrine Dope Craze Hits Jail" was a typical headline at the time. "What appears to be a harmless medication for clogged-up noses has started a new dope craze that is creeping across the country," another newspaper reported. By 1954, more than half of all U.S. convictions of pharmacists for illegal sales of prescription items involved amphetamine.

Nonprescription Benzedrine tablets were particularly popular among truckers who needed to stay awake at night to finish long hauls. Previously, caffeine tablets and ephedrine tea (so-called Teamster Tea) had done the job, but then drivers started to switch to the amphetamine pills that were freely available from all-night truck stops and gas stations along major trucking routes. While some truckers adamantly refused to touch the stuff, a measure of the popularity of Benzedrine pills among drivers was the number of slang names they used for the drug. "West Coast turnarounds" were so called because a trucker could drive from the one coast to another and back without stopping for sleep. Other slang terms for Benzedrine included "cartwheels," "coast to coasts," and "copilots," the last term supposedly derived from an accident that happened when a driver dozed off, believing his "copilot," actually a sleep-deprived hallucination brought on by the amphetamine, was driving the big rig.

Crisscrossing the country on Benzedrine, truckers effectively started a mobile transcontinental distribution system for the drug, spreading its illicit use across the nation, much like peripatetic "circuit parties" would later spread the use of methamphetamine in the gay community.

Benzedrine had become such a problem in the trucking industry by 1956 that *Time* magazine, in an article entitled "Benny Is My Co-Pilot," reported that many trucking companies were posting signs saying, GET YOUR REST. BENNIES CAN KILL. The same article detailed how two Food and Drug Administration officials posing as truckers and driving a repainted army trailer, spent six weeks making buys of Benzedrine at gas stations, truck stops, and pharmacies in the Charleston-Charlotte-Atlanta area. Forty-two individuals in six states were arrested because of the sting.

The commissioner of the Food and Drug Administration commented in a press release announcing the arrests: "Use of these drugs by truck drivers is particularly dangerous because they so stimulate the driver that he stays on the job long beyond the point of normal physical endurance. His brain tires, his driving judgment and his vision are finally impaired, and a tragic accident sometimes follows."

Nevertheless, amphetamine now became firmly intertwined with the romance of the open road. The drug developed an association with freedom and mobility, an idea that would reach its apotheosis with Jack Kerouac's *On the Road,* a story about an amphetamine-fueled road trip that was written in twenty-one days during a Benzedrine bender. This notion was expanded by pill-popping outlaw biker gangs and was continued throughout the 1960s when the drug became better known as "speed," eventually flaming out in the 1971 cult movie *Vanishing Point,* the tale of a former race car driver who loads up on bennies and leads the police on a cross-country car chase.

The 1950s saw Benzedrine's dominance in the marketplace being challenged by a whole slew of new amphetamine and methamphetamine products, many of which targeted suburban housewives. This was a period of rapid social change, as America became increasingly mobile and hundreds of thousands of people deserted the cities in search of a new life in the suburbs. There was a naïve belief that science and technology could solve all our problems. "Better living through chemistry" was a popular slogan of the time. Everyday items like automobiles and home appliances seemed to hold the promise of utopia. Television and magazines bombarded consumers with images of a perfect lifestyle, especially for women, a number of whom felt trapped and alienated by this often lonely new reality. Amphetamine appeared tailor-made for this new way of living—a synthetic drug for a synthetic environment. It was during this time that amphetamine developed a reputation among psychiatrists as a valuable tool to enforce social conformity, a soft form of mind control.

Leafing through the medical journals of the 1950s, you can't help but be amazed at the sheer number of amphetamine and methamphetamine preparations on offer. There was:

- Smith, Kline and French's Dexedrine, the dextro-isomer of amphetamine isolated from the levo isomer to create the twice-as-powerful dextroamphetamine ("Dexedrine's gentle stimulation will provide the patient with a new cheerfulness, optimism, and feeling of well-being that may again make her life seem worth living").

- Norodin, from the Endo company—just like Burroughs Wellcome's Methedrine, it was pure pharmaceutical-grade methamphetamine designed to cash in on the dieting craze then sweeping the country ("Norodin is useful in reducing the desire for food and counteracting the low spirits associated with the rigors of an enforced diet").

- Desoxyn, from the Abbott Laboratories, more pure methamphetamine ("When she's ushered by temptation").

- Syndrox, another meth product, this one produced by McNeil ("For the patient who is all flesh and no will power").

And then there were the drug cocktails:

- Ambar, a combination of methamphetamine and the barbiturate phenobarbital, courtesy of the Robins Company ("An appetite suppressant strong enough to do the job").

- Obedrin, a mixture of meth, pentobarbital, Vitamin B, niacin, and ascorbic acid from the S. E. Massengill Company ("She calmly sets her 'appestat' [a pun on 'thermostat'] with one daily Obedrin").

- Coricidin Forte, a cold remedy that contained methamphetamine and caffeine, along with the analgesic phenacetin, a substance that was finally removed from the market in 1983 because it was said to cause kidney damage.

Smith, Kline and French even targeted expectant mothers with yet another product, this one called Dexamyl, a mixture of dextroamphetamine and the sedative amobarbital. "You could help her enjoy pregnancy," proclaimed one advertisement with a picture of a sad-faced, visibly pregnant woman standing in front of a refrigerator with a mop and bucket at her feet.

Clearly, these products offered more than just weight loss and extra energy. The real agenda being promoted here had as much to do with women's mental health as their physical girth or stamina. Psychiatrists had known since the mid-1930s that amphetamine was a powerful antidepressant. Indeed, years before Prozac, Benzedrine was the first widely prescribed drug for this purpose. The practice of mixing amphetamine with barbiturates originated with psychiatrists who believed the two taken together were a more effective treatment for depression than amphetamine alone.

Moreover, as well as banishing the blues and boosting energy, amphetamine has another interesting quality—the ability to make boring and repetitive mechanical work seem fascinating and meaningful. Anybody who has spent any time around serious methheads is bound to notice the way they fixate over seemingly trivial tasks. They're happy to spend hours and hours disassembling and reassembling electronic equipment, or cleaning the same spot over and over, or shuffling and organizing the contents of their apartments. Psychologists have a name for this type of obsessive behavior—"punding." Under the influence of amphetamine, the Desperate Housewives of the 1950s were supposed to be transformed into smiling Stepford Wives, eager to cook, clean, and polish all day long without complaint.

In the 1950s, doctors dispensed amphetamines to men, women, and children as if they were Halloween treats. By 1958, the legal production of amphetamine pills had reached an astonishing 3.5 billion, enough to supply every person in America with twenty standard doses. The ones who first turned America onto methamphetamine in a big way weren't the Hells Angels or Mexican drug traffickers, but doctors and psychiatrists working in tandem with the pharmaceutical industry in the 1950s and early 1960s: the same people who transformed amphetamine from an obscure, forgotten substance into one of the most widely prescribed drugs in the history of Western medicine.

"The notion that mass-scale, nonmedical drug use was born in the counterculture of the sixties isn't really true," says Craig Reinarman, professor of sociology at the University of California, Santa Cruz. "Prior to that, the combination of the pharmacological revolution and psychiatry in the nineteen fifties and early nineteen sixties popularized the notion that you could change how you felt, change your view on the world, change your mood, and change your consciousness by ingesting a pill. So, long before marijuana and LSD became part of the counterculture, that idea was out there and it came from medicine."

Beginning in the mid-1950s, however, attitudes had started to change about amphetamine. Public concern about the abuse of the drug was on the rise. Responding to this concern, Senator Price Daniel of Texas held hearings about the drug and commented about reports he'd received concerning "young waitresses who have taken amphetamines and traveled with transport-truck drivers; of older people furnishing them to teenagers, and having sex relations with them; thefts by gangs of teenage boys who used these drugs to bolster their courage and keep them sharp; as well as professional peddlers supplying the amphetamine."

The growing outcry forced the federal Food and Drug Administration to act. While Smith, Kline and French had voluntarily withdrawn Benzedrine inhalers from the market a few years before, a number of other pharmaceutical companies continued to sell over-the-counter amphetamine inhalers under different brand names. In 1959, such inhalers were banned by federal law. Strangely, though, the law applied only to amphetamine and dextroamphetamine, not to the strongest drug in the class, methamphetamine. Within months, the Pfeiffer Company in St. Louis debuted the first ever over-the-counter methamphetamine inhaler, Valo, which contained 200 mg of high-grade meth. Almost immediately, reports surfaced about teenagers in Oklahoma and Missouri who had learned how to extract the meth from the Valo inhaler and inject it into their arms with hypodermic needles.

In the early days of amphetamine production, social disapproval was minimal, whether in America or elsewhere. Smart, successful people—politicians, scientists, musicians, actors, writers, and intellectuals—took Benzedrine. From 1938 onward, the poet W. H. Auden started each day with Benzedrine, a practice he kept up for twenty years. By his own admission, the British prime minister Anthony Eden was on Benzedrine during the Suez crisis. The composer Leonard Bernstein took the drug to stay up all night to write music. The philosopher Jean-Paul Sartre once observed: "The amphetamines gave me a quickness of thought and writing that was at least three times my normal rhythm."

Amphetamine was so socially acceptable in the 1950s that even a confirmed alcoholic like the fictional British secret agent James Bond popped the occasional "benny." "Benzedrine. It's what I shall need if I'm going to keep my wits about me tonight," Bond mused to himself before a card game with the book's villain in Ian Fleming's *Moonraker*.

As late as 1955, Dr. Halsey Hunt, the nation's assistant surgeon general, told the House Ways and Means Committee that amphetamine "is not addicting in the true sense of the word." But as the 1950s turned into the 1960s, the political mood had shifted decisively in Washington. President John F. Kennedy sounded the alarm in 1962 when he identified the abuse of so-called thrill pills—a confusing term that lumped together both barbiturates and amphetamines—as a growing problem among the young. Meanwhile, behind the scenes, Kennedy's personal physician, Max Jacobson, the infamous "Dr. Feelgood," was administering booster shots of methamphetamine mixed with steroids and vitamins to the president to treat an adrenal condition. Singer Eddie Fisher, a friend of Kennedy's, once recalled: "Looking back on it, it's amazing how we all just accepted the fact that the president was taking Dr. Feelgood with him to a meeting that would affect the entire world. The fate of the free world rested on Max's injections. I can still see Max taking a little from this bottle, a little from that one, and 'pull down your pants, Mr. President.'"

Heading the president's call, Senator Thomas J. Dodd of Connecticut launched a crusade against amphetamine pill abuse and estimated that there were 100,000 "seriously addicted pill-heads" in America, with millions more taking amphetamine without medical supervision. Dodd called rampant pill abuse "an unsuspected time bomb ready to go off in every community." The same sort of rhetoric we hear today when politicians talk about the so-called meth epidemic sweeping the nation.

Before the mid-1960s, practically anybody could order huge amounts of amphetamines from wholesale mail-order companies whose only addresses were usually P.O. Box numbers. And practically anybody could sell them to you. The pharmaceutical companies were pumping out so many pills, it was almost impossible to keep track of them all, and large numbers were being diverted to the black market at all points in the supply chain—from factories to wholesalers to pharmacists to doctors. In 1962, one wholesale dealer was found to have forged thousands of prescriptions and managed to obtain over nine million amphetamine and dextroamphetamine tablets from a variety of drug manufacturers all over the country.

The scandal came to a head in 1964 when the news show *CBS Reports* ran an exposé that showed how easy it was to secure large supplies of amphetamine and barbiturate pills. Producer Jay McMullen rented an office and a mailbox, and set up a bogus company. Then he managed to purchase from legitimate drug suppliers over a million pills, worth half a million dollars on the black market, all for the price of six hundred dollars.

Congress cracked down in 1965 when it passed the Drug Abuse Control Amendment, but not before the American Medical Association complained "in the United States at this time, compulsive use of amphetamines and barbiturates constitutes such a small problem that additional legislation to control such abuse does not seem necessary." Some products such as Methedrine and Desoxyn were eventually removed from the market. And companies were required to keep better and more detailed records about where and to whom they were shipping their products, all measures bitterly resisted by pharmaceutical lobbyists and medical organizations. It's no different from today when the pharmaceutical companies fiercely resist all measures to restrict the sale of over-the-counter cold medicines which can be used to manufacture meth.

The law did possess some teeth. Doctors tightened up their prescribing practices. Pill poppers found it more difficult to secure significant amphetamine supplies on the black market and some of them started traveling across the border to Mexico to buy amphetamine. In the same year the law passed, singer Johnny Cash was arrested at the El Paso airport after he returned from Juarez, Mexico, with hundreds of Dexedrine pills in his luggage. Shady operators followed suit. Amphetamines were now shipped to front companies in foreign countries and then either smuggled in or mailed back to the United States. The Chicago Crime Commission reported in 1969 that one small company had shipped 15 million amphetamine tablets to a post office box for a nonexistent drugstore in Tijuana, Mexico. Congress at the time estimated that 60 percent of amphetamine pills legally exported to Mexico returned to the United States via illegal channels, often through Tijuana, which was dubbed Pill City.

But the law did nothing to stop the overproduction of the drug by pharmaceutical companies. In 1967 alone, doctors wrote 31 million amphetamine prescriptions, most of them to women. Amphetamines accounted for almost 5 percent of the total prescriptions written by physicians in the United States. In 1969, two years before amphetamine was outlawed for general use, pharmaceutical companies produced roughly 8 billion amphetamine tablets. The drug companies must have known that these numbers far exceeded the amount needed for legitimate medical purposes, but presumably profits came first.

"There is a pattern in the medical community of optimism about new psychoactive drugs followed by disillusionment," wrote Lester Grinspoon and Peter Hedblom in *The Speed Culture*:

A drug is introduced as "non-addicting"; its capacity to produce dependence is not observed. When evidence of abuse gradually accumulates, legal controls and sanctions are applied, whereupon an illegal traffic arises. Meanwhile, physicians begin to debate whether or not the drug is "truly addictive." In 1898 heroin was introduced as a "non-addictive" cure for opium and morphine addiction, its name derived from the word "hero." Twelve years later, it was already considered more dangerous than the other opiates. Claims of panacea-like powers, harmlessness, and capacity to "cure" other kinds of drug abuse were made at one time or another for morphine, cocaine, and barbiturates.

Yet, what is most astonishing about this deluge of pharmaceuticals that swamped America in the postwar era is how little long-term damage the various pills and potions ended up inflicting. Pre-1970, untold millions of Americans consumed billions of doses, and only a relative handful got into serious trouble on account of their amphetamine use because most people took the drug in moderation. The lesson of this mass-scale chemistry experiment—see what happens when you introduce huge amounts of a powerful and potentially addictive psychoactive substance into the general population—appears to be that amphetamine and methamphetamine taken in calibrated doses are not particularly dangerous.

"It's the dose that makes the poison," said the sixteenth-century Swiss chemist Paracelsus. His point was about to be hammered home as a far more troublesome mode of amphetamine use started to take hold, one that combined the most potent form of amphetamine with the most dangerous way of taking the drug. This new pattern of high-dose abuse signaled the end of amphetamine as a socially sanctioned high, not much different from alcohol or cigarettes, and the beginning of its transformation into one of the most reviled substances in the whole pharmacopeia.

The historical roots of America's current methamphetamine crisis can be traced directly to the Bay Area in the late 1950s, when local doctors began prescribing liquid ampoules of Methedrine and Desoxyn (brand names for methamphetamine) to help heroin addicts, among them a number of Korean War veterans, kick their addiction. Burroughs Wellcome started to manufacture Methedrine tablets, America's first commercially available form of methamphetamine, in 1946 and later introduced an injectable form of the drug.

Crazy as it may sound to the layman today, many physicians and researchers sincerely believed that a suitable treatment for heroin dependency was to substitute a powerful depressant with a powerful stimulant, on the basis that if the patient was going to inject something, methamphetamine was less harmful than heroin.

Other physicians were more motivated by money than medicine. For the price of a visit, unscrupulous doctors—called script writers—would write prescriptions for methamphetamine to practically anybody who wandered in off the street, without even examining them for needle marks. Typically, for less than ten dollars, the intravenous addict would receive a hundred Methedrine ampoules—plus hypodermic needles and sedatives to help with the comedown afterward. A single San Francisco doctor reportedly prescribed twenty-four thousand ampoules of Methedrine to a hundred patients in a single year.

In *Marketplace of Speed,* one intravenous meth user recounted to criminologist Dr. Roger C. Smith how easy it was to get hold of Methedrine in that period:

> *There was a doctor . . . who would write anything for anybody at any time and he was making $7 a visit and on the day we went down there he wrote almost 400 prescriptions at $7 a head. So you can imagine how much money he was making. . . . They used to make caravans down there . . . to his place. You'd get within two blocks of his office and you'd start seeing people you knew from all over.*

In 1968, Dr. Smith, who headed the Amphetamine Research Project at the Haight-Ashbury Free Clinic, conducted a study among local intravenous meth users. Entitled "The Marketplace of Speed: Violence and Compulsive Methamphetamine Behavior," the study explored the early history of mainlining speed, as liquid methamphetamine was fast becoming known.

Up until the 1950s, shooting up methamphetamine for kicks was pretty much unheard of in America, though the practice probably existed in some small form. Intravenous drug users tended to be hopheads or coke fiends. The vast majority who took any type of amphetamine ingested it orally. The drug came in pill or tablet form and was swallowed or dunked into coffee or beer. Injectable Methedrine radically altered the rules of the game. The risk-benefit ratio for amphetamine dramatically changed. The pleasure associated with the drug increased, but so did the danger.

According to Dr. Smith, the first report of intravenous methamphetamine abuse among Americans came from servicemen stationed in Korea and Japan in the early 1950s—not surprising, since the region was awash in supplies of liquid meth left over from World War II. A number of them started experimented with a new type of speedball: instead of mixing heroin with cocaine, they substituted the latter with the less expensive, longer-lasting methamphetamine, which they nicknamed "splash." Servicemen brought the habit home with them when they reentered civilian life.

Smith's study revealed for the first time the underground economy that had sprung up in San Francisco surrounding the trade in Methedrine. Heroin addicts who used to make a living by burglary or bad check writing or credit card scams could now support themselves solely by selling meth. Addicts would get the drug from their doctor, keep half the meth for themselves, dilute the other half, and sell the rest on the street. Some San Francisco pharmacists even sold meth injections over the counter without a prescription, or on the basis of forged prescriptions, or on a telephoned "prescription" from a user posing as a physician. We're used to thinking of heroin addicts and so-called speed freaks as two distinct types. But in the Bay Area at the time, heroin users and methamphetamine users crossed over all the time, since much of the intravenous meth use was in the form of speedballs.

The New York Times reported in a story headlined "Addicts Turning to New Narcotic: Officials in San Francisco Cite Methedrine Use," written in the early 1960s: "Among many of the narcotics in the San Francisco Bay Area a new brand of poison is partially supplanting the opium derivatives . . . Methedrine."

The injectable methamphetamine scandal hit the headlines in 1962, when a crackdown resulted in the arrest of a number of doctors for illegally prescribing the drug to patients. During the first six months of 1962, doctors had prescribed over half a million hits of injectable meth. The next year, California's Attorney General urged the pharmaceutical companies to voluntarily withdraw injectable meth from the market in his state. Both Burroughs Wellcome and Abbott Laboratories complied and stopped distributing the Methedrine and Desoxyn ampoules to Californian pharmacies, though injectable meth was still available in area hospitals, which now became the target of thieves.

The crackdown inadvertently helped create the modern-day meth lab. In 1962, or thereabouts, a group of ex-servicemen who had picked up a taste for speed in Korea supposedly set up the first illegal laboratories in the Bay Area. They correctly anticipated there would soon be a shortage of the drug in West Coast cities because of the withdrawal of Methderine and Desoxyn ampoules from the market. It wouldn't be the last time that well-meaning efforts to restrict methamphetamine usage would end up opening the door for black market racketeers.

These original laboratories were relatively sophisticated operations. Skilled chemists produced pounds of the drug at a time. A regular source of the precursor chemicals used to make methamphetamine was a necessity. One informant in the Smith study described how he procured the key chemical phenyl acetone (P2P):

I just walked into this store. Two old people work there who are about fifty years old and they look at you and smile and say "what would you like?" and you would say that you want P2P and so on, and you would run down the list and they would say "fine, come back in two days." These two people knew what was going on, because one time we went in there and they asked how the crank was coming. It completely blew my mind seeing this sweet old lady asking how the crank was coming.

Clandestine speed production also received a boost from 1965's Drug Abuse Control Amendment, which made it more difficult to divert legal amphetamines to the black market. As Edward M. Brecher noted in his 1972 book, *The Consumers Union Report on Licit and Illicit Drugs*:

> *Before . . . 1965, illicit speed labs had to compete with diverted legal tablets priced at wholesale as low as thirteen or fourteen tablets for a penny—75 cents per thousand. When enforcement of the Drug Abuse Control Amendments at least partially dried up those low-priced legal supplies, the door was opened for profitable illicit manufacture on a far larger scale.*

Methamphetamine achieved much notoriety in the late 1960s as the substance that soured the counterculture dream. "The drug that even scares hippies," claimed *Life* magazine. Meth was blamed for destroying the peace-and-love vibe in San Francisco's Haight-Ashbury district, the world capitol of hippiedom. As early as 1965, poet Allen Ginsberg called methamphetamine "a plague on the whole dope industry" and complained that "all the nice gentle dope people are getting screwed up by the real horror monster Frankenstein speed freaks who are going around stealing and bad-mouthing everybody."

The year 1967's fabled Summer of Love catapulted Haight-Ashbury's population of Flower Children to national prominence. Mainstream magazines were full of stories about this new radical antiestablishment movement that preached free love, protested consumer society by living in communes, listened to mind-bending music, and smoked pot and gobbled LSD with abandon. Busloads of middle-aged tourists on six-dollar "hippie hop" tours—billed as "the only foreign tour within the continental limits of the United States"—began to descend on the area, where they would briefly disembark to snap photos of the residents, as if a new type of exotic wildlife had just been discovered. As one journalist at the time put it, the Haight-Ashbury went from "scene to seen."

All this publicity also had the effect of encouraging a new generation of young people to flock to the Haight to experience the lifestyle for themselves. These kids—often from working-class backgrounds, unlike the mainly middle-class hippies—didn't arrive wearing "flowers in your hair," as the famous Scott McKenzie song "San Francisco" advised. To outsiders they resembled hippies, with their long hair and shabby clothing, but they shared little of their political idealism or spiritual concerns. These newcomers—dubbed "hoodies" to distinguish them from genuine hippies—took any drug they could get their hands on, but generally favored Methedrine over more introspective substances such as pot and LSD. Unruly in their ways and sometimes prone to violence, they scared the hell out of the original Flower Children, many of whom escaped by decamping to the countryside.

Dr. David E. Smith, the medical director of the Haight-Ashbury Free Clinic, described the hoodies in his 1971 book, *Love Needs Care*:

> *Hoodies consisted of young whites in their late teens and early twenties . . . most of these youths had criminal records . . . and were known in the Haight only by aliases and nicknames. They were uneducated and lacking any religious or mystical interest and had traveled from across the country to exploit the Flower Children they assumed were still living there. These young people were tough and aggressive. Instead of beads and bright costumes, they wore ankle chains, leather jackets and coarse, heavy clothes. Instead of ornate buses, they drove beat-up motorcycles and hot rods. Although they used many drugs on occasion, they dismissed*

*the hallucinogens as child's play and preferred to intoxify them-
selves with opiates, barbiturates and amphetamines.*

The mood changed dramatically in the Haight as so-called crystal palaces—filthy flophouses where speed freaks went to shoot up
Methedrine—began to replace the original communes. Recipes for
making the drug circulated in the neighborhood. By 1968, it was
estimated there were five to ten large-scale methamphetamine laboratories operating in the Bay Area, each pumping out about twenty-
five to a hundred pounds of product per week. They were
supplemented by a larger number of small-scale kitchen labs, which
had also started to spring up. An upsurge in gang rapes, drug
ripoffs, and murders were all blamed on Methedrine, even if other
drugs such as heroin, alcohol, and barbiturates were involved. A
gang called the Methedrine Marauders appeared on the streets,
whose sole purpose was to stick up speed dealers. By the end of
1968, the area had turned into what the Free Clinic's David E. Smith
called "a teenage slum."

In late 1968, a crime occurred that seemed to sum up all that had
gone wrong with the Haight. Two days after Christmas, nineteen-
year-old Ann Jiminez, who had traveled to the neighborhood from
Washington State to be part of the hippie scene, was raped and murdered in a crystal palace on Waller Street by a group of speed freaks.
David E. Smith described the murder in *Love Needs Care:* "There she
was accused of either knick-knacking or intentionally stealing a
pair of boots. She was then beaten, forced to have anal sex with six
bikers while three girls looked on, had her hair clipped, her body
shaved—and was left to die with obscenities scrawled on her body
in lipstick."

By now, meth had spread beyond its West Coast stronghold, and
was becoming increasingly popular in the rest of the country. In
New York, shooting up Methedrine became a popular pastime
among the coterie of trendsetters at Andy Warhol's Factory. In 1967,

the double murder of a hippie couple in the basement of a Lower East Side tenement was widely blamed on a meth deal gone wrong. Methamphetamine was demonized as much in the underground press as in the mainstream media. An editorial in the Boston alternative newspaper *Avatar* opined: "Speed kills. It really does. Amphetamine, Methedrine, etc. can, and will, rot your teeth, freeze your mind and kill your body. The life expectancy of the average speed freak, from the first shot to the morgue, is less than five years. What a drag." (This spurious assertion is still repeated today.) *The Village Voice* described speed freaks as "a distinct group, semi-quarantined and often regarded with apprehension by fellow hippies."

"At the end of the 60s," writes the historian Philip Jenkins in *Synthetic Panics: The Symbolic Politics of Designer Drugs,* "methamphetamine already had the distinction of being one of the very few drugs stigmatized within a drug culture of seemingly limitless tolerance."

In 1968, in response to what many hippies saw as a blight on their community, the Do It Now Foundation launched the famous "Speed Kills" campaign designed to educate young people about the dangers of methamphetamine. A number of musicians were enlisted to speak out in radio commercials, among them Frank Zappa, who said: "It will mess up your liver, your kidneys, rot out your mind. In general, this drug will make you just like your father and mother." The campaign alerted youths to the dangers of the drug, but ignored the possibility that in publicizing the dangers, the adverts might be increasing the drug's attractiveness. The idea that you were dancing with death when you did meth only served to heighten the appeal for some. In 1970 a report on the problem by Canada's Commission of Inquiry underscored the point:

Some "speed users" who inject almost suicidal doses of methamphetamine into their veins without any regard for their safety and health, may actually be trying to test the truth of the youth slogan

"Speed Kills." The role of the doomed person who is at once a martyr sacrificing himself, a hero braving the confrontation with certain destruction, and a gambler playing dice with death, is a role that seems to have a strong seductive pull for some young people who are morbidly hungry for compassion, admiration, and excitement.

By the end of 1969, all the avenues for securing amphetamines for recreational use—doctor's prescriptions, the diversion of legal drugs at the wholesale level, methamphetamine labs—were coming under growing scrutiny by various authorities. Then, in 1970, after a ferocious battle with the American Pharmaceutical Association, the United States Congress passed the Controlled Substances Act, which divided drugs into different schedules depending on their perceived potential for abuse. Liquid methamphetamine became a Schedule II drug and was eventually moved into the Schedule I category, the most restrictive grouping. Regular amphetamine was initially listed as a Schedule III drug, but then was recategorized as Schedule II. The law had the effect of severely curtailing licit amphetamine production making it illegal to possess without a prescription and effectively outlawing the drug as a recreational high. In 1958, American pharmaceutical companies produced approximately 165,000 kilograms of amphetamine. Because of the law, by 1973 that number had dropped to roughly a thousand kilograms. Doctors continued to prescribe some types of amphetamine, but in greatly reduced amounts, and they stopped prescribing Benzedrine altogether.

The pharmaceutical companies could no longer make enough amphetamine to supply the black market, so outlaw biker gangs, who had been involved in the meth trade since the 1960s, stepped up production. Throughout the 1970s, students continued to use what they thought were amphetamine pills to stay up at night and study, but in reality what were sold as speed pills were more often than not look-alike tablets in the shapes and colors of the original drugs but which contained no amphetamine, only caffeine or ephedrine. Moreover, as often happens in the drug world, cultural fashions shifted. Downers, not uppers, became the new fad. Many Methedrine addicts rediscovered heroin. And barbiturates and sedatives became the preferred way to get high.

By the end of the 1970s, an old drug had started to make a comeback. The war against speed opened the door for the resurgence in cocaine, which became the new stimulant of choice. And methamphetamine became associated with the rural poor and with gay people in San Francisco, many of whom continued to use the drug throughout the '70s and '80s.

After the arrival of crack cocaine in the 1980s, which was linked to inner-city minorities, cocaine started to lose its allure. Then, as cocaine slipped down the social scale, methamphetamine began to come back into fashion again. A drug that possessed in the 1970s a distinctly unglamorous reputation as a cheap high for badass bikers and rough-hewn hillbillies started to slowly regain its popularity among the middle class.

CHAPTER FIVE

CHEMICAL CONTROL

WASHINGTON, D.C.

Flying home from a meeting in Europe one day with his boss, Gene Haislip was thirty thousand feet above the Atlantic, comfortably cocooned in first class, when the idea struck him: a comprehensive plan to attack the illegal drug trade in America at its source by curtailing the supply of raw materials needed to both process and synthesize the drugs. The year was 1985 and Haislip, a well-groomed if understated figure sporting windowpane glasses, whose soft features made him look more like a kindly uncle or a college professor than the number three man at one of the most feared agencies in the U.S. government, headed the Drug Enforcement Administration's Office of Diversion Control. His main job was to prevent the theft and diversion of prescription drugs onto the black market, but he saw an opportunity to expand his role by taking on illegal drugs as well. Haislip was that rare thing—an intellectual in an agency known more for its brawn than its brains. A strategist rather than a tactician, he had long been interested in the regulatory control of dangerous substances ever since he studied international law and atomic energy at George Washington University in the mid-1960s.

Haislip was perfectly aware that nearly every illegal drug, with the notable exception of marijuana, needed some sort of chemical to process the product before it was finished. Take cocaine as an example. The extraction of the active ingredient in the coca leaf to produce coca paste, and then the purification of the paste into cocaine base, and the subsequent conversion of the base into the final product requires large amounts of common industrial chemicals, including potassium permanganate, hydrochloric acid, ethyl ether, and acetone, most of which at the time were exported to South America from the United States. In 1982, the DEA had discovered hundreds of barrels of ether being shipped to cocaine laboratories deep in the Amazon jungle of Colombia. Similarly, poppies are converted into heroin using acetic anhydride, a commonly used chemical in the manufacture of plastics and synthetic fibers. The way Haislip figured the situation, if drug manufacturers found it more difficult to secure these chemicals, less of the product would be produced, prices would rise, and as a consequence demand would fall. At least in theory, you could stop drug abuse before it even happened.

Haislip drew up two lists. One list catalogued so-called essential chemicals—substances essential to the manufacture of plant-derived drugs like cocaine and heroin but which do not become part of the molecular structure of the drug in question. The other list contained precursor chemicals—substances used to make synthetic drugs such as PCP, LSD, and methamphetamine and, unlike essential chemicals, do become part of the finished product's molecular makeup. There were at least two hundred different chemicals used in the manufacture and processing of illegal drugs and Haislip knew he couldn't control them all. But he was convinced that if he could persuade Congress to pass a law restricting the dozens he had identified, that would go a long way toward seriously disrupting in one fell swoop the entire drug trade in America. Two of the chemicals Haislip targeted were methamphetamine precursors: ephedrine and pseudoephedrine.

Once back in his office at the DEA's headquarters, directly across from the Pentagon, Haislip called a meeting with his top staff and informed them: "Gentleman, today we're going to make a new law and this is what it's going to look like."

Haislip's idea was not entirely new. The government had previously tried this type of supply-side intervention when they attempted to close down the biker meth labs by making P2P a scheduled substance, though with mixed results. Also, the feds already monitored from the factory to the pharmacy potentially dangerous prescription drugs such as morphine. But what Haislip was proposing was far more wide-ranging than anything tried before. Instead of a war on drugs, Haislip envisaged a kind of bureaucratization of drugs: In place of quasi-military tactics, he proposed driving drug dealers out of business by wrapping their chemical suppliers with red tape. By making manufacturers and sellers keep detailed records of the sales of bulk amounts of these chemicals, the government could create a paper trail that would allow them to track any illegal diversion directly to the drug dealers. Much as the Banking Secrecy Act of 1970—which first required banks to start reporting deposits over $10,000—had allowed the feds to detect laundered drug money. But what on paper seemed like an elegant and simple solution to a vexing and complex problem proved in practice far more difficult to implement than Haislip imagined.

As he tells the story today, Haislip's ambitious recommendations were met with scant enthusiasm by many in the agency. Some of his colleagues were worried that they would be inundated with clerical work. In their opinion, busting drug dealers in the field, not filling out forms, was what the agency did best.

"The reactions in many quarters were pretty negative at first," Haislip recalls in his chirpy, Virginia-honed drawl. "DEA people are often focused primarily on tactical tasks. Identify, collect evidence, and arrest. That was the way to do things. When I started this, chemical control was virtually unheard of. But luckily there were a few senior people at the agency who thought broader than that."

Haislip had already achieved some success with this approach when he won an undisputed victory in the fight against drug abuse by cutting off the street supply of a sleeping pill that today is largely forgotten because of his efforts. The 1970s is often remembered as the disco decade, the time when cocaine became affluent America's recreational stimulant of choice. But the 1970s was as much a decade devoted to the abuse of prescription sleeping pills and sedatives. Quaaludes—and to a lesser extent barbiturates like Seconal and Tuinol, not to mention Valium, the so-called housewives' heroin—were just as popular as well as being considerably cheaper to purchase than cocaine. Roughly four million Quaalude prescriptions were written each year, a large proportion of which ended up being sold on the streets, where the drug was popular among teenagers too young to drink alcohol. *New York* magazine writer Julie Baumgold testified before a Senate committee in 1973 and described scenes she had witnessed at New York "juice bars" with names like the Zoo, the Inferno, and the Fudge Factory, where zombielike youngsters zoned out on Quaaludes and heavy metal music, clung to the walls, or collapsed on the floor.

As a result of the congressional hearings on the abuse of the drug, methaqualone—the powder used to make Quaaludes—was reclassified as a Schedule II controlled substance. Doctors wrote fewer prescriptions. Quaalude abuse appeared to decline for a while, but then shot up again with the appearance of so-called stress clinics. After legitimate medical practitioners began to shy away from prescribing the drug, shady operators skirted the law by setting up storefront operations in major cities such as New York, Miami, Boston, and Chicago. They employed barely qualified doctors who gave patients cursory physical examinations and then issued them prescriptions for Quaaludes.

Popular initially with rock and roll fans, by the middle of the decade the drug had migrated onto the disco scene, where it was used both as an aphrodisiac (it was said to make some women exceptionally horny) and to help smooth the comedown after snorting too much cocaine. "Luded out" became a popular phrase to describe the drowsy high and loss of motor coordination, similar to being drunk, that the drug induced. The drug drew further infamy in 1977 when it was revealed that the film director Roman Polanski plied a thirteen-year-old girl with champagne and Quaaludes before having sex with her in Jack Nicholson's whirlpool.

In the late 1970s and early 1980s, the Drug Abuse Warning Network (DAWN) reported dramatic increases in methaqualone-related emergency room visits and fatalities. "We got regular reports from DAWN, and from month to month there were three drugs that kept changing places as number one: heroin, cocaine, and methaqualone," says Haislip. "That's how serious it was."

Haislip wondered where all these Quaaludes were coming from. The raw powder was manufactured in a number of plants in Europe and China. But there was only one pharmaceutical firm in the entire country that made the pills and tablets—the Lemmon Company of Sellersville, Pennsylvania. In 1981, the United States imported less than ten tons of methaqualone powder for legitimate medical purposes, yet in the same year over fifty-seven tons of the powder was seized in or en route to the United States. Haislip was surprised to find out that most of the Quaaludes being consumed recreationally weren't being diverted from legitimate medical supplies in this country, as was the case with the first wave of Quaalude abuse in the early 1970s, but were actually counterfeit tablets being manufactured by Colombian cocaine cartels in labs in the Caribbean and then smuggled into the United States. They looked like the real Quaaludes produced by the Lemmon Company, complete with the firm's logo—but unlike the fake amphetamine pills also common at the time, which often contained little more than caffeine or ephedrine, they were just as potent as the originals.

"What I found out was that about ninety percent of the global production of methaqualone was for the illicit drug trade," says Haislip. "The Colombians had discovered that there was a growing market for the drug in the United States that could be pumped up. It was about a two-billion-dollar-a-year business for the Colombians. They were buying hundreds of tons of this stuff from the manufacturers using go-betweens in Switzerland, and it was all perfectly legal."

Hailsip and his staff traveled to Colombia. In the old port city of Barranquilla, they unearthed a major shipment of methaqualone, complete with paperwork that indicated the powder came from Hungary. Next, they flew to Budapest and after presenting the evidence to top government officials there, they managed to convince them to stop exporting methaqualone altogether. The Hungarian authorities even recalled a shipment of the powder that was already on its way to the United States via Switzerland. In Germany, however, the reception was chillier.

"In Germany, methaqualone wasn't even listed as a controlled substance," says Haislip. "When I went to the Germans, they just said, 'What do you think we can do? It's not against the law here. We can't help you.' Well, after a while, they found out they could help us."

Working in tandem with the State Department, Haislip eventually managed to convince the five major source countries for methaqualone production, including Germany, to place stringent controls on the export of the powder. Meanwhile, back in America, the Lemmon Company voluntarily withdrew Quaaludes from the market, citing as the reason "the increasingly adverse legislative climate surrounding the product and the resulting unjustified negative publicity." In 1984, methaqualone was reclassified yet again, this time as a Schedule I drug, meaning that what was previously available as a prescription drug could now be used only for research activities sanctioned by the government. By the following year, there were so few methaqualone emergency room mentions reported by DAWN (down 80 percent from 1980 levels) that the drug no longer made it onto the top twenty list of most commonly abused controlled substances. Thanks to Gene Haislip, Quaaludes had all but disappeared from the streets and nightclubs of America.

"We beat them," says Haislip. "We turned off the faucet. By using diplomacy and control techniques, we drove the Colombians out of the methaqualone business."

Buoyed by his success in cracking down on Quaalude abuse, Haislip became convinced he could repeat this triumph, but this time on a much bigger scale. He and his staff wrote a first draft of the proposed law and submitted it to Congress in 1986. Haislip's timing was just right. This was the era of "Just Say No," as official hysteria about drugs reached new heights. A powerful tide of antidrug sentiment was sweeping the nation. "Zero tolerance" became the new law enforcement mantra. Worried about crack cocaine, Republicans and Democrats alike competed with each other to see who could come up with the toughest drug laws. This was also the time when the phrase "designer drugs" first entered the public consciousness, along with the fear, stoked by exaggerated reports in the media, about a new wave of sinister laboratory-made concoctions ready to be unleashed on the American public. No wonder the response to Haislip's law was so broad and enthusiastic.

"The legislation whipped through the White House in record time," says Haislip. "President Reagan bought the idea almost immediately. I thought, Hell, they'll be big trouble on the Hill. To my great surprise, there wasn't. There emerged immediately a lot of congressional support on both sides. I had worked a lot in legislation and this was not the way it usually went, especially when dealing with a pioneering law."

Then he adds with a mischievous chuckle, "Well, the pharmaceutical industry didn't like it too damn much, I can tell you that."

The first thing that Allan Rexinger did every day when he got to his office on the twelfth floor of the American Express building on Connecticut Avenue in the heart of Washington, D.C., was to read the *Congressional Record,* the daily account of the proceedings in the House and the Senate. One morning in September 1986, the low-key lobbyist was plowing through the bulky document when he noticed that a new bill sponsored by the powerful Senate Majority leader Bob Dole had just been introduced. One of the provisions of the proposed legislation was the first-ever attempt to turn ephedrine and pseudoephedrine into a law enforcement issue by making them regulated substances. At the time, both chemicals were perfectly legal to sell in unlimited amounts under the Food, Drug and Cosmetic Act. The new law would have made unsanctioned commerce in ephedrine and pseudoephedrine a crime similar to trafficking in methamphetamine. At the time, ephedrine was widely used both as a diet aid and to treat asthma. More significant, pseudoephedrine was the chemical cornerstone of the three-billion-dollar-a-year cold-medicine industry.

Rexinger was perturbed. As the chief lobbyist for the Nonprescription Drug Manufacturers Association, it was his job to know what was coming down the legislative pipeline. But this was the first time he'd heard of the bill. Normally, the Food and Drug Administration, the agency that usually deals with over-the-counter medicines, would have given him advance notice of any pending legislation, but the DEA was behind this law. This was an arm of the government he'd never dealt with before.

"The first thing I did was call Gene Haislip's office," says the now-retired Rexinger, twenty years later. "He didn't return my calls. It was obvious from the start the DEA weren't interested in meeting with us. The legitimate pharmaceutical industry was always willing to cooperate with the DEA; it was the DEA that didn't want to cooperate with us."

If Haislip thought he could get around the pharmaceutical industry's objections by simply ignoring them, he would soon find out otherwise. The big drug firms constituted one of the most powerful lobbies in Washington, with friends and allies in high places. Then, as today, the industry spent millions of dollars on campaign contributions and lobbying efforts to sway public policy. Unable to make any headway with the DEA, Rexinger went to see staffers at

Bob Dole's office and told them if Haislip's bill passed as it was written, there was a real danger that common household products such as Sudafed, Actifed, and Dimetap would become illegal.

"They [Doles's staff] were absolutely appalled," says Rexinger. "They had no idea that this law would wreak such havoc on the legitimate pharmaceutical industry. They felt they'd been hoodwinked by the DEA. Our argument at that point was that there was nothing happening with pseudoephedrine to justify regulating it. It was a legitimate pharmaceutical product being used in legal drugs approved by the FDA that was taken by millions of people to control cold symptoms. To put burdensome and unnecessary regulations on pseudoephedrine in our opinion was an overreaction on the part of the DEA."

Rexinger managed to engineer a temporary delay. Haislip's legislation was initially folded into an omnibus bill, the Anti-Drug Abuse Act, but when the legislation passed in 1986 the chemical control provisions were absent. "I thought it was going to pass that session, but it didn't," says Haislip. "The pharmaceutical industry had some objections. It was really too late to successfully deal with the issues they brought up that late in the Congress, so the bill expired. However, it expired with all sorts of promises on the Hill: 'Don't worry, it's going to be picked up and we're going to run with it in the first part of next year.'"

It took a call from the White House to finally convince Haislip to sit down and talk with Rexinger. "There were some things they [the lobbyists] were doing and I remember I got called over to be confronted," Haislip recalls. "Certainly, they saw the bill as having the potential to hurt their profit margins. It's kind of hard to go before a board of directors and say, 'This year, we're going to make less money so we can help the DEA.' On the other hand, their knowledge of the illicit traffic in methamphetamine was about zero. They didn't know a damn thing about it. They didn't know what we were telling them was the truth. There was a knowledge-communications problem. There's also these strange rules that

Washington plays by. You back somebody into a corner and they say, 'Look, I'm representing an interest, that's my job. Your job is something else. I'm doing my job, you do your job, and let's see what happens.' A lot of these lobbyists know how to do business, they know who to call, they know what to say, they know how to make it have weight."

Neither side got exactly what they wanted, but over a series of meetings Haislip and Rexinger eventually hammered out a compromise that was called "the legal drug exemption." While sellers of bulk supplies of ephedrine and pseudoephedrine powder would be required to report transactions to the DEA, pills and tablets were left unregulated.

"At this point, making meth from over-the-counter medicines wasn't a major problem," admits Haislip. "Most of the meth made was produced from ephedrine powder. I had hoped that it would never happen, but I knew that it could because I had a team of chemists who told me so."

The behind-the-scenes maneuvering that accompanied Haislip's bill as it passed through Congress was first revealed by *Oregonian* reporter Steve Suo in his 2004 Pulitzer Prize–nominated series "Unnecessary Epidemic." Suo argued that the so-called meth epidemic of the 1990s could have been stopped in its tracks, if only the pharmaceutical companies hadn't thwarted the DEA's plans to regulate ephedrine and pseudoephedrine pills. The evil drug companies, by putting profits above public safety, helped turn a local drug trend confined to a handful of Western states into a national crisis.

"If all of Haislip's initial ideas had actually been implemented back in the nineteen eighties when meth was a small problem, it may never have gotten out of hand," Suo told the television show *Frontline*. "This is in many ways an unnecessary epidemic in the sense that the government had numerous opportunities to stem the supply of the drug and has pretty much missed each of those opportunities along the way, both due to industry lobbying and due to its own wavering interest in the problem."

Haislip's law as originally written might have thrown up a temporary roadblock for home labs but would have done little to halt the spread of Mexican-produced meth, since the cartels purchased their drug-making materials from international sources, not from within the United States.

"It's sometimes said that the pharmaceutical industry puts profits above public safety," says Haislip, who now, having retired from the DEA, works as a consultant to the industry. "I've even been known to say that myself sometimes. But the truth is there was more than one side to the story."

Adds Rexinger: "The media likes to portray the pharmaceutical industry as the bad guys and make the DEA look like wonderful people: The big bad pharmaceutical industry blocked the DEA from controlling meth, and but for the pharmaceutical industry we wouldn't be where we are right now. Well, it wasn't quite that simple."

In the end, both sides expressed satisfaction with the outcome of their extended negotiations. The law was delayed by less than a year because of the efforts of the pharmaceutical lobby. It wasn't easy, and he had to make some compromises, but Haislip finally got his bill passed in Congress.

"Overall, we got the big score," says Haislip. "Some of the meth aspect was watered down, but we got the law through relatively intact, with maybe ten to fifteen percent difference. If you have tight controls over bulk ephedrine pills and powder, you've accomplished a lot, even if a door has been left open."

The Chemical Diversion and Trafficking Act (CDTA) came into effect in 1989, and with the implementation of the law, the United States became the first major chemical-producing country to adopt mandatory controls over the ingredients that are used to make illegal drugs.

The CDTA placed twelve precursor chemicals and eight essential chemicals under tight regulation, a list expanded the next year to include eleven additional chemicals. Anybody who handled these chemicals—importers/exporters, manufacturers, wholesalers—was required to register with the DEA, and purchasers of supplies had to show IDs. Each chemical was allocated a threshold amount, and any transaction above that set limit had to be reported to the government, along with instances of lost chemicals or irregular sales. The DEA had the power to stop shipments it regarded as suspicious and to suspend the license of any supplier suspected of not complying with the new regulations. Because of the law, most of the major ingredients used in the manufacture of a wide variety of drugs—heroin, cocaine, methamphetamine, ecstasy, LSD, PCP—now came under federal control.

The effects of Haislip's law were immediate and dramatic. During the 1980s the tonnage of chemicals such as acetone, ethyl ether, and toluene exported to South American countries doubled. In the first six months of 1990, this amount was slashed by more than half, as the DEA denied permission to seventy percent of new customers for these chemicals. Colombian traffickers found that it was increasingly difficult to secure the supplies needed to process the product and so less cocaine was produced. In the United States, cocaine prices spiked and consumption plummeted. Within a year of the law coming into effect, cocaine-related emergency room mentions nationwide declined by roughly a third. The Colombians were forced to turn to other sources, especially in Germany, which increased exports to South America fourfold.

The CDTA also caused a major disruption in the methamphetamine trade. After increasing steadily throughout the 1980s, the number of meth labs busted by the DEA nationwide declined from 852 the year the law came into effect to 549 the year after to 408 the year after that. This drop was the first time that meth-lab seizures had fallen appreciably since 1981. In California, the law halted a seven-year rise in meth-related hospital visits. Across the country,

DAWN methamphetamine mentions dipped from 8,732 in 1989, to 5,236 in 1990, to 4,877 in 1991.

However, the Rand Institute's Peter Reuter warns that additional factors other than the CDTA may have helped drive down these numbers. In August 1989, the Medellin cartel assassinated in broad daylight a leading candidate for the Colombian presidency. The first George Bush was outraged by the brazen killing and ordered a law enforcement crackdown in America. Domestic arrests skyrocketed, not just for cocaine but for all drugs. Reuter suggests that may also have helped drive down cocaine and methamphetamine numbers.

Either way, it was difficult to deny that Haislip's law had helped cause a substantial interruption in the supply of illegal drugs in America. But by the last half of 1992, just as dramatically as the statistical indicators had fallen, they started to rise again. Between November 1992 and April 1993, meth-related ER visits jumped 52 percent nationwide. By the end of 1993, they had surpassed pre-intervention levels. Meth-related deaths also rose sharply. In Phoenix, Arizona, medical examiners reported only twenty deaths in 1992. Two years later, the number had risen to over 120, indicating that meth was no longer just a Californian problem. Meth purity also spiked. After declining to 34 percent in the wake of the law, it shot up again to 68 percent in 1994. Clearly, meth manufacturers must have discovered new chemical sources.

"It seemed like a great success story, and then it started to fall apart and we didn't know why," says Haislip.

In 1989, the CDTA had been in effect for less than a month when the DEA busted a meth lab in Southern California, the first one ever discovered using ephedrine tablets. At first, the CDTA hurt Californian meth cooks. But they quickly discovered the exemption in the law and made the switchover from ephedrine powder to tablets. As it turned out, the supplier of the tablets was San Diego resident

Ronald Lee Henslee, who bought wholesale quantities from Nationwide Purveyors, a crooked Pittsburgh mail-order chemical company that sold ephedrine tablets ostensibly as "herbal energizers" or diet aids via advertisements in the back pages of adult magazines. Just like Benzedrine in the 1950s, ephedrine in its own right was a common and legal drug used by college students, professional athletes, and truck drivers as a performance enhancer. But the bulk of Nationwide's business was supplying California's clandestine meth labs. Nationwide sold White Cross thins—a favorite brand among meth cooks—in thousand-count bottles at discount prices on a sliding scale depending on how much was purchased: ten dollars a bottle for less than six thousand bottles, eight dollars a bottle for more than six thousand, and dropping to five dollars a bottle for more than twelve thousand. After the filler was extracted from the tablets, each bottle yielded about 25 grams of ephedrine that could be converted, depending on the expertise of the cook, into half to three-quarters an ounce of pure methamphetamine worth three or four thousand dollars. Ephedrine tablets were not technically illegal under the CDTA, but if the DEA could prove that Nationwide knew their products were being turned into methamphetamine, then the company's owner could be arrested and charged. In 1992, a San Diego federal grand jury indicted Nationwide's president. The indictment alleged a conspiracy between Nationwide and Ronald Lee Henslee to supply approximately nine thousand pounds of ephedrine tablets to meth labs in California. Nationwide's president denied any knowledge that his products were being illegally diverted, but he was eventually found guilty of "conspiracy to manufacture and distribute a listed chemical" and sentenced to twenty years in prison.

The Nationwide case spurred Haislip into action. Marshaling support among his allies in Congress, Haislip proposed amending the CDTA to close the loophole left open by the legal drug exemption that left ephedrine and pseudoephedrine tablets unregulated. Under the new law—this one called the Domestic Chemical Diversion Control Act (DCDCA)—ephedrine and pseudoephedrine tablets would become listed chemicals. Suppliers would have to register with the DEA and keep scrupulous documentation of domestic sales and exports, just as handlers of bulk ephedrine powder were required to do. Under the proposed changes, the DEA would have the power to revoke or deny registration without proof of criminal intent if the agency suspected any distributor wasn't legitimate. As was the case with the CDTA, the pharmaceutical industry strongly objected. And once again, after more testy negotiations, a compromise was engineered. Ephedrine tablets were subject to new regulations, but pseudoephedrine tablets were allowed to remain unburdened by bureaucracy.

The DEA used the new powers granted under the DCDCA to launch its most aggressive campaign yet to shut down businesses supplying ephedrine and pseudoephedrine tablets to meth labs. On May 31, 1995, the DEA raided the Atlanta offices of X-Pressive Looks (XL), a mail-order distributor, and confiscated five hundred cases of pseudoephedrine tablets. The DEA investigation revealed that in a sixteen-month period the company had distributed 830 million tablets to head shops, truck stops, and minimarts across the country. This was enough pseudoephedrine to make thirteen tons of methamphetamine. According to testimony at his subsequent trial, X-Pressive Looks's owner, Vernon Prather, continued to supply customers, even though he knew some of them were being investigated by the DEA for selling pseudoephedrine to meth manufacturers. Indeed, he advised one of them to be careful how large a quantity he bought since "cops would be hot on your trail." Even after the raid, Prather, after raising his prices, continued to sell hundreds of cases of pseudoephedrine until the DEA shut down his place for good three months later.

Earlier in the same month, the DEA also raided the warehouse of Clifton Pharmaceuticals, a Pennsylvania company that bought bulk supplies of ephedrine and pseudoephedrine powder and turned them into tablets, which were then sold to mail-order companies that in turn sold them to meth cooks. After drug agents kept finding the company's products in meth labs in California, the DEA set up an undercover sting operation and purchased from Clifton twenty million pseudoephedrine tablets for $180,000. The subsequent raid netted twenty-five metric tons of pseudoephedrine and ephedrine powder, which was enough to make sixteen tons of meth. So great was the load that the DEA needed five tractor trailers to haul it away. This was at a time when, according to the White House Office of National Drug Control Policy, the estimated annual national consumption of methamphetamine was only just over thirty-four tons. Later in the year, a third raid took place when the owner of another mail-order distributor, this one in Arkansas, was busted with two million ephedrine tablets at his home and nearly nine million in his warehouse.

The amount of ephedrine and pseudoephedrine seized by the DEA in these three raids was truly enormous. The agency had taken down the biggest domestic suppliers of methamphetamine precursors in the country. Drug researchers Carlos Dobkin and Nancy Nicosia characterize the campaign as "probably the largest 'supply' shock that has occurred in any illegal drug market in the United States." Dobkin and Nicosia's 2005 study, "The War on Drugs: Methamphetamine, Public Health, and Crime," examines in detail the combined effects of the DCDCA and the takedown of XL and Clifton Pharmaceuticals on methamphetamine consumption in California. Using DEA seizure statistics and lab reports, emergency-room data from local hospitals, drug tests from criminals, and treatment admission numbers, the duo documents a startling reduction in nearly every major statistical indicator of meth use. On the streets of San Diego and in other Californian cities, Dobkin and Nicosia estimate the supply of methamphetamine was reduced by half. The price of a gram of methamphetamine more than tripled, from thirty dollars per gram to a hundred dollars. As the drug became harder to find, dealers stepped on the product, and the average purity of the drug dropped sharply from 90 percent to 20 percent. The drug grew so scarce that some users switched to cocaine. Hospital admissions declined by half, halting a four-year rise. Drug treatment admissions fell by 40 percent. Arrests for possession and sales of methamphetamine also plummeted: felony arrests by 50 percent, misdemeanor arrests by a more modest 25 percent. The number of criminals testing positive for methamphetamine when arrested declined by 60 percent. The only set of numbers they examined that wasn't affected was property and violent crime rates, which showed no appreciable change. The researchers concluded that Haislip's new law and the concomitant crackdown that accompanied it, had "disrupted the methamphetamine market and interrupted a trajectory of steadily increasing usage" and was "quite possibly the DEA's largest success in disrupting the supply of a major illegal substance."

Clearly, this was looking like another big win for Haislip. Then, just as with the Chemical Diversion and Trafficking Act, the numbers started to go awry. Hospital admissions started to rise again. Methamphetamine prices returned to their original levels within four months. Other indicators—the purity of the drug, the number of treatment admissions, drug arrests—followed suit so that within twenty months they had all returned close to the original levels.

The impact of this supply shock proved fleeting. Just as with any other business, markets either adapt to disruption or they die. The DEA had given its best shot but the meth trade had managed to absorb the blow. Dobkin and Nicosia wrote: "The fairly rapid recovery of the methamphetamine market after the massive intervention in the precursor market suggests that the operators of illicit laboratories were able to find other sources of precursors."

The spur for this latest recovery in the meth market was the switchover that manufacturers had quickly made from ephedrine tablets to pseudoephedrine pills. Even before the law had come into effect, manufacturers anticipated the rule change; in 1994, the DEA shut down twenty-eight clandestine labs that were using pseudoephedrine pills to make meth, a figure that would rise exponentially in the coming years. This was the period when meth manufacturing became less like a science experiment and more like a culinary class, when chemists turned into cooks, and all you needed to successfully make meth was the ability to read a set of instructions, which could easily be downloaded by anyone from the Internet. Once the knowledge got out that you could make meth using Sudafed, the number of labs really started to head into the stratosphere. DEA meth-lab seizures nationwide shot up from 299 in 1995, to 734 in 1996, to 1,321 in 1997, at the same time as imports of pseudoephedrine into the United States increased by 50 percent.

In 1997, the DEA finally gained the power that Gene Haislip had long sought to regulate the wholesale distribution of pseudoephedrine pills, but by this time it was too late. After a decade of trying, he succeeded in convincing Congress to cancel the exemption for pseudoephedrine. The Comprehensive Methamphetamine Control Act of 1996 was intended to counter the traffickers' response to the DCDCA. Sponsored by California senator Dianne Feinstein, the CMCA not only stiffened penalties for manufacturing meth and trafficking in precursor chemicals but made it illegal to sell laboratory equipment to meth manufacturers. But its most important provision—after years of Haislip's efforts—now made pseudoephedrine a listed chemical.

President Bill Clinton addressed Congress after the signing of the bill and said hopefully: "We have to stop meth before it becomes the crack of the nineteen nineties, and this legislation gives us a chance to do it."

But Congress had left one last loophole—the so-called blister pack exemption—which allowed unlimited sales of pseudoephedrine products as long as they came encased in blister packs. Lawmakers incorrectly assumed that meth manufacturers would have neither the time nor the patience to pick open hundreds of foil wrappers. The big-time makers reacted by buying deblistering machines.

In what by this time had become a familiar pattern, once again statistical gauges of meth use started to decline, but the effects of the CMCA was even less durable than previous interventions. Hospital admissions and other indicators dropped but were back to their original levels within six to twelve months. By late 1998, all the signs indicated that meth was on the march again. Mexican traffickers had found a new source of precursors. The focus of pseudoephedrine smuggling switched from America's southern border to its northern border, as millions of pills started to be smuggled in by Middle Eastern middlemen from Quebec through Detroit, eventually ending up in Mexican superlabs in California.

Haislip retired in 1997 just before the latest law came into effect. "Things somehow didn't continue on the best, most forceful track after I left," he says a little wearily. "We had them on the run. It wasn't perfect but we were getting there. When I retired, some momentum must have been lost somewhere.

"I've wrestled with this problem my whole damn career. My approach was to try to do only what seemed to be necessary based on the evidence we had and the hope that traffickers wouldn't go beyond that. Well, that just didn't work too well. What I learned from the whole experience is that you have to chase this problem, you have to be aggressive. You have to be the hawk on the hunt. You can't do one big thing and say, Okay. I've done my job, I'm going home."

And then he laughs. "We all learned in Bible school as little children that the conflict between good and evil is a constant struggle."

Do chemical controls work? The lessons of the 1990s suggest that chemical controls do work, but only in the short term. Three major laws—the Chemical Diversion and Trafficking Act, the Domestic Chemical Diversion Control Act, and the Comprehensive

Methamphetamine Control Act—were imposed in 1989, 1995, and 1997, respectively. After each law was passed, supply declined, prices spiked, and meth purity fell for a while, just as Gene Haislip had predicted. But within a year or two, meth indicators rose again, often surpassing their previous levels. If you were to track the spread of methamphetamine during the decade on a graph, you'd see a number of transitory downturns coinciding with the implementation of each new piece of legislation, but in general the trajectory was upward.

Hospital admissions are a good example. In their 2003 research paper, "Impacts of Federal Ephedrine and Pseudoephedrine Regulations on Methamphetamine-Related Hospital Admissions," James K. Cunningham and Lon-Mu Liu examined the effect of the CDTA, the DCDCA, and the CMCA on hospital admissions in three states—California, Arizona, and Nevada. What they found was that in California the CDTA stopped a seven-year rise in admissions, reducing them by 35 percent; the DCDCA stopped a four-year rise in all three states, driving them down on average by more than half; and the CMCA cut admissions by 38 percent, 61 percent, and 41 percent in California, Nevada, and Arizona, respectively. But in each and every case, admissions rose again within a relatively short period of time, as little as six months in some instances. Overall, methamphetamine emergency room visits tripled nationwide during the 1990s.

Cunningham and Liu concluded: "The repeated rise and fall of methamphetamine-related hospital admissions speaks to producers' ingenuity and adaptability regarding precursor regulations."

What about the number of people trying the drug for the first time? After all, the main argument for precursor controls is that by choking off the supply of chemicals to drug traffickers, prices will rise, which will cause some users to quit and deter others from starting to use the drug in the first place. According to the National Survey on Drug Use and Health, in 1989, the year the Chemical Diversion and Trafficking Act came into effect, methamphetamine attracted an estimated 253,000 new users, a figure that dropped to 211,000 the next year, presumably because of the CDTA. Ten years later, in 1999, after three significant legislative attempts to curb meth use and despite a massive deployment of law enforcement resources, an estimated 308,000 chose to begin taking the drug. In that same time frame, the price of a gram of pure uncut meth adjusted for inflation had gone down from $350 to $210.

The one area where you would expect chemical controls to have a lasting impact is on the purity of the drug. Meth purity did decline in the 1990s. According to the numbers issued by the White House Office of National Drug Control Policy, average meth purity at the gram level in 1989 stood at 65 percent. Ten years later it was 46 percent. Maybe chemical controls forced some dealers to step on their product. But even that may be a hollow victory. Just because a drug is weaker doesn't necessarily mean that less people do the drug. Users simply react by upping the dosage.

The most conspicuous failing of Haislip's laws was their inability to stop the increase in the number of meth labs. In 1989, the DEA discovered 852 labs, the beginning of a six-year decline in busts. But in 1995, the number of labs started to skyrocket. In 1998, the DEA seized 1,627 labs, a figure that continued to increase well into the next decade. To be fair, a big part of that increase was due to the wave of mom-and-pop labs that started up after amateur cooks discovered they could make meth using over-the-counter cold medicines. Regardless, it's clear that there were significantly more labs operating at the end of the decade than at the beginning. And, remember, these are the federal numbers and do not include seizures made by state and local law enforcement.

Not only did precursor regulations fail to halt the rise in meth use during the 1990s, in some instances they actually encouraged it. Just as drugs can have unpredictable side effects, so can drug laws. Precursor laws often end up boosting the meth trade by disproportionately hurting small and midlevel manufacturers but leaving the big guys relatively unscathed. Such laws oftentimes give major-league criminals a perverse incentive to expand their business into new territories. Just as Prohibition consolidated the hold of organized crime over the alcohol industry, so precursor laws helped the Mexican cartels increase their market share by stifling domestic competition.

Proponents of supply-side controls, preeminent among them *The Oregonian* reporter Steve Suo, acknowledge the long-term failures of these regulations but insist the solution is even tighter restrictions. Suo argues that the meth trade is highly susceptible to supply-side disruption. Because ephedrine and pseudoephedrine are manufactured in only a handful of factories abroad, and because these precursor chemicals are too technically complex for the traffickers to make themselves, it should be relatively easy to cut off the pipeline and choke off meth production.

"The meth trade's enormous demand for an ingredient that only a limited number of producers can supply makes it uniquely vulnerable," Suo writes in *The Oregonian*, "Because the traffickers lack the specialized expertise and equipment to make pseudoephedrine—a far more exacting process than cooking meth—they must rely on the legitimate marketplace."

Not according to chapter seventeen of Uncle Fester's *Secrets of Methamphetamine Manufacture,* which details how to make ephedrine by fermenting yeast with benzaldehyde in a five-gallon plastic bucket, a process that sounds not much more difficult than brewing beer. But if pseudoephedrine became impossible to obtain, the most likely scenario is that manufacturers would simply revert to making meth the old-fashioned way—with P2P, the method most commonly used prior to 1980. As long as the demand is there, someone will figure out a way to supply it. Cutting off the supply of chemicals is one thing. Figuring out why people take methamphetamine in the first place and what can be done to depress that appetite is something else altogether.

CHAPTER SIX

METH CAPITAL OF AMERICA

SAN DIEGO, CALIFORNIA

As dawn broke on a quiet Sunday in March 1989, 350 officers from state, local, and federal agencies fanned out across the San Diego area and descended on dozens of homes. Twenty-nine meth labs were shut down. Nearly a hundred meth manufacturers were arrested and taken to the Metropolitan Correctional Center in downtown San Diego. More than a hundred guns were confiscated, along with a cache of explosives. One gun was emblazoned with a Nazi swastika and the words "Hits 1989," accompanied by twenty notches that drug agents believed signified the number of people killed by the weapon's owner. Also seized was 830 pounds of ephedrine, more than 10 percent of the total legal imports of the decongestant into the United States that year.

Operation Crankcase was a major blow against the meth trade in California. A DEA spokesman boasted that the agency had pulled off "the single biggest roundup of methamphetamine manufacturers in the country's history."

The success of the operation was due in large part to the efforts of one man, an undercover police officer code-named Chuck, a fifty-year-old ex-marine and martial arts expert with a passion for motorcycles, who worked at Triple Neck Scientific, a chemical supply house named after the three-neck, round-bottomed flasks commonly used in meth labs. The store was located in Kearny Mesa, an industrial area to the north of San Diego. The owner of Triple Neck Scientific was a DEA informant who had previously worked with the agency on a similar but smaller sting in Texas three years before. He offered the use of his firm as a front to capture meth manufacturers buying chemicals and let agents set up hidden cameras and plant concealed microphones in his establishment. He also allowed Chuck to work there, posing as a security guard whose job was to check customers for weapons and narcotics.

Chuck, who was always armed during the undercover sting in case his life was threatened, was a tough-talking character dressed in denim and leather. He sported long, unkempt hair and a scraggly beard that made him look like an outlaw biker, which was what he was pretending to be. Over time, Chuck befriended many of the regular customers, and unbeknownst to them he made note of their license plates and the serial numbers on the weapons they checked with him at the front door. He would then phone in this information to a nearby command post, where DEA agents had set up surveillance. Chuck became so friendly with Triple Neck's clientele that they openly snorted methamphetamine and discussed drug transactions in front of him, bragging about the quality of the meth they made in San Diego—a reputation that made it easier for them to distribute their product in places as far away as Hawaii and New England—while all the time the video cameras were rolling. As he revealed to the *Los Angeles Times*, when any customer questioned his identity, he sternly told them: "I don't ask for references and I don't give them." Quizzed about his lack of tattoos, he said that he didn't like them because it made it easier for the police to track down criminals. On the numerous occasions he was offered methamphetamine, he declined to snort the drug himself, claiming he was a recovering heroin addict, but said he would take it and give it to his wife later. In reality, the drugs were shipped straight to the DEA lab for analysis.

One time, a customer who suspected Chuck was a narc patted him down and felt a lump in the back of his shirt; it was actually a tape recorder that was recording the confrontation. The quick-thinking Chuck told him it was a gun, and if he didn't back away, Chuck was ready to use it. On another occasion, to further establish his bona fides, he falsely accused a customer of being an undercover cop and forced him to strip naked to show he wasn't wearing a wire. The customer was so shaken by the encounter that he left the state for good soon afterward.

During his nine-month stint at Triple Neck Scientific, the under-cover cop managed to identify more than five hundred people in-volved in meth manufacturing. About half of them were outlaw bikers, mostly Hells Angels; the other half were freelance cooks, like the pharmacist and nurse he met who cooked the drug to feed their own habits, or the seventy-year-old grandmother who he found out distributed meth in Illinois. Chuck even discovered whole families involved in the meth trade. One father taught his sixteen-year-old son to cook the drug and often sent his eleven-year-old daughter to pick up chemicals from the store. More than seventeen hundred illegal purchases of meth-making ingredients were eventually recorded. Agents stationed at the nearby command center used a fleet of cars to tail hundreds of vehicles as they drove away with the chemicals. Of all the customers he befriended, only three were identified as le-gitimate purchasers.

This major victory in the war on meth was somewhat sullied, however, when it was later revealed that the government had not only paid for advertisements in trade magazines to help generate business for Triple Neck but had allowed Triple Neck's owner to keep nine million dollars in proceeds from the illegal transactions and had failed to recover most of the chemicals that had been sold to meth manufacturers. The government was forced to admit that the precursors had most likely been turned into thousands of pounds of methamphetamine that had been sold on the streets of San Diego and elsewhere across the nation.

———

t took until 1995 for San Diego's crystal meth problem to become national news after local resident Shawn Nelson, an unemployed plumber who was high on the drug, stole a sixty-ton National Guard tank and went on a Mad Max–style rampage, turning his quiet suburban neighborhood into a scene from a demolition derby. The incredible live camera footage of the tank plowing through lampposts and fire hydrants and crushing parked cars like they were beer cans captivated the television audience. After twenty minutes of slow-motion mechanical carnage, the chase ended when the tank got stuck on a concrete highway divider, and cops forced open the hatch and shot Nelson to death. The incident became emblematic of the horrific effects on the human mind of this "new drug," as the media insisted on calling methamphetamine. The incident cemented in the public imagination the impression of tweakers as dangerous psychotics who might flip out at any moment.

But ten years earlier, at a time when crack cocaine was garnering all the headlines and crystal meth barely registered as a national trend, local law enforcement officials were already calling San Diego—where during World War II the navy produced industrial-scale amounts of Benzedrine to supply to troops heading out to fight the Japanese—"the meth capital of America." At the same time, Hawaii suffered from a similar problem. There, after a crackdown on locally grown marijuana (called pakalolo) that sent locals looking for a new way to get high, a form of smokable meth known as ice, imported from Taiwan and South Korea, was devastating native communities on the island. "The locals were told, 'Here's another drug; you smoke it and it does the same thing as pakalolo.' But it didn't," says University of California, Berkeley's Patricia Morgan, who has done extensive research on meth in Hawaii. "The Hawaiians thought that meth was like pot. They were tragically naïve."

But Hawaiians didn't make the drug themselves. San Diego, however, was already the meth laboratory for the rest of the country. According to the *Los Angeles Times*, roughly a quarter of all the meth labs seized nationwide in 1988 were discovered in San Diego County, 137 in all, up from only five years before. While cocaine was still the city's top killer when it came to illegal drugs, in the last half of the 1980s the number of meth-related emergency room visits shot up from 112 mentions to 778, and during this same time frame, meth-related deaths rose from 9 to 64. By 1988, in a measure of how far San Diego was ahead of the curve compared to the rest of the country, 28 percent of local felons tested positive for the drug when they were arrested, contrasting with 4 percent in Los Angeles and 1 percent in New York. As the decade ended, methamphetamine accounted for nearly 40 percent of all drug treatment admissions in the area. The city's police chief was only slightly exaggerating when he complained that San Diego was "to crystal what Bogota is to cocaine."

There were a number of reasons why San Diego became such a happy home for meth manufacturing in the 1980s. In the immediate aftermath of World War II, returning troops took jobs in San Diego's defense plants, and some of them who had picked up the habit while serving their country continued to use amphetamine to help them work longer hours and earn overtime pay. So there was already a well-established blue-collar market for the drug that stretched back decades. In the 1960s, after Methedrine was effectively banned from the state, many of the first-ever clandestine meth labs constructed in America were located in rural areas outside the city. The proximity to the Mexican border was another factor. Downtown San Diego is only twenty miles from its poor stepsister city, Tijuana. The Tijuana–San Diego corridor—the busiest border crossing in the world—has been a major pipeline for the smuggling of illicit goods into America since at least the days of Prohibition. But the major reason why the San Diego area became such a focal point for meth activity in the Reagan years was the presence of the Hells Angels Motorcycle Club, which was founded in 1948 in San Bernardino, California, by a group of ex-servicemen who had grown bored with the slow pace of civilian life.

The Hells Angels dominated the meth trade in the San Diego area, as they did in the rest of California. The outlaw biker group wasn't the chaotic rabble portrayed in the famous Hunter S. Thompson book. By this time, the Hells Angels had reorganized themselves, kicked out some of the heroin-addicted veterans, and modernized their operation so they more resembled a Mafia-on-wheels than the marauding mechanical Visigoths of legend. The Angels were now a business, operating one of the largest criminal networks on the West Coast. They had their fingers in a number of pies—fencing stolen goods, pornography, prostitution, extortion, gun running, contract murders—but the group's main profit center was its control of California's clandestine drug laboratories. While the Angels had been involved in the distribution of methamphetamine since the 1960s, it wasn't until the early 1970s that they started manufacturing the drug. According to Yves Lavigne's book *Hells Angels: Into the Abyss*, the group recruited a trained chemist from Shell Oil who taught members of the Oakland chapter how to cook crank. Soon, dozens of Hells Angels all over California were making meth. By the mid-1980s, law enforcement officials alleged that the Angels controlled about three-quarters of the state's multimillion-dollar meth trade. The business was so profitable that some Angels lived in expensive homes and drove luxury cars. When the group's biggest meth manufacturer, Kenny Owens, was busted in San Francisco by the DEA in 1987, he was found with a million dollars in cash in his possession. Like the Italian mob, the Angels maintained their stranglehold on the illegal goings-on by intimidation. Typically, they would approach a freelance chemist and offer him tens of thousands of dollars on the condition that he now work only for the group. The Angels' fearsome reputation ensured that anybody who valued their safety took the deal.

"They went from a loose-knit bunch of guys to an organized crime family," one San Diego narcotics detective said half-admiringly.

What was so puzzling about this dramatic upkick in methamphetamine activity was that just a few years earlier, it had seemed as if the biker meth labs were going out of business. Not just in San Diego, but in other meth-manufacturing outposts such as San Francisco, Dallas, and Philadelphia, the number of meth labs uncovered by law enforcement showed a marked decrease after 1980, when a federal law listed phenyl acetone (P2P)—the main ingredient in biker meth—as a Schedule II controlled substance. A workaday brown liquid used mainly to clean swimming pools, P2P achieved a second, more exciting, existence as the immediate precursor needed to make biker meth, also called prope dope. All the most popular methods of methamphetamine synthesis at the time involved P2P. Biker gangs killed people over jugs of the stuff. In certain roughneck circles, the chemical was more valuable than gold. (P2P is what the bad cops steal in the Harrison Ford movie *Witness*.)

After the new law came into effect, supplies of the precursor chemical grew so scarce that P2P was fetching as much as five thousand dollars a gallon on the black market. As a consequence, less product was made. And the purity of meth on the street tumbled. Some of the small-time manufacturers grew so desperate that they resorted to trying to make meth by breaking open Vicks nasal inhalers and dissolving the contents in muriatic acid, a crude one-step recipe that did produce a type of methamphetamine called kitchen crank, but in its weakest form.

In Philadelphia, as a direct consequence of the new federal law, the Pagans—the East Coast equivalent of the Hells Angels—were forced to forge an alliance with the South Philly Mafia, who supplied the motorcycle club with large amounts of illegally diverted P2P imported from Germany via the Caribbean. In California, the Hells Angels imported the chemical from Australia disguised as wine. They also manufactured their own P2P using phenyl acetic acid, a substance sometimes found in perfumes, which at that time wasn't a regulated chemical. When phenyl acetic acid became difficult to procure, they synthesized the precursor of the precursor using ethyl benzene.

It soon became clear that lawmakers had underestimated the

ingenuity of the criminal mind. Banning P2P on its own wasn't going to work. After a temporary dip in production, biker meth labs rebounded. Such were the many synthetic routes leading to the successful manufacture of the drug, you would have to place literally dozens of chemicals on the watch list to cut off all avenues of production. Moreover, the legislative attempt to curb biker meth had fallen prey to another kind of law—the law of unintended consequences.

Beginning in 1981, a new type of methamphetamine started turning up at the DEA's lab busts in Southern California. This type of meth was made from a recipe that would fundamentally alter the nature of the meth business. Some resourceful chemist was casting around for a way to bypass the new federal law when he figured out he didn't need P2P to make meth, that he could successfully synthesize the drug by reacting the unregulated substance ephedrine with iodine and red phosphorus. Not only did this new method have the advantage of being simpler than the P2P route, but the chemicals needed were readily available. Prior to 1987 in California, anybody could buy any amount of ephedrine without being asked any questions. Purchasers weren't required to show ID and sellers weren't obligated to keep any record of the business deal.

But perhaps the biggest advantage of the ephedrine reduction method from a purely commercial viewpoint was that it produced a more powerful drug. Biker meth is what chemists call a racemic mixture, meaning it consists of two isomers—the active "d," or dextro-isomer, and the less active "l," or levo-isomer. Ephedrine reduction produces only the more potent d-isomer, which creates an edgier, more intense experience in the user. Now you had a drug that was not only easier to make but was twice as powerful and potentially twice as dangerous, an unwelcome development inadvertently spurred by the federal crackdown on P2P.

Slowly at first, but then with increasing regularity, the ephedrine reduction method caught on with clandestine chemists throughout southern California. Then the recipe spread north to other Californian cities and after that into Oregon and Washington. In the early 1980's, the vast majority of the labs seized in California were fairly sophisticated setups that used P2P. By the end of the decade, 90 percent of the labs had made the switchover to ephedrine. The relative simplicity of this method opened the door for a new breed of independent operators, enthusiastic amateurs who produced small amounts of the drug in suburban garages and apartments and who weren't controlled by the Hells Angels. It was these amateurs who were largely responsible for the rash of explosions and fires that started to be reported with alarming regularity in the San Diego area. In a pattern that would be repeated again in coming years, a well-meaning law meant to choke off the supply of chemicals needed to make meth ended up making the problem worse, unintentionally abetting rather than curbing the spread of the drug.

The twentyfold increase in the number of meth labs discovered in the San Diego area in the mid-1980s—due in large part to the increasing popularity of the ephedrine reduction method—set alarm bells ringing at the Drug Enforcement Administration's regional office. Field agents knew that for so many labs to exist, somebody had to be supplying the Hells Angels with a steady stream of precursors. The DEA set its sights on half a dozen rogue chemical supply companies in the area that they believed were selling the bulk of the ingredients to fuel these labs.

One of those targeted was Robert J. Miskinis, who was suspected of being the biggest purveyor of ephedrine and other drug-making chemicals in the San Diego area. He was a former UCLA chemistry student who had been charged in 1978 with making methamphetamine. Miskinis's company, RJM Laboratories, sold precursors and lab equipment to methamphetamine and PCP manufacturers not just in San Diego but all over the country. The DEA gathered evidence that beginning in 1982, RJM had supplied more than two thousand meth labs in five different states—California, Texas, Tennessee, New Jersey, and Washington. Miskinis was a difficult target to pin down. Ninety-five percent of his business was cash-and-carry. He kept limited records of his business transactions, and he wasn't legally required to do so for many of the chemicals he sold. For the DEA to make a case, they had to prove that Miskinis sold the supplies knowing they would be used to make meth.

Miskinis was such a smooth operator that in 1986, when the state legislature was considering a law imposing new controls on ephedrine and a number of other chemicals used in the manufacture of methamphetamine, he paid a lobbyist twenty-two thousand dollars to get lawmakers to agree to delay implementing the restrictions by six months. The proposed bill required that bulk purchases of ephedrine be reported to California's Department of Justice. The lobbyist successfully argued that RJM Laboratories was a legitimate chemical house that would be stuck with large amounts of unsold ephedrine if the law wasn't rewritten. The bill's sponsor, Assemblywoman Lucy Killea, explained to the media that the postponement was necessary to aid small businesses that needed ephedrine to produce prescription drugs. The law was amended, but the delay was later revoked by angry and embarrassed politicians after Miskinis's past was revealed in the local press.

In August 1988, the DEA raided and seized three chemical supply plants that comprised RJM Laboratories. One of the plants was located in an industrial park in Lakeside, an inland suburb of San Diego, where the DEA allegedly found a gigantic two-hundred-liter flask capable of manufacturing eighty pounds of meth, as well as drums of ephedrine powder and enough chemicals to make fifty tons of the drug. In a follow-up raid the next year, a ninety-member task force seized three other chemical houses allegedly belonging to Miskinis, one of them in the picturesque coastal town of Carlsbad, where agents reportedly discovered already-assembled meth laboratory kits, complete with instruction books that ranged from simple setups suitable for producing a few ounces of the drug at home to the sort of glassware appropriate for industrial-scale production. Miskinis was charged under a new federal "drug kingpin" statute with conspiring to aid and abet the manufacture of methamphetamine with intent to distribute. He was eventually convicted and sentenced to forty years in federal prison by a judge who during sentencing lambasted Miskinis as one of the main reasons why San Diego had earned the title of "methamphetamine capital of America." "A great deal of the methamphetamine problem in San Diego can be placed at the doorstep of RJM Labs," a DEA agent told the *Los Angeles Times*. Miskinis was released after four years when an appeals court held that he might have been inadequately represented by his attorney at trial.

As a new decade dawned, politicians and law enforcement officials were congratulating themselves on a job well done. The meth problem in San Diego hadn't gone away, but it appeared to have been contained. Nearly all the major indicators of meth abuse were heading in the right direction. According to the Drug Abuse Warning Network (DAWN), the number of meth-related emergency room visits, which had risen steadily throughout the 1980s, declined from 778 in 1988 to 516 in 1991. More dramatically, meth-related deaths also dipped from sixty-four in 1989 to thirteen in 1991. In addition, the proportion of local criminals testing positive for meth dropped to 18 percent from close to 30 percent at the end of the 1980s. The number of people entering treatment also declined, albeit only slightly, from 1,280 in 1990 to 1,140 in 1991. Fewer meth labs were discovered by the DEA. In 1990, there were 79 lab busts, a significant decline from 114 the year before and 134 the year before that.

The combination of high-profile drug sweeps like Operation Crankcase and the 1987 state law restricting ephedrine and other meth-making chemicals appeared to have worked. The Hells Angels, battered by a string of RICO (Racketeering Influenced Corrupt

Organizations) indictments that targeted not just their drug business but the whole range of the group's criminal enterprises, were losing their grip on the meth trade. For a brief moment, it appeared as if San Diego was winning the war on meth.

Then, in a development that initially baffled law enforcement, meth indicators started to rise again. Seemingly out of the blue, meth emergency room visits more than doubled between 1991 and 1994 and meth-related deaths nearly tripled. The number of people seeking treatment spiked upward. For the first time ever in San Diego's history, there were now more admissions for methamphetamine than for alcohol. The proportion of male inmates booked at county jails who tested positive for the drug also rose to 42 percent in the same period. And, most startling of all, the amount of methamphetamine seized by local law enforcement skyrocketed— from 1,409 pounds in 1991 to 13,366 pounds in 1994.

The reason for this alarming surge in the amount of meth turning up on the streets of San Diego lay just across the border in Mexico, where some of the drug cartels had also discovered the ease with which ephedrine could be turned into methamphetamine. Mexican polydrug organizations, who were already smuggling marijuana, cocaine, and heroin into the United States, realized that the crackdown on meth in California provided them with an opportunity to further diversify. They quickly moved to establish themselves in the meth trade, elbowing the Hells Angels out of the way, and setting up superlabs in Mexico as well as in isolated areas in San Diego and throughout California's farm belt. Sophisticated, large-scale production lines, these superlabs were capable of churning out unprecedented amounts of the drug that dwarfed the output of the bikers. If small freelance cooks could produce ounces of methamphetamine and the Hells Angels could produce pounds, the Mexicans could produce tons, which were distributed through the cartels' extensive and well-established cocaine and heroin networks. A single superlab could produce as much as a million dollars' worth of product per week. And the drugs that came out of these labs were top quality. On the streets of San Diego, meth purity almost doubled. Soon, the Mexicans had replaced the Hells Angels as the number one source of meth in California. Local DEA agents began to make fun of the bikers for allowing foreigners to come in and take over their business.

CHAPTER SEVEN

THE KINGS OF METHAMPHETAMINE

PIHUAMO, MEXICO

A small cowboy town in the western state of Jalisco, even by Mexican standards Pihuamo has a reputation as a macho place. Approached by a winding road, this dusty mark on the map lies huddled beneath the steep peaks of the Sierra Madre. At the center of the town lies a Catholic church the size of a cathedral that resembles a giant rococo wedding cake. Matters of family pride and honor are taken seriously among the local *charros* and *rancheros*. A couple of years back, two cousins, one aged seventy and the other eighty-five, shot each other to death in a duel intended to resolve a long-standing dispute over water rights.

José de Jesús Amezcua-Contreras was born in 1965 on his family's hardscrabble cattle ranch on the outskirts of Pihuamo. He had an older brother, Luis, and a younger brother, Adan, as well as four sisters. Theirs was a meager existence that entailed a lot of work for little reward. They literally lived hand to mouth; their father, Ignacio, slaughtered pigs and cows in the barn for the family table. He also sold meat on the weekend at a marketplace in the city of Colima, about twenty miles away. Jesús was the more serious and ambitious of the brothers, even though he never finished school. Luis was the joker and ladies' man, Adan the ugly duckling. There was nothing about them in their early days to distinguish them from the millions of other poor Mexican peasants trying to scrape out a living or to suggest that they would one day go on to create a global drug trafficking empire—*reyes de la metanfetamina* (the kings of methamphetamine), as the Mexican media would dub them.

There is next to no biographical information about the Amezcuas in the English-language press, but from scouring Mexican newspapers and magazines it's possible to piece together the story of the brothers' formative years. According to an account in the Mexican magazine *Contenido* by journalist Maurizio Guerrero, the fortunes of the Amezcua clan started to change for the better in the mid-1970s when the clan moved to El Moralete, a neighborhood on the outskirts of Colima. They had inherited a tiny bodega and allegedly started to sell small quantities of marijuana out of the store. Soon, Luis was driving around in his first-ever car, a secondhand jalopy bought with pot profits.

From the start, Jesús was determined to move up in the world. He was only thirteen when he made his first trip to the United States in 1978. Dodging border patrols, he tramped through the hills to the east of the San Ysidro border crossing and then made his way to Los Angeles, where he helped his uncle Arnaldo Amezcua Díaz by sweeping floors and taking tickets at the movie theater the uncle managed. By the age of seventeen, Jesús was working as an assistant at a law center for undocumented aliens in San Diego. He put this experience to good use the next year when, after inviting Luis to join him, he and his brother went into business smuggling *pollos* (literally, "chickens," a slang term for illegal immigrants) through the desert. In 1996, President Ronald Reagan signed an immigration reform bill that legalized 2.7 million migrants, but the law failed to stem the flow of poor Mexicans looking for a better life. The human trafficking business was so good that the brothers were able to buy a car repair shop in San Diego. However, tightened border security did result in the 1988 arrest of Luis, who was sentenced to six months in prison for trafficking illegal aliens.

During this period, according to confidential files compiled by the Procuraduria General de la Republica (PGR), details of which were released to Mexican newspapers, Jesús met a number of Californian meth cooks who asked him if he could supply them with ephedrine powder from Mexico. There was an ephedrine drought in California, thanks to the new federal law regulating bulk amounts of the drug. In addition, there was an ongoing state crackdown on meth makers. Local meth cooks were having trouble getting their hands on the chemicals needed to manufacture their drugs and were clamoring for new sources. Ephedrine was perfectly legal to buy in whatever amounts purchasers wanted at the time in Mexico. Jesús drove to Mexico City and there bought two hundred kilograms for fifty thousand dollars. He transported the ephedrine to San Diego, broke up the consignment into kilogram batches, and sold the sought-after chemical on the black market for five times what it cost him to buy.

The brothers were fairly minor players in the drug trade at this point. In addition to smuggling ephedrine, they also traveled back and forth between Tijuana and San Diego carrying modest amounts of marijuana and pound bricks of cocaine. They were making good money, but they were hardly drug kingpins. That would change after a visit home to Colima in 1990, when they met an important figure in local political circles known as El Ingeniero ("the Engineer"), who would propel the brothers into the major leagues. He called himself Don Pedro Orozco and posed as a wealthy businessman and philanthropist. Under that identity, he counted among his many influential friends the governor of the state, Elias Zamora Verduzco. But El Ingeniero led a double life. His real name was Manuel Salcido, one of the most violent drug lords in Mexico's history, who smuggled huge quantities of cocaine and marijuana into the United States. Back in his home state of Sinaloa, he was known as El Cochiloco ("the Crazy Pig") because he didn't just kill anybody who crossed him, but had his men slaughter them as if they were farm animals, gouging out their eyes, pulling out their fingernails, chopping off their hands and, in some cases, castrating them.

Salcido was impressed with the Amezcuas' organizational skills as well as their cool under pressure. The brothers had a reputation for never raising their voices, even in moments of high tension. Salcido thought the young men showed promise, and he introduced them to his important friends in politics and law enforcement. After Salcido was shot to death in August 1991 near his horse ranch in Guadalajara by men firing M-60 machine guns, the Amezcua brothers took over the Crazy Pig's old smuggling routes.

Jesús soon realized that he could turn an even bigger profit smuggling ephedrine if he bought the chemical directly from the manufacturers. In 1993, he traveled all over Asia scouring the continent for factories producing the chemical. He found places in India where he could buy ephedrine wholesale for forty-eight dollars a kilogram, an eighth of what he paid in Mexico. He rented an office in Bangkok, Thailand, and allegedly put a trusted lieutenant, José Osorio-Cabrera, in charge of setting up an ephedrine pipeline from India to Mexico. After obtaining import permits from the Mexican embassy in New Delhi, Osorio allegedly used an American Express card to buy tons of the chemicals from the Indian factories, which were then flown to Mexico City, where customs officials who had been bribed in advance quickly released the consignments without inspection.

Not satisfied with just importing ephedrine, the Amezcua brothers hired a team of chemists and started producing methamphetamine themselves. By 1993, the brothers had set up factory-size methamphetamine laboratories, not just in rural parts of California but also throughout the Sierra Madre Mountains, in isolated areas in the western states of Jalisco, Colima, and Michoacan. Once the meth was manufactured, the product was transported to the frontier cities of Tijuana and Mexicali and then smuggled into California. Mexican police started to come across peasants in pickup trucks transporting sacks of methamphetamine and barrels of ephedrine. After one truck was stopped in Michoacan in April 1995, the police discovered seven hundred pounds of ephedrine. Inside the vehicle was Roberto Amezcua del Toro, one of Jesús' cousins, who led them to two nearby methamphetamine laboratories.

Family was important to the Amezcuas, but not just because of sentimental reasons. They tried to insulate themselves from law enforcement efforts to infiltrate their ranks by keeping a low profile and using only relatives and longtime friends from back home as top-echelon employees. In this respect, they were no different than the Italian Mafia, who also used linguistic and cultural ties to protect themselves from outsiders. But in June 1993, the Drug Enforcement Administration arrested one of the Amezcua brothers' top aides at a house in Chula Vista, California. Jesús had planned to buy fifty kilograms of cocaine from the Cali cartel and had sent the aide to negotiate the deal, when DEA agents came bursting through the door. San Diego federal prosecutors slapped Jesús with cocaine distribution charges, but he fled back to Mexico before he could be arrested, and for a while he fell out of sight.

Prosecutors and agents who tailed Amezcua back then saw little about him to suggest that he was a major drug trafficker, except his strong drive to succeed in his chosen profession, according to a 1995 *New York Times* report. "He was sassy and arrogant," an assistant United States attorney in San Diego who helped indict Jesús told the *Times*. "He had the BMW, the braggadocio, the gold jewelry. He was a young guy looking to come up in the drug world." At this point, the DEA had no idea just how extensive the Amezcua brothers' methamphetamine empire had already become. But they were about to find out.

O ver the years, drug crackdowns in the United States have often proved a boon to Mexican traffickers. Anybody with an eye for history shouldn't have been surprised that the Mexican cartels had by the early 1990s found a way to exploit the DEA's attempt to squash meth manufacturing in California. Flexible and resilient, Mexican drug smugglers—whose exploits were often celebrated in songs known as *corridos* and who were regarded by some Mexicans as practically folk heroes—had eight decades' worth of experience dealing with the vagaries of gringo drug-war politics and had proven more than once their ability to adapt to both shifting cross-border law enforcement tactics and the changing tastes of their customers.

The American appetite for opium in the early twentieth century and the subsequent attempt to suppress the habit more or less created the modern-day Mexican drug trafficking trade. After the passage of the Harrison Narcotics Tax Act in 1914, which was intended to curtail what was then a serious drug problem in America, groups in Mexico, where opium was still legal and where poppies had been grown since the late nineteenth century, began smuggling large amounts of the narcotic across the border. No different from today, these so-called *gomeros*, as opium traffickers were known, were protected by powerful political figures. Colonel Esteban Cantú, the governor of Baja California from 1914 to 1920, was suspected by the American authorities of controlling much of the opium trade from Tijuana into San Diego.

"Drug trafficking in Mexico began as a response to U.S. opium demand," the sociologist Luis Astorga, a researcher at the National Autonomous University of Mexico, has written. "Prohibition on one side of the U.S.-Mexican border and legal commerce on the other created the conditions for drug trafficking."

The subsequent passing of both the Volstead Act in 1919, which ushered in an era of alcohol prohibition in the United States, and the Marijuana Stamp Act of 1937 provided Mexican smugglers with further windfalls, until by 1960 San Diego narcotics detectives were estimating that as much as 80 percent of the heroin and nearly all the marijuana imported into the United States came from Mexico. By the end of the decade, according to some estimates, as much as five tons of pot per week was coming across the border.

The pot boom among American middle-class youth that began in the 1960s turned many a poor Mexican peasant into a rich man. But beginning in 1975, a joint military-style U.S.-Mexico drug crop eradication program called Operation Condor (not to be confused with the assassination campaign of the same name and time period that was waged by various South American dictatorships against Marxist dissidents) seriously disrupted the pot trade. Tons of drugs were destroyed as acres of marijuana and poppy fields were sprayed with the toxic herbicide Paraquat. A batch of the tainted pot found its way into the American market where it made some customers sick. American marijuana smokers began to steer clear of Mexican pot, fearing it was contaminated. By 1979, Mexico, which used to be the source of the vast majority of marijuana that came into the country, accounted for only 11 percent of the trade, and that dropped to 4 percent two years later.

Temporarily forced out of the pot business, the Mexican cartels then turned to Colombian cocaine producers, with whom they struck a deal. The Colombians delivered the cocaine to Mexico and then paid the local cartels a thousand dollars per kilogram to smuggle the drugs across the border. The Colombians picked up the drugs on the other side and distributed them throughout the rest of America. Increasingly, as trafficking routes through the Caribbean were shut down by the DEA, the Colombian cartels came to rely more and more on the Mexicans to deliver their product to the American consumer. Sensing a shift in power, the Mexicans renegotiated their deal in 1992 and now insisted that the Colombians give up half the cocaine shipments. In return, the Mexicans would not only smuggle the drugs across the border but would use their by-now extensive distribution networks in California, the Southwest, and the Midwest to sell the drug themselves. In this way, the Mexicans would soon come to eclipse the Colombians as the primary importers of illegal substances into the United States.

"This deal was a major turning point in the fortunes of the Mexican cartels," wrote University of Nebraska's Chris Eskridge in his 1999 paper "Mexican Cartels and Their Integration into Mexican Socio-Political Culture." "With this new business arrangement, the power and wealth of the Mexican drug cartels exploded."

But there was a problem. Demand for cocaine was starting to

decline in the United States. The great crack boom of the 1980s was petering out. The Mexican cartels needed a new drug to boost their bottom line. Methamphetamine proved attractive to the Mexicans because, unlike cocaine, they didn't have to split the profits with the Colombians. Instead of acting as middle men, they could control every aspect of the business from the production to distribution to sales. In addition, labor and manufacturing costs were low. Because methamphetamine is a synthetic drug produced in a laboratory, there was no reliance on growing seasons and the vagaries of nature. The cartels didn't need to employ armies of peasants to harvest the drug, as they did with marijuana. And methamphetamine was so inexpensive to produce in bulk—with a cost-price ratio of ten to one—that they could afford to lose up to half their product and still make a sizable profit.

The Mexicans' ability to produce massive quantities of high-quality product practically overnight—as much as a hundred pounds per cooking cycle—and have it delivered to practically any state in the union within days revolutionized the meth trade in America. Within less than five years, the Mexican cartels had claimed the major share of the market, wresting control of the trade from the outlaw biker gangs to become far and away America's biggest source of methamphetamine. Now the roles were reversed. In a humiliating turnaround, the Hells Angels, who used to buy precursor ingredients from the Mexicans to make their own meth, were now forced by circumstances to accept a diminished role as little more than delivery boys for the Mexicans. Today, the DEA estimates that 65 percent of the methamphetamine consumed in America comes from labs operated by Mexican criminal groups.

"The shift . . . was a brilliant business decision by these organizations," the then DEA head Thomas Constantine said in a 1997 speech. "Unlike the cocaine business, where traffickers from Mexico are just one link in a chain, meth is one rung they can control from beginning to end. And because they are in complete control, they can keep 100 percent of the profits."

A number of different Mexican cartels moved into the methamphetamine business during the 1990s, each with its own distinctive way of doing business. There was the Tijuana Cartel operated by the Arellano-Felix brothers, reputedly the most violent of the groups, who employed Latino gang members in the United States to act as local distributors. In 1993, in what seemed like a replay of the crack cocaine turf wars of the mid-1980s, Nico Marron, an associate of the organization and one of the biggest meth traffickers in San Diego, unleashed a wave of bloody retribution against a rival methamphetamine gang after his brother was murdered execution style. When the smoke cleared, twenty-six people were left dead. That same year the Tijuana Cartel gained international notoriety when, in what the brothers later claimed to the Vatican was a case of mistaken identity, one of their gunmen assassinated Cardinal Juan Jesús Ocampo at Guadalajara Airport. Other than a reputation for gruesome violence, such as breaking open suspected informants' heads in a vise, the Arellano brothers' other claim to fame was the pay-to-play system they initiated in Tijuana, whereby for a fee rival cartels were allowed to use their territory to ship methamphetamine and other drugs into the United States. The Tijuana Cartel alone was estimated to have shipped between fifty and a hundred pounds of methamphetamine across the border each month.

Then there was the Juárez Cartel, the most politically powerful group, run by Rafael Aguilar, a former police commander, and Amado Carrillo-Fuentes, known as a mediator who advocated cooperation rather than violence between the different Mexican smuggling groups and who did everything in his power to consolidate the Mexicans' control of the cocaine trade in America by cutting out the Colombians. Fuentes earned the nickname "Lord of the Skies" because he owned a fleet of 727 and DC-3 jets on which he flew multiton loads of cocaine directly from Peru and Bolivia into Mexico. His organization, by far the wealthiest of the cartels, was said to gross as much as two hundred million dollars a week from overall drug sales and boasted assets in the billions. Fuentes reportedly had plans to take over the methamphetamine trade in America, just as he had done the cocaine business, and he set up meth-distribution pipelines from Hermosillo into Arizona and from Juárez into Texas. In 1995, in Las Cruces, New Mexico, the DEA seized fifty million dollars' worth of Fuentes's methamphetamine that was headed to the Midwest. The Juárez Cartel allegedly had a wide array of politicians, military officers, and policemen on the payroll, including even Mexico's drug czar, General Jesús Gutiérrez Rebollo. Through Gutiérrez, Fuentes had access to every last scrap of confidential intelligence detailing the joint U.S.-Mexico government effort to shut down the cartels. The organization's plans to monopolize the meth business were only partially implemented when Fuentes died of complications from plastic surgery in 1997, trying to change his appearance to throw off the DEA agents hot on his trail.

But when it came to methamphetamine, the most important trafficking organization—the Mexican group that first saw the immense commercial possibilities of the expanding demand for the drug in the United States—was the Amezcua brothers. If you used meth at a rave or a circuit party in California during the early 1990s, there was a good chance it came from one of the Amezcua brothers' labs.

January 1994 was a busy month for Jesús Amezcua as he embarked from Mexico to Thailand to India, and then on to Holland, arranging ephedrine transactions. In Amsterdam, he met with a new supplier of the chemical, an Arab contact, and a deal was struck. The following month in Guadalajara Jesús gave José Osorio $100,000 to give to the supplier from the Middle East as a down payment. He was supposed to send the ephedrine, which came from a factory in Madras, India, directly to Mexico City, but a shipping agent in Frankfurt, Germany, put the load on the wrong plane, which made a stopover at the Dallas/Fort Worth International Airport. U.S. Customs agents boarded the plane, and inside they found 120 barrels of what was listed in the paperwork as fertilizer.

The Customs agents had been alerted to be on the lookout for large consignments of smuggled ephedrine, and the inspectors were suspicious of the consignment because of its size. Adding to their suspicions, the name of the chemical manufacturer on the labels attached to the drums was blacked out. Prying open the cardboard barrels, the agents found fine white powder inside. They took a sample and sent it to the DEA to be analyzed. What the customs agents had discovered almost by chance turned out to be three and a half metric tons of ephedrine, which at the standard 70 percent conversion rate was enough to make about two and a half tons of pure methamphetamine.

Customs and the DEA were still in the middle of investigating the matter when, three months later, eighty more barrels of ephedrine arrived at the airport. This second consignment had originated in Pakistan, been routed through the United Arab Emirates, and was headed to its final destination, a front company that Jesús had founded in Guadalajara. Three months after that, Dutch authorities seized another huge haul, this time nearly seven tons of ephedrine at Amsterdam's Schipol Airport that was also bound for the Amezcuas.

Sitting in his office in DEA headquarters, Gene Haislip was astonished at the international scale of this ephedrine diversion operation. The DEA had seized less than four hundred kilograms of ephedrine the previous year. Fifteen times that amount was discovered in Dallas alone. "I was even more surprised when the number of tons kept getting bigger and bigger," he says. "That was a hell of a lot of ephedrine. It got to be that it looked more like the methaqualone picture than anything else."

The worldwide exports of bulk supplies of ephedrine and pseudoephedrine, along with other chemicals used to make illegal drugs, were supposed to be regulated by Article 12 of the 1988

United Nations Convention Against Illicit Traffic in Narcotic Drugs and Psychotropic Substances, a treaty signed by all the major chemical manufacturing countries and an agreement that Haislip, as the head of the DEA's Office of Diversion Control, had a major hand in drafting. Haislip understood early on that controlling domestic supplies of precursor chemicals wouldn't succeed without global cooperation. "I realized the necessity to go international right away," he says. "I organized the first-ever international conference on chemical control in 1987 in Quito, Ecuador, to educate the rest of the world about this important new tool in the fight against drug traffickers."

European countries were initially reluctant to go along with Haislip's ideas, reasoning that it wasn't their problem if Americans turned legal chemicals with legitimate uses into illegal drugs. But the U.S. government managed to convince the United Nations to adopt the recommendations. Similar to the Chemical Diversion and Trafficking Act, Article 12 listed twenty-two chemicals used to make illicit drugs, including such other meth-making materials as phenyl acetone, toluene, and phenylacetic acid. Signatories to the treaty were obliged to monitor exports of listed chemicals to make sure that the materials didn't end up in the hands of drug dealers. This system of worldwide controls that Haislip helped put in place apparently hadn't worked in this case.

The Dallas discovery sparked an international probe, as Gene Haislip tried to track down who was buying all these chemicals. He sent investigators to India to follow the paper trail back to the original factories where the ephedrine was produced. They soon found out that a Mexican national was buying huge quantities of the chemical and having the consignments shipped back to his home country via circuitous routes, an obvious ploy to disguise the final destination of the cargo.

The DEA determined that between June 1993 and December 1994 Jesús had arranged shipments of ephedrine involving a total of seventy tons. Stop orders were issued to halt another hundred tons that Jesús has also purchased but had yet to be shipped to Mexico. What the DEA had stumbled upon was nothing short of extraordinary—the largest methamphetamine precursor trafficking network that the agency had ever uncovered. They now had the answer why, after the initial spectacular success, the Chemical Diversion and Trafficking Act had so conspicuously failed to halt the spread of meth in America. But more than that, they also understood for the first time the full scope of the Mexican cartels' involvement in the American meth business.

Haislip launched a diplomatic offensive. Working with the United Nations International Narcotics Control Board, he visited India, met officials there, and succeeded in getting them to crack down on the sales and exports of ephedrine to the Amezcuas. In eighteen months, the D.E.A. in cooperation with foreign countries seized up to two hundred tons of ephedrine bound for Mexico. The Amezcuas immediately felt the effect. A twenty-five-kilo barrel of ephedrine, which normally sold on the black market for about forty-five thousand dollars, began selling for as much as eighty thousand dollars. By early 1996, Haislip thought he had managed to largely eliminate the diversion of ephedrine from foreign sources to the Amezcua brothers using the same tools he had used to cut off the supply of methaqualone powder to the Colombians a decade earlier.

In November 1995, at a meeting in Tijuana, a police wiretap caught the Amezcua brothers grumbling to their subordinates about the disruption of their ephedrine pipeline. But not to worry, they assured their associates. They'd already discovered new sources of ephedrine, this time from factories in China and the Czech Republic.

The Amezcua brothers quickly recovered from the temporary setback, when the DEA shut down their Indian connection, and were busily consolidating their empire even as the United States was pressing the Mexican government to arrest them. As was the case with domestic cooks, the brothers made the switchover from bulk ephedrine powder to easier-to-obtain pseudoephedrine pills. Most of the methamphetamine that the Amezcuas produced used to be consumed in California and adjoining states. But as their labs stepped up production, meth flowed eastward out of California along migrant worker routes, across the Rockies, and into the Midwest. Latino immigrants who traveled to the Midwest to work on farms and in meatpacking plants were paid thousands of dollars to act as mules to transport the drug. The seasonal ebb and flow of immigrant farm laborers provided convenient cover for the Amezcua brothers to hide their expanding operation.

"The Mexicans do it so simply, so quickly and their network is so mobile and tight that they can make meth today and have it sold in the Midwest tomorrow," a top official from California's Bureau of Narcotic Enforcement told the Los Angeles Times in 1995.

One of the things that distinguished the Amezcuas from the other cartels, and one of the reasons why they were so successful, was their ability to get along with their rivals. They formed an alliance with the Arellano-Felix brothers, who ran the Tijuana Cartel, and paid fees to them to be allowed to ship their product through the Tijuana–San Diego smuggling corridor that the Arellano brothers controlled. The Amezcuas were happy to pay tribute to the Arellano family just as long as the flow of meth into the United States remained uninterrupted. Other cartels, however, resented this toll system, sparking violent clashes with the Arellano organization.

The Amezcua brothers also enjoyed the friendship of the Arellanos' archrival, Amado Carrillo-Fuentes, the powerful boss of the Juárez Cartel. When Fuentes died unexpectedly under the surgeon's knife in 1997, the Amezcua brothers wisely stayed on the sidelines and waited for the bloodshed to subside, as competing factions within the cartel went to war with each other for control of the organization, a vicious struggle that left hundreds dead. The Amezcuas were more than willing to use violence when necessary. Luis was suspected but eventually cleared in the 1997 murder of the popular television host Paco Stanley, who was machine-gunned to death outside a Mexico City restaurant. Prosecutors charged that Luis had ordered the execution supposedly over a drug debt that Stanley refused to pay. The prosecution's key witness was one of the brothers' meth cooks, who claimed to have overheard Luis plotting the killing. But he changed his story on the witness stand and the case fell apart. In general, though, the Amezcuas tended to shy away from the gruesome displays of sadism that brought so much unwelcome scrutiny to their fellow drug lords.

The Amezcua brothers stayed out of the spotlight in other ways. In their early years as drug traffickers, they adopted the flashy lifestyle that went with the job. But as their organization grew bigger, they realized this was a mistake. Instead, they dressed humbly and drove around in beat-up automobiles so as not to draw attention to themselves. Constantly moving from city to city to elude their captors, they always seemed to stay one step ahead of law enforcement. The Mexican media dubbed them "men without faces." The rumor was that the brothers were protected from on high. Just how high their influence reached was hinted at during the trial of General Jesús Gutiérrez Rebollo, Mexico's disgraced ex–drug czar, who was arrested in 1997 and accused of accepting money from Amado Carrillo-Fuentes in exchange for confidential information. Rebollo's lawyer presented as evidence a series of secretly recorded phone conversations, one of which featured the Amezcua brothers discussing their supposed friendship with the father-in-law of then president Ernesto Zedillo. Zedillo's office issued a statement denying any connection between his family and the Amezcua clan.

While all this was happening in Mexico, back in the United States, the DEA was getting ready to deliver another blow to the Amezcuas' organization. In the early morning hours of December 4, 1997, drug agents swooped down and arrested 121 suspects, including the Los Angeles and Dallas cell leaders of the brothers' cartel. Three working meth labs were seized, including one in a public stable in Acton, California, and another close to a day care center. Operation Meta (*meta* means "goal" in Spanish, a slang word for meth) led to the seizure of 1,765 pounds of marijuana, 1,100 kilograms of cocaine, 90 gallons of chemicals, and 133 pounds of methamphetamine. Through wiretaps and surveillance in seventeen different cities, the DEA had managed to uncover the Amezcuas' distribution network, through which precursor chemicals were shipped across the Mexican border to Los Angeles, where they were made into methamphetamine. The drugs then were hidden in secret compartments of vehicles and then transported to Dallas to be distributed throughout the rest of the United States.

"These arrests are the result of an unprecedented effort to shut down methamphetamine labs and disrupt the meth trade," said the then attorney general Janet Reno. "We are sending a clear message to the meth merchants. Your days are numbered. We will not tolerate your threat to our children and our neighborhoods, and we are not going to let methamphetamine spread across America the way crack did in the nineteen eighties."

Operation Meta was a major setback for the Amezcua brothers' organization, followed the next year by an even bigger shock.

By the late 1990s the Amezcua brothers had moved their headquarters to Mexico City in the hope that they could lose themselves in the teeming metropolis. But the pressure from the United States was building on the Mexican government to do something about the drug-dealing clan. In June 1998, Jesús Amezcua was shopping for materials for a Santeria ceremony at the Sonora witchcraft market in Mexico City, when special agents from an elite antidrug team pounced upon and arrested him without incident. Hours earlier and three hundred miles away, his brother Luis was apprehended while looking at a secondhand Chrysler Shadow in a car showroom in downtown Guadalajara. The third brother, Adan, had been arrested by the Mexican army the previous November at his ranch in Jalisco, while he was milking a cow. All three were held at the same high-security federal prison in Mexico City.

The capture of the three Amezcua brothers was celebrated on both sides of the border as a crushing defeat for the *reyes de la metanfetamina*. "The Government of Mexico should be commended for the actions of their law enforcement agencies," said the then DEA head Thomas Constantine on hearing the news. "The arrest and removal of these two key leaders should significantly disrupt the established methamphetamine trade."

Oddly, though, the brothers weren't charged with drug trafficking but with money laundering. The Mexican equivalent of the IRS was looking into seven years of financial dealings involving thirty-two members of the organization, all said to be involved in managing businesses for the Amezcua clan. Their empire included factories, pharmacies, gas stations, Laundromats, strip clubs, restaurants, travel agencies, and construction firms. The Mexican authorities identified at least 125 properties bought with drug money, all of which were subsequently confiscated.

The investigation also uncovered a sophisticated money-laundering scheme involving *cajas ahorros*—the small savings accounts used by poor Mexicans who don't have enough money to bank with major financial institutions. Beginning in 1995, the authorities claimed that Cirilo José Ocampo Verdugo, known as the financial brain of the Amezcua organization, had set up credit unions (*cajas populares*) first in Colima and Jalisco, then in twenty-three other states, and had lured legitimate customers by offering them up to 45 percent annual interest on their accounts. Ocampo then allegedly commingled these legal funds with the Amezcuas' dirty money and used the cleaned-up proceeds to purchase luxury hotels and condominiums in Mexico and Miami. Eventually, some five hundred accounts were traced to the Amezcuas containing a total of eight hundred million pesos (about eighty million dollars). The Mexican authorities estimated the Amezcuas' annual income at about five hundred million dollars.

The celebration over the arrests of the Amezcua brothers proved short-lived. In October 1998, a Guadalajara judge ordered that all criminal charges be dropped against Jesús and Luis because the money-laundering statute was not in effect when the crime was alleged to have been committed. But under intense criticism from the U.S. government, which wanted to extradite the brothers to face methamphetamine trafficking charges in San Diego, the Mexican authorities refused to release them from prison. Adan, though, was released in May 1998. At a press conference afterward, Adan's lawyer claimed all the ephedrine the Amezcua brothers had imported into the country was for the purpose of feeding the cows on their cattle ranch. For his part, Adan declared to the assembled reporters: "I will dedicate my time to growing corn, buying and selling cattle, which has always been my business. All that I want is to be left alone." Adan didn't get his wish and was rearrested the next year, this time charged with drug trafficking.

Mexican judges repeatedly refused to extradite Luis and Jesús to the United States on the grounds that under American law, the two brothers faced the death penalty as drug kingpins. But the three brothers were eventually charged under Mexican law as drug traffickers and received long prison sentences. Even that was subject to controversy when Jesús' sentence was slashed in half on appeal.

By 2000, the Mexican government declared that the Amezcua brothers' organization had been officially disbanded. But skeptical voices in the Mexican media questioned that assertion and wondered whether this was all an elaborate publicity stunt to please the gringo politicians. Some journalists speculated that the Amezcuas weren't really the kingpins they were made out to be by the DEA. Their rise to the top was a little too easy for some to swallow. How could three dirt-poor peasant brothers have come from out of nowhere and in such a short space of time become some of the biggest drug traffickers Mexico has ever produced? Citing anonymous law enforcement sources, they raised the possibility that the Amezcuas were merely front men for more powerful political figures as yet unnamed. Either way, even with the Amezcua brothers behind bars, the flow of Mexican meth into the United States continued unabated.

B y the end of the 1990s the good news was that San Diego was no longer the crystal meth capital of mainland America. The bad news: The drug had become so prevalent thanks to the Mexican drug families that no one city or location could claim that title anymore. What started out as a drug concentrated mostly among lower-income white males on the West Coast had by the end of the decade spread throughout much of the rest of the country and was just as popular with middle-class women and among affluent gay men.

Today, Mexican meth is as plentiful as ever on the streets and in the neighborhoods of America, even more so because of all the new precursor restrictions. At the time of writing, forty-four states have passed laws restricting the sale of pseudoephedrine and ephedrine products. This, combined with the federal Combat Meth Act, has had a dramatic effect in curbing domestic production, especially among small-time cooks, cutting the overall number of meth labs discovered according to El Paso Intelligence Center's National Clandestine Laboratory Seizure System from 10,015 in 2004 to 5,846 in 2005 to 2,159 for the first nine months of 2006. In California, once the home of the superlabs that powered the explosion of meth use in the 1990s, the number of large-scale production facilities seized has dropped from 244 in 2001 to less than 20 in 2006. The cartels still operate a small number of superlabs in this country, but increasingly the manufacturing of the drug has moved back across the border into Mexico, where since 2000 the imports of pseudoephedrine into the country have nearly quadrupled in amount—from 66 tons to 224 tons.

Yet, what should be a spectacular success story, a shining example of the efficacy of precursor laws in stamping out meth production, has turned out to be anything but. Just as Uncle Fester predicted, the demise of the small mom-and-pop labs has only served to further bolster the power and influence of the Mexican drug families, who now control the methamphetamine trade in markets where only a few years back independent operators ruled the roost.

This the National Drug Intelligence Center acknowledged in its National Drug Threat Assessment 2007, released in November 2006: "Marked success in decreasing domestic methamphetamine production through law enforcement pressure and strong precursor chemical sales restrictions has enabled Mexican DTOs [drug trafficking organizations] to rapidly expand their control over methamphetamine production—even in eastern states—as users and distributors who previously produced the drug have sought new and consistent sources. These Mexican distribution groups (supported by increased methamphetamine production in Mexico) are often more difficult for local law enforcement agencies to identify, investigate, and dismantle because they typically are much more organized and experienced than local independent producers and distributors."

Even more troubling than the Mexicans' increased market share from a public health point of view is the unsurpassed potency of the product that the cartels are managing to deliver to the American consumer. I'd been hearing about this new turbocharged version of meth called "Mexican ice" for some time. Superexpensive at $240 a gram, but worth every cent, according to aficionados, it was said to be the purest type of meth available and made other forms of the drug pale in comparison. Typically, the purity of meth emanating from home labs varies widely, anywhere from 20 to 80 percent, but this new form of the drug was said to be 98 percent pure. Fifteen years is a long time to not have taken a particular substance, but I was curious to see how it compared to the biker meth I used to sample back in the day, which if I remember correctly came from a group of Hells Angels in Oakland, Calfornia. This new stuff, which is customarily smoked, certainly looks different, not powdered, but similar to shards of broken windshield glass. Taking what I presumed was a modest amount, half a gram, which barely covered the bottom of a small plastic baggie, I ground up the chunks into a fine powder and separated them into eight lines, which were to be taken twice a day over four days, to be accompanied by the occasional nap and lots of fluids. At least, that was the plan. I had a pile of boring fact-checking work to do and I figured meth would make the task easier.

Right from the first line, I could tell this was as different from the old biker meth I used to do as the biker meth was from the adulterated amphetamine sulfate of my teenage years. Some new plateau of intensity had been reached here. This was powerful, maybe too powerful. Still, for the first twelve hours, I managed to stay on an even keel, working at the computer, dropping off dry cleaning, going to the Korean deli to pick up some beer and cigarettes. Then, as night fell on Sunday evening just before Thanksgiving 2006, I was sitting at my desk in my twenty-second-floor midtown Manhattan apartment when I was startled by a fierce blast of music that filled up the whole room: "O Tannenbaum, O Tannenbaum." Looking out of my window to check the source of the racket, I saw two plastic discs with blinking red lights hovering outside, which I surmised were some sort of surveillance cameras peering into my room. Strange, I thought. It's a little early for the onset of sleep-deprivation hallucinations. Ignoring the discs, I sat back down at the computer and continued working, only to be interrupted a short while later by a tapping sound. A young man with long hair had appeared at the window and was gesturing for me to look out of the other window, where on a hydraulic metal stage half a dozen bondage babes in rubber and fishnets were cavorting in various stages of erotic undress. On further inspection, it became obvious that the figures were actually holograms being projected by a shadowy figure sitting at a console in the background, the only thing clearly visible being the red tip of his cigarette glowing in the darkness. This was amazing, I thought. How was this possible? Even more amazing things followed, as the figure at the console proceeded to beam indecipherable messages—scientific equations, Latin quotations, Egyptian hieroglyphics—onto every bare surface in my bedroom.

At this point, I became determined to find out who was behind this mind-boggling spectacle and managed to open up a line of communication with the figure in the shadows by typing questions onto my computer, which were then beamed as if by magic onto a giant screen hovering high in the air over Thirty-fourth Street.

At around 4 A.M. on Monday morning, my reverie was interrupted by an unexpected visit from two FBI agents who informed me that I was under arrest. The charges: aiding and abetting terrorists. According to the FBI agents, the underground organization I had been communicating with had stolen the technology they were using from a top-secret military installation and had set up a string of bondage parlors as a front operation to hide their attempt to sell the purloined government property to the highest bidder. Seeing my alarm at the possibility of spending the next twenty years in federal prison, the agents offered me a way out: infiltrate the organization and report back with my findings, and the FBI would forget the terrorism charges, not to mention the meth residue all over my desk. The agents then broke off the conversation to set up a boom box. Opening up all the windows in the apartment, they blasted at top volume: "O Tannenbaum, O Tannenbaum." As neighbors banged on the front door complaining about the noise, the agents explained that the song was really a tracking signal they used to force the flying bits of machinery to return to the military base they originated from.

After the agents left, what followed was days of wild sex with the holograms floating outside my window, strange couplings involving these half-human, half-animal creatures. A recurring element was one of the dildo-wielding bondage girls who would transform in front of my eyes into a horse which would then proceed to fuck one of the other girls, who herself would turn into a leopard. Periodically, I would break off from the kinky goings-on to jot down notes in my computer that I planned to give later to my FBI handlers. In between, I would attempt to quiz the Wizard of Oz who was lurking in the background. What was the name of his company? In what part of the country was he based? Where did this technology come from? How come I'd never heard about this before?

On the fifth day, as the drug started to wear off and I returned to a semblance of normality, it became obvious to me what had just taken place. There was no secret techno-sex cult. And there were no FBI agents. It was all a figment of my imagination. The meth was so powerful that it had given me this extraordinary ability to surrealize reality, animate my surroundings like a cosmic cartoonist. Looking around my apartment, all the elements of the hallucination were readily at hand. The frisky stallion that kept appearing in the sadomasochist scenes was a leather statue of a horse that sits atop a Chinese dresser in my bedroom. The flying saucers hovering outside my window were modeled on an Apple AirPort wireless router I use to connect to the Internet. The blaring music—"O Tannenbaum, O Tannenbaum"—was coming from the department store Christmas display across the street. And the plotline of the fantasy—the sadomasochist episodes, the hallucinations, the futuristic technology, the secret organization—was lifted straight from the sci-fi classic *Videodrome*, a movie I saw as a college student and which had an enormous impact on me at the time. In effect, the fantasy elements were so seamlessly intertwined with reality, I had spent the last four days living in a David Cronenberg movie and I couldn't tell the difference.

I can't deny the experience was an exhilarating one, but it was also deeply scary and one I vowed not to repeat anytime soon. I had experienced meth hallucinations before, but never with such intensity or duration. If a half a gram of Mexican ice spread out over four days could do this to me, imagine what an eight ball could do.

CHAPTER EIGHT

SEX AND THE CITY

CHELSEA, NEW YORK CITY

ighth Avenue between Fourteenth Street and Twenty-third Street
is the gayest stretch of real estate in New York City. Lined with
coffee shops, boutiques, and bars, this formerly run-down working class neighborhood is the home of the stereotypical "Chelsea
boys," muscular men in tight jeans and T-shirts who on warm eve-
nings parade up and down the avenue holding hands or checking
each other out. This is the epicenter of gay life in the city, the place
to see and be seen. This is also an area that has been hard hit by
crystal meth. Plastered on walls and attached to phone booths, you
see posters with a pink triangle over which is superimposed the slogan SILENCE =METH, a deliberate echo of the famous SILENCE =DEATH
campaign organized by the protest group ACT UP in the 1980s to
raise awareness about AIDS. Below the slogan, the posters read: "25
years ago, our community refused to be silent about AIDS. Today,
we must not be silent about crystal meth."

Just off Eighth Avenue is an AIDS hospice, where Lee, a former
musician and a descendant of English aristocracy, sits on the bed in
his tiny cell-like room. A genealogical tree and pictures of the family
castle decorate the walls. Lee, a rotund, middle-aged, recovering
meth addict dressed all in black, lets out a long sigh as he recalls the
history of his disease.

In 1996, Lee, who had been diagnosed as HIV positive in the late
1980s, was getting ready to die. His doctor told him he had only six

months left to live. "I was a walking skeleton," remembers Lee. "My body had gotten to the point where it wasn't even absorbing food or medication anymore." He had already visited his family in Texas to say one final farewell and had written the music for his own memorial service when his doctor prescribed protease inhibitors, the anti-HIV retroviral drugs that had just been introduced. Almost immediately Lee felt better, but he was still physically weak from a chronic wasting syndrome. His doctor wrote out another prescription, this one for steroids, which bulked up Lee's body, radically changing his appearance. For the first time in many years, he felt fully masculine again.

"Suddenly in gay society," he says, "there were these people who used to be sickly and thin and now they were muscular, who used to feel tired and now they felt virile and vibrant, who used to feel unattractive and now they felt sexy. So naturally, they wanted to go out and party and have sex."

Lee felt miraculously reborn and began attending late-night parties and sex clubs where crystal meth was freely available, and where he would often engage in intercourse with numerous partners while under the drug's influence. Meth is said to have a particular attraction to gay men because it boosts the libido and loosens inhibitions. (As early as 1946, an article in a medical journal commented on the "homosexually toned perversion of their [methamphetamine users'] sex lives.")

"Crystal made me feel smart, energetic, powerful, hungry, desirable, and very, very slutty," says Lee. "One of the side effects of protease inhibitors is lethargy. But the crystal picked me right up. It felt like all the switches in my body and my brain finally got turned on." The meth also temporarily held at the bay the crippling depression he had suffered from ever since he was a child, the feelings of "being less than, of not being wanted, of being an outcast."

But there was a snag. Despite its reputation as an aphrodisiac, meth can sometimes make it difficult to sustain erections, leading to what is referred to as "crystal dick." The advent of Viagra, which

combated the deflating effect that meth can have on the male geni-
talia and which is often taken by gay men in combination with
meth, not only reversed this predicament but added fuel to the fire.
Now, thanks to the little blue diamond-shaped pills, Lee was free to
engage in marathon sex binges that lasted anywhere from ten to
fourteen days and involved as many as three sex partners a night. "I
wasn't a sex pig, I was the entire fucking barnyard," he says. "The
thing that always drove me was I needed to have sex with you because when you have sex with me it validated me as a person. The
problem with that was as soon as I got the validation from you, I
needed to get more validation."

In the wake of 9/11, Lee—who saw the Twin Towers fall from
the bedroom window of his Midtown apartment—kicked up his
crystal use in a dramatic fashion. "From my apartment I watched
the second plane hit," he says. Every time he got high after that, he
would imagine airplanes crashing into his building. He put up
black curtains to block out the hallucinations and he slept under the
bed or in the bathroom because it was the only room in the apartment without a window.

Under the influence of meth, he also forgot to take his medicines
on a regular basis, sometimes for weeks. In December 2001, Lee's
CD4 count, a measure of immune system health, was over 800,
which is in the normal range. Five months later, it was down to 53.

"You have to take the medicines regularly for them to work," he
says. "I knew that if I wasn't adhering to the medications, I would
develop a resistance to them and that in fact did happen. I'm now
on the last protease inhibitor I don't have a resistance to because of
my crystal meth use. It was more important for me to get high than
take my medicines."

Lee's story is typical of a number of HIV-positive gay men I
talked to who, having been given a second lease on life, ended up
ruining their health with crystal meth and other drugs. The advent
of the first combination protease inhibitors in the mid-1990s made
HIV a manageable disease. AIDS was no longer an automatic death

sentence. The tide of doom and gloom subsided. By the late 1990s, many HIV-positive men were in relatively good physical shape. As they put on weight and began to feel well again, many of them went back to the sort of hedonistic nightlife that had declined at the height of the AIDS era. So-called circuit parties proliferated: the peripatetic dance marathons that often stretch over several days and attract gay men in the thousands who fly in from all over the country to attend them. They initially started out as fund-raisers for AIDS organizations but soon developed a reputation as orgiastic affairs where many attendees engaged in wild sex while high on drugs. While all manner of illegal substances were available at these events, the signature drug was and remains crystal meth. As these parties gained in popularity and spread across the country, a national market for the drug was created among gay men, whereas previously meth had been confined largely to scenes on the West Coast. In the process, meth underwent a glamorous image makeover as gay men, who often pioneer nightlife trends, turned a blue-collar high ("poor man's cocaine") into a fashionable club drug.

Much of the sexual antics that Lee used to indulge in at parties and in clubs were done without the benefit of condoms. "The desire for intimacy is ultimately greater than the desire for self-preservation," he says by way of explanation. Beginning in the late 1990s, the phenomenon of "barebacking"—indulging in anal sex without condoms—began to rise alarmingly in the gay community. A July 2006 survey of ten thousand gay men by the Centers for Disease Control and Prevention (CDC) revealed that nearly half of them had engaged in unprotected anal sex in the previous twelve months. Medical experts say that many gay men suffer from something called safe sex fatigue. Weary of using condoms, their common sense compromised by meth, and lulled into a false sense of security that HIV medications will save them if they contract the disease, many men today are engaging in the sort of dangerous sexual practices that the previous generation of AIDS activists railed against. It's even said that a small segment of gay men actually welcome the AIDS virus—having become infected, they no longer have to worry about contracting the disease and can indulge themselves in unlimited sexual pleasures.

While the number of new HIV infections diagnosed annually in America (roughly 40,000) has not increased since 1990, the proportion of gay and bisexual men diagnosed with the illness has grown every year since the beginning of the decade. According to the CDC, in 2004 (the last year for which figures are available) new cases of HIV infections increased 8 percent from the previous year. This news came after a 2003 CDC report that estimated that HIV infections had jumped 18 percent nationwide among gay and bisexual men since 1999. And it's not just HIV that has undergone a resurgence. Syphilis rates have skyrocketed. In 1999, gay and bisexual men accounted for only 5 percent of new syphilis cases diagnosed nationwide. By 2004, they made up nearly two-thirds of the total. In New York, syphilis rates among gay men have quadrupled in five years.

Many of those involved in HIV prevention place the blame for this frightening renewed spread of the AIDS virus and other sexually transmitted diseases in the gay community firmly on crystal meth, which has been associated with high rates of unprotected sex. A 2005 joint study of gay men in San Francisco conducted by the CDC in collaboration with the University of California, San Francisco reported that those who use meth were three times as likely to be infected with HIV as nonusers were. Doctors at Callen-Lorde, an AIDS treatment center in New York, estimate that three-quarters of their patients who are newly diagnosed with HIV each month admit that crystal meth played a role in their contracting the disease. While in terms of sheer numbers, many more straight people—eight or nine times as many—take meth than gay people, percentagewise, the rates of usage among homosexual men is anywhere from four to six times compared to the general population.

But Lee thinks it simplistic to blame the situation solely on crystal meth: "Safe sex is a myth in the gay community," says Lee. "The reason why HIV infections are on the rise again isn't crystal meth but having unprotected sex with multiple partners."

Though crystal meth is not a new drug on the gay scene—in San Francisco, gay men and women have used crystal meth since the 1960s—for a long time New York City seemed immune to the meth problem sweeping the rest of the country. New York was a cocaine and Ecstasy town, and crystal meth was difficult to obtain. But New York could not stay crystal free forever. Beginning in the mid-1990s, demand for meth rose as local gay men who were introduced to the drug on trips to West Coast circuit parties came back with stories about how the substance not only enabled them to stay up and dance all night but made sex a breathtaking experience. The drug was especially appealing to men in their thirties and forties who attended these events, many of whom were affluent professionals with demanding day jobs, yet they were still expected to dance for twelve hours straight and then engage in marathon screwing bouts afterward. Meth taken through the nose proved the ideal pick-me-up on both fronts.

When New York University psychology professor Perry Halkitis conducted his first survey on New York gay men and meth in 1999, about 12 percent of the sample were regular crystal users. Today, he says, an estimated 20 percent of gay men in the city use the drug.

The social effects of the drug have been most strongly felt in New York's gay club world, where, according to a 2004 study by the Center for HIV/AIDS Educational Studies and Training in New York, 62 percent of those who use any club drugs reported "significant and frequent use" of crystal meth. I spent August 2004 reporting and writing an article for *The New York Times* Styles section on the ripple effect that meth was having in the wider world of gay men in the city, even among those who didn't use the drug. Talking to aficionados of the scene, it wasn't difficult to find partygoers who said they hated what the drug was doing to their social world and who complained that dance clubs had become sterile settings filled with monotonous music and detached dancers thanks to its influence. Crystal meth "turns people into antisocial zombies," Trip Zanetis, a young nightclub publicist, told me. "It makes people hostile and delusional. The vibe is much more negative and colder than in the past, thanks to this drug." This sentiment was echoed by Max Wixom, a theatrical publicist and production designer, who said, "Even the way gay men look at each other is different. In nineteen ninety-six, when I first arrived in New York and started going out, you could easily get to know people. It felt like a community or a brotherhood." But with the rise of crystal meth, Wixom said, gay nightlife had turned "more predatory and dehumanized."

"I've been in this business for twenty-five years, and I've seen four or five different sets of people come and go," said John Blair, New York's leading gay party promoter. "Each group of people goes through a similar experience with different music and different drugs. But crystal is by far the worst drug I've ever seen happen to night life. It not only takes over people's lives, but it really negates what the whole scene is supposed to be about."

Dr. Steven Lee, a New York psychiatrist who specializes in treating crystal meth addicts and who in 2006 published a guide to beating the drug entitled *Overcoming Crystal Meth Addiction*, told me there is now "a much harder edge in New York gay clubs than in the past." This change is largely because of the drug: In addition to its sexual and stimulant effects, crystal meth can promote aggression. "Some of my patients talk about how they feel on crystal meth as akin to being robots programmed with the sole purpose of doing more crystal and having more sex," Dr. Lee said.

On a sticky afternoon in the city, I went to visit Dr. Lee at his office in one of those recently constructed deluxe apartment buildings that have turned Chelsea from a seedy neighborhood into a desirable location for the well-to-do. A smooth-faced, soft-spoken Asian man sporting a Tin-Tin coiffure and wearing a stylish off-white summer suit, he wouldn't look out of place ordering a bottle of champagne at a trendy lounge. As a humidifier hummed in the background, Dr. Lee told me that he has been treating gay men who take meth ever since he started to practice psychiatry in 1996. But the pattern of use a decade ago was different. "There was this East Coast–West Coast drug culture divide," he says. "In New York people really preferred cocaine, whereas on the West Coast they really wanted crystal. On the East Coast, at clubs and circuit parties, crystal was always there but it was more of an occasional drug, an add-on. So if people got tired dancing, they would sniff a little to fuel themselves to go on."

But that started to change around 1999, according to Dr. Lee. "What happened was in New York people started to smoke it," he says. "And once people started to smoke it, everything changed completely. That's when meth really caught on. The amount that your brain is suddenly exposed to in a short period of time is exponentially greater when you smoke it. That, compared to snorting it, really altered people's behavior."

The switchover from snorting meth to smoking the drug coincided with the emergence of Internet sex sites such as manhunt.net, gay.com, and m4m4sex.com. Gay men flock to these sites where they post explicit sexual profiles of themselves—whether they are a top or a bottom, the lengths of their appendages, whether they are HIV positive or not—and, usually within minutes, other gay men reply to them. If the poster likes what he sees, he invites one or more of them over to his apartment for "pig sex," frenzied animalistic trysts that can last for days and which are often fueled by smoking crystal meth. Not all men who advertise on these sites smoke the drug. Many of them adamantly kept their distance from those who do. The rift is apparent in the language people use, coded references like "PNP" (for "party and play," meaning drugs with sex) or "No PNP," "chem friendly," or "absolutely no tweakers" (a reference to people strung out on the drug).

Because of these sites, the way many gay men interact with each other has been transformed. Rather than going to nightclubs to pick up partners, men now have sex delivered to their doorsteps like Chinese takeout. This isn't just a matter of convenience. Before the Internet, gay men who went out to clubs couldn't appear too obviously stoned if they wanted to get past the velvet ropes. As wild as these clubs can be, there were limits to the debauchery. You couldn't just take out a pipe on the dance floor and start smoking, unless you wanted to be ejected from the premises. But with the shift in the action from clubs to apartments, "people can do things in the privacy of their own homes that they would be embarrassed to do in a nightclub," says Dr. Lee.

This has led to the phenomenon of "crystal meth shut-ins." As people become heavier users, they turn increasingly reclusive and spent long hours focused on Internet sex liaisons, barely leaving their apartments, their only visitors men they meet online and invite over for sex. What started out as a party drug, a social lubricant to facilitate dancing and sex, over time has turned some users into virtual hermits.

Dan Carlson, a founder of an anti-crystal-meth organization called the HIV Forum NYC, tells the story of one club promoter who offered to help with the group's work. "I said, 'Great, but what's in it for you?'" Carlson says. "And he's like, 'This Internet stuff is killing my business.' People stay home and they do crystal and they're on the Internet all the time and they don't go to clubs."

Three highly addictive phenomena—the Internet, crystal meth, and casual sex—have combined to wreak havoc in the lives of many gay men who might otherwise lead quite normal lives; one addiction feeding the others, according to Dr. Lee. "The Internet, sex, and crystal meth; on their own, each of them has addictive and compulsive potential," he says. "When you put them together and they become associated with each other, the addictive potential is extremely high and it's that much harder to stop."

Dr. Lee gives an example of one patient he treated, a highly successful banker with a steady lover:

He and his partner partied occasionally, and got involved with crystal and started smoking it. So they started having sex with other people they met online and then it became having unsafe sex, then his lover became HIV positive. They were watching all this happening and saying, "Oh my God, what are we doing, this is not good for us, this is terrible for our health, we have to stop." But they didn't. Then he too became HIV positive. And then he lost his job. He ended up becoming sober and getting a temporary midlevel job, but he watched all these things disappear one by one and intellectually he told himself, "My life is going down the tubes, I have to stop," but he couldn't. Statistically speaking, people who are well educated, who are employed, people who are partnered, all of these things increase people's chances of being able to pull away from a drug and achieve sobriety. And despite having all these things, this person was not able to resist it.

"This is not an uncommon story," Dr. Lee adds.

When gay men who use crystal meth complain that the drug brings out some primal urge inside of them to keep on having sex, they're not speaking in metaphorical terms, according to Dr. Lee. He locates the source of this compulsion in a chain reaction of events that occur when meth stimulates the release of the pleasure chemical dopamine in a neurological pathway, called the brain-reward circuit, located deep in the primitive part of the brain.

"The deeper you go into the brain, the more primitive the function, and the less voluntary the control is," he says. "The particular circuit that meth affects is the same part of the brain that we share with animals. It is nature's way of trying to trick an animal into doing something again and again like sex and eating because that's going to keep it alive and keep the species going. Compared to the normal rate of dopamine stimulation in the brain-reward circuit, cocaine will raise the dopamine rate about four hundred percent; meth is about fifteen hundred percent. That gives you an idea how powerful meth is. If sex and eating are things we feel we need to do again and again, imagine fifteen times that reinforcement to repeat the behavior. When people say, 'Meth is ruining my life, I need to stop,' that's the logical outside surface of the brain talking. The reason they can't stop is because meth affects a much deeper level of the brain. The longer that you use it, the more the primitive brain takes over and the less control you have."

Dr. Lee says sexual compulsion among gay men who use meth is not just a matter of brain chemistry, however. It also has to do with growing up in a homophobic society.

"I want to be very careful how I phrase this because I've been misinterpreted before," cautions Dr. Lee. "But many gay men growing up in a society, where from the time you're very little you're ostracized, you internalize the views of everyone around you so that you not only are hearing other people say you're bad for being gay, you actually think of yourself as bad. So you grow up hating yourself and it's very hard to get rid of that inner voice that says, 'You're terrible, you're a pervert, you're disgusting.' And so even when they come out and say, 'I'm comfortable with being gay,' the reality is that many, if not most, have internalized views of themselves as less than fully human. If you're gay, sex is that much more complicated because every time you do it you have these very strong messages inside your head saying, 'This is dirty. This is disgusting. You're evil and you're going to go to hell.' What happens when gay men use crystal, it elevates their self-esteem and silences the voices in their head and they can actually enjoy the sexual act. It's one of the few rare times that many gay men can actually experience unconflicted sex."

In February 2005, the New York City Department of Health and Mental Hygiene made a dramatic announcement. "We've identified this strain of HIV that is difficult or impossible to treat," New York City health commissioner Dr. Thomas Frieden bluntly told reporters. "Potentially, no one is immune." A rare strain of rapidly progressing HIV had been detected in a gay man who participated in meth-fueled orgies with hundreds of people he met on the Internet and at sex clubs. The so-called supervirus had supposedly proved resistant to nineteen of the twenty-one drugs used to treat HIV. "It's a wake-up call to men who have sex with men, particularly those who may use crystal methamphetamine," Frieden said. The Department of Health believed the man was infected in October 2004; he was diagnosed with HIV two months later. By January, his illness had progressed to full-blown AIDS, the onset of which usually takes years to happen. The doctor who diagnosed the new strain called it "a silent tsunami" that could well signal a return to the days when AIDS was a terminal illness.

The day after the announcement, New York mayor Michael Bloomberg issued a warning to those engaged in unsafe sexual practices. "I think some people thought, 'Well, it's probably not going to happen to me,'" he said. "'And if it does, there are drugs that can stop it, or control it, or let me continue to lead a life.' And that's not true with this new strain."

The news set off a panic in New York's gay community, as well as in other cities. Journalist David France wrote in *New York* magazine: "Physicians across the country reported a crush of visits from worried patients; the Gay Men's Health Crisis Website experienced a 63 percent surge in hits. At two heated community meetings in Manhattan, gay men and AIDS service providers swapped accusations with rancorous outbursts reminiscent of early ACT UP meetings." A measure of the alarm was that *The New York Times* ran twelve articles about the so-called supervirus within a week of the story breaking.

In the coffee shops along Eighth Avenue, gay men discussed this worrying development. Was this an isolated case or the harbinger of a resurgent epidemic? Was this man a new "patient zero," the first case of an even deadlier mutated form of the disease? And was meth the reason the virus progressed so rapidly? The anonymous patient, a middle-aged man, had used crystal sporadically for a long time, but in the two years prior to being diagnosed he had started using at least every week. Studies have been done that suggest meth may increase the amount of the virus in the brain.

Seeking to calm public fears, some scientists professed skepticism about the Department of Health's findings. This was not the first time that doctors had come across a rapidly progressing AIDS virus that had at first proved impervious to drugs, they said. Two similar cases had been diagnosed in Vancouver, Canada, in 2001, and despite the initial fear that these cases could signal the beginning of the spread of a new type of untreatable AIDS, the concern proved unfounded. The right combination of drugs was eventually found that effectively combated the virus in the men, and today the two of them are still alive and supposedly in relatively good shape. It is estimated that as many as 10 percent of new HIV patients are resistant to some retroviral drugs. World-renowned AIDS expert Dr. Robert C. Gallo, who helped discover the HIV virus, even questioned whether the man really had full-blown AIDS. An early stage of HIV called acute infection can imitate the symptoms of AIDS, but typically it passes. Questions were also raised about the host as well as the virus. Was there something about the man's immune system that made him unable to fend off the disease?

Within six weeks of the initial announcement, the Department of Public Health began to back away from its original, unnerving assessment. The department put out a press release informing the public that the patient's health had improved and he was responding well to antiviral medications. In addition, medical investigators were unable to find anybody that the man had infected. It seems that the supervirus wasn't so super after all.

Exaggerated or not, the case did serve to intensify the already heated debate about the link between meth and HIV that burst into the open in early 2004 when posters began appearing on phone booths in Chelsea saying, HUGE SALE! BUY CRYSTAL, GET HIV FREE. The posters were the work of a former bond trader and recovering meth addict named Peter Staley who used $6,000 of his own money to print and distribute them. The posters set off a storm of controversy in

Chelsea. One school of thought welcomed them as a long overdue warning to irresponsible party boys who were threatening the health and well-being of the wider community with their out-of-control lifestyle. Others, however, took offense at the message that crystal meth use inevitably leads to unsafe sex, believing the posters were merely the latest chapter in an ongoing antisex, antidrug argument that has been going on for years in the gay community.

In the May 2004 issue of the gay magazine *Genre*, a writer who called himself Diabolique lambasted people like Staley as "nanny nelly liberal activists" and accused them of helping spur a continuing police crackdown on gay nightlife.

"It combines the worst aspects of over-the-top anti-drug hysteria with the best of 'get press at any cost' '80s-era AIDS activism," Diabolique wrote. "The ads don't work on drug-taking hedonists, they work on riling up the news media, public health and law enforcement officials."

In an interview I conducted with him soon after the article came out, Diabolique expanded on his criticism. "There's a total split in the gay community about this issue," Diabolique said. "Most gay men I know thought the 'Buy crystal, get HIV' ads were ridiculous.

"Crystal meth is a problem," he continued. "It's the worst drug problem I've seen in all my years of clubbing. But hysterical antidrug, antisex propaganda does nothing to solve that problem."

Diabolique's target, Peter Staley, is one of a growing number of vocal antimeth activists in New York, many of them former users themselves, who have banded together to fight what they see as the greatest health threat to hit their community since the height of the AIDS epidemic in the 1980s. Staley's friend, Dan Carlson, started the HIV Forum NYC/Crystal Meth Working Group in July 2003 with Dr. Bruce Kellerhouse, a psychologist, after they became enraged at the news that HIV infections were once more on the rise among gay men, an increase they blame largely on crystal. Having lived in New York for over a decade, the thirty-six-year-old Carlson is no stranger to the Chelsea party scene. Before he became an activist, he frequented nightclubs and sex establishments—including the infamous West Side Club, where the anonymous man who was diagnosed with the "superbug" supposedly contracted the disease—and engaged in "drinking and drugging nearly every night."

After he cleaned up in 2002, he continued to be very sexually active and often surfed the Internet looking for partners. But now sober, he became increasingly alarmed at the demands being placed on him. "A lot of the guys I would meet over the Internet were insisting on having unsafe sex with me," he says. "I'm HIV negative, thank God. But there were no public messages out there to help me stay that way. I started wondering who's protecting HIV negative men like myself."

He adds, "There's a shocking complacency in the gay community about this issue, an attitude that says, 'I don't want to talk about HIV. I don't want to talk about drug addiction. I just want to have a good time.' But the truth is we have to."

Carlson and Kellerhouse have hosted a string of well-attended public forums in Chelsea intended to raise awareness about the issue of meth and HIV. Doctors, drag queens, city officials, clubbers, law enforcement officers, and recovering addicts come to these meetings to discuss the negative impact that the drug has had on the gay world and what can be done about it. In addition, Carlson, who works in advertising, personally designed a public education campaign intended to deglamorize the drug. One of the adverts he produced featured a buff young man clad only in briefs, looking at a computer screen and sucking on a glass crystal-meth pipe filled with smoke. The caption underneath read, "Another night on the A List?" and the tagline said, "Crystal meth: Nothing to be proud of."

"For many years," Carlson says, "crystal has built this reputation as being glamorous, being fun. Anyone who's edgy is doing crystal meth. And if you're not, you're not cool—you're not part of the 'in' crowd, not part of the scene. What we're trying to do is change the social norm and say that crystal meth is not cool."

Carlson worries about the wider political implications of all of this rampant barebacking and crystal meth use. He's concerned about a right-wing backlash. At a time when many same-sex couples are trying to normalize homosexuality—getting married, taking out mortgages, adopting children, doing all the things straight couples do, but with one crucial difference—Carlson frets that the Jerry Falwells and Pat Robertsons of the world will use the stories about some gay men destroying themselves with sex and drugs to stigmatize gay men in general.

"I'm not antisex or antipartying, but what does it say about our community that we glamorize a drug like crystal meth?" asks Carlson before adding, "How can we make a case for gay marriage and more equality when we behave in this reckless manner? We're killing ourselves. Politically, it's a disaster."

In June 2006, the HIV Forum took out a full page ad in *The New York Times* to publicize an anticrystal manifesto that was signed by, among others, the writers Andrew Sullivan and Larry Kramer, the musician Rufus Wainwright, and the deejay Junior Vasquez. (The last signatory drew guffaws from cynics, since the parties at which he performed were notorious for unbridled crystal use.) Five points were highlighted:

- "We will take responsibility for our lives and for the health of our community."

- "We will not be silent."

- "We will show compassion for those who are addicted."

- "We will fight for more money for drug treatment."

- "We won't let crystal meth destroy another generation of gay men."

"Crystal meth poses a very important question for gay men," says Carlson. "Are we going to evolve from an identity defined by sex and drugs to a multifaceted community that offers so many other things? Those who argue that they have the right to have as much sex when they want to, do as much drugs as they want to, how they want to, and how often, to me are holding back the evolution of our community."

Not all gay men think crystal is a pox on their community. And not all gay men regard meth as a surefire prescription for HIV. During Sunday brunch in a diner on Eighth Avenue, Jay is brandishing one of the many advertisements produced by Carlson's organization, the HIV Forum, and he's hopping mad.

"Look at this, it's ridiculous," Jay says. He holds up an ad that depicts a shirtless bartender with a can of paint stripper in one hand and a bottle of Drano in the other pouring the fluids into a cocktail glass, under the headline: "How to Make Crystal Meth." The caption reads: "Three parts sinus medication. Two parts drain cleaner. One part antifreeze. One part paint thinner."

"Whoever designed this ad doesn't know anything about chemistry," Jay mocks.

It is true the chemicals discussed in the ad are used as solvents and reagents to *synthesize* methamphetamine; they're not simply mixed together like a margarita. If ingesting meth was like drinking paint thinner and bleach, then thousands of party people would be dropping dead on the dance floor every weekend.

"Why this drug?" Jay asks. "Why not alcohol? Why not tobacco? Why not all the things that are killing gay people instead of this drug that kills only a handful of people a year?"

But it's not really the faulty science that has Jay's dander up. It's the overall message of the campaign that gay men who use crystal meth inevitably engage in unsafe sex.

"I'm personally insulted by these adverts," says Jay. "I regard them as a slap in the face. I've been HIV positive for twenty-three years and I've not had unprotected sex once since I was diagnosed. I don't care how high I get, I will always use a condom.

"Crystal meth makes you horny; it doesn't make you stupid," he says.

Jay is the quintessential weekend warrior. During the workday, this ivy league graduate has a high-powered job as the comptroller of a medium-size corporation. But every third weekend or so, this forty-four-year-old buys an eight ball of meth, injects himself with the drug before he goes out to the Roxy or Crobar, where he strips off his shirt and turns into a combination dancing machine and sexual superman. After coming home from the clubs, he shoots up again, and then he and his lover go online to hunt for men. He estimates he sleeps with four to six different partners a weekend, which by Chelsea standards is not a huge number.

Jay spent ten years in a 12-step program because of a cocaine addiction. After a decade of sobriety, he moved to Chelsea and threw himself into the party scene. "I decided to see if I could do meth responsibly, in a way the program said I wasn't able to do, and I think I have," he says. "I don't want to spend the rest of my life hearing the same sad people telling the same sad stories over and over again. Think of all the fun I would have missed. I love my life, really."

Jay is one of an unusual breed in the gay world—so-called slammers, a subculture within a subculture of men, who inject crystal meth. Injecting meth is still relatively rare among gays. It's a practice more closely associated with heterosexuals. A lot of gay men like to show off their bodies, and track marks tend to spoil the effect. "I can't really explain it, but injecting seemed like the right method of delivery for this drug," he says. "I don't have to stop every thirty minutes during sex to smoke meth to keep the high going."

Jay says his experience with meth has been almost uniformly positive. Despite his disease, he says he feels no lasting ill effects from the drug, at least not yet. He doesn't suffer from hallucinations. He's never undergone any psychotic episodes. And he's never experienced "suicide Tuesday," the crashing comedown following a crystal binge that many users report plunges them into a pit of depression. "You know what," he says, "when I go to work on Monday morning a little hung over and tired, I'm in complete harmony and at peace with the universe. Hedonism is my religion."

Jay sees no harm to anybody but himself in what he's doing. That's why he's angry that he and his kind have been portrayed as traitors to their people, spreaders of disease, irresponsible individuals who put their own selfish pleasures ahead of the welfare of everybody else.

"Leave Chelsea alone," he protests. "I'd like to think that the gay world has progressed further than blaming a drug for the spread of HIV. That we haven't is quite disappointing to me."

It's not just party boys who complain that this exclusive focus on meth as the cause of new HIV transmissions may be clouding the wider picture. At least one prominent researcher is expressing reservations about his previously held view that the two are inextricably connected. Perry Halkitis, a psychology professor at New York University, was one of the first experts to sound the alarm about meth use among gay men in New York City. In a well-known column which he wrote for *Newsday*, he called HIV and meth "twin epidemics." But today, he's backing off from some of the claims made in that piece.

"We're always looking for a simple excuse for why HIV continues to exist in the gay community," he says. "Crystal is the simple excuse: Methamphetamine causes you to take risks and you become HIV positive. Well, it's not that simple."

Halkitis is a well-built man in tight clothing who looks not unlike one of the Chelsea boys whose mating and drug habits he studies, which must prove useful in persuading his interview subjects to spill intimate details about their lives. Sitting in an office crammed with books and papers and overlooking Washington Square Park, Halkitis says the gay community doesn't have a crystal meth problem as much as a polydrug problem. Few tweakers do only meth. More often than not, meth is combined with other drugs.

"If you look at our data," says Halkitis, "you see meth gets introduced to a larger repertoire of drug use. There are very rare circumstances among gay men where people are using this drug in isolation. It's all about polydrug use. It's not that cocaine has gone away. It's meth with cocaine with Ecstasy with alcohol.

"People want us to show that there's a simple x equals y relationship between crystal and HIV, and we can't do it," he says. "We can't find these men who are just using meth and having risky sex."

Meth doesn't cause AIDS, unsafe sex does. An obvious point, but one the anticrystal activists in their zeal sometimes seem to forget. While meth clearly plays a role in passing on the AIDS virus, the answer to why some gay men behave in such a self-destructive manner is not just the drug on its own. As well as the extensive list of other illegal drugs that party boys do, legal drugs like Viagra, steroids, and alcohol play a role. So do the highly sexualized environments in which gay men take the drug and the depression about their HIV status that some gay men suffer from. All these factors have contributed to the worrisome spike in new infections.

Halkitis has been studying the effect of meth on New York's gay population for eleven years. He's conducted thousands of interviews and released numerous papers on what he calls "the intersection between mental health, drug addiction, and sexual risk taking." He oversees with colleagues two ongoing research projects: Project TINA, a study of meth users; and Project BUMPS, a study of general club drug use among gay men. He first noticed meth in 1995 when a drug dealer he knew, who used to work the street between two leather bars on the West Side of Manhattan, added crystal to his menu of offerings. "I felt there was a potential for increase in use," he says. By 1998, he says he was warning the New York City Department of Health—the same city agency that hyped the supervirus scare—about the likelihood that meth was about to hit the local gay community hard, but they scoffed, "Well, cocaine's the problem. Meth is a West Coast problem. It's never going to come here."

From the beginning, the gay men that Halkitis talked to cited sexual enhancement as the most common rationale for taking meth. But he soon came across a significant number of people who told him they used it for another reason: in addition to its libido-boosting properties, meth is also a potent mood elevator. "Depression is definitely one of those factors that brings people to this drug," Halkitis says. "Rates of depression are much higher among gay men than in the general population, and that's been documented for more than a decade now. Being raised gay in a hetero society could cause anyone to become depressed. Even if it is the twenty-first century and we have *Will and Grace* and all that crap, it's still a struggle to be a gay man. HIV-positive men talk about the drug combating feelings of being lonely and blue and disconnected from the world, while negative men talk about the drug overcoming feelings of insecurity and self-doubts. People talk about the drug as something that alleviates those anxieties and helps them fit in."

The problem comes over time when users develop a tolerance for the drug. They need more and more meth to feel the original uplift, and the subsequent comedown from the drug becomes progressively harsher. "They use the drug to mask their feelings of depression," says Halkitis, "eventually to find out that they are even more depressed. You have this vicious cycle—HIV, meth, depression."

Halkitis says the relationship between meth and dangerous sex is a complex one. He believes that men with certain psychological profiles—those who are often sensation seekers and risk takers to begin with—are drawn to the drug, take it in erotically charged contexts, and as a result put themselves in a prime position to engage in unsafe sexual practices. Rather than the drug causing men to take sexual risks, he sees people actively using meth as a tool to facilitate hazardous hookups.

So is there any solid evidence to suggest that crystal meth really makes men more likely to have unprotected sex? "It's completely ludicrous for people to think that this drug is causing all this risk taking to go on," says Halkitis. "Even when sober these guys are having unprotected sex. My studies suggest that the men who are going to have unsafe sex are going to do it with or without crystal meth. It's psychological states that ultimately cause this type of behavior to go on. People think, 'I'd like to have unsafe sex. If I do meth, I might not worry about it so much.' But there's got to be a desire there ahead of time to engage in that behavior."

That's why Halkitis is critical of the HIV Forum NYC/Crystal Meth Working Group's approach. "People would have you believe that because of these public education campaigns there is less meth use," he says. "I believe that they've raised awareness and promoted dialogue about meth use. Potentially, that discussion has caused people to think twice before they use. But I don't know if those ads are necessarily effective that they're putting up all over the place. I think the message is wrong linking HIV to meth because you're losing sight of the big picture. And I think it's possible you're causing meth users to go underground by having Larry Kramer come to your meeting and scream at the top of his lungs, 'Do your meth, do your sex and die.'

"I'm also pretty sure that these ads sometimes act as triggers for people to use," he continues. "At one point, the Crystal Meth Working Group produced a set of ads, the 'Crystal Free and Sexy' campaign [which featured buff young men who were supposedly drug free] that they never published. Inside information reveals that they actually acted as a trigger for people to use. The guys they interviewed in a focus group were looking at the pictures of the perfectly cut bodies and perfectly cut abs, and it made them want to do meth."

Halkitis currently sees the drug expanding its demographic, spreading from its traditional enclave in Chelsea to elsewhere in New York City. The latest data from Project BUMPS shows that 20 percent of the sample do meth on a regular basis. Of that 20 percent, 15 percent are white, 28 percent black, and 29 percent Latino. (The remaining percentage are either of mixed race, of other races, or did not report their race.) And they come not just from Chelsea but from all five boroughs of the city. "To say that this is a phenomenon confined to middle-class white men in Chelsea is false," Halkitis says.

Yet at the same time, Halkitis also detects a certain turning away from the drug in New York's gay community. Dan Carlson's campaign may be having some effect. Either that or the social learning curve that accompanies any new drug trend has kicked in. As any drug gains in popularity, the horror stories start to accumulate and users begin to see more and more negative effects associated with its use and less of the positive attributes that drew them to the substance in the first place. From talking to people in the community, one finds a general sense that meth is not the chic substance it once was. Using crystal is not something to brag about anymore.

"Everything in life cycles," Halkitis says. "Civilization cycles. Popular television shows cycle. Drug use cycles. It was A-list to be doing crystal in the gay community a few years ago, now it's 'ugh.' Five years from now, it will be some other drug."

CHAPTER NINE

MOTHER'S LITTLE HELPER

COOKEVILLE, TENNESSEE

Ashley Sanders was barely eleven when she tested positive for methamphetamine, the result of years spent living in a house that doubled as a meth lab. Picking at a salad in a bustling restaurant filled with chattering families on the outskirts of Cookeville, she pauses between bites of food as she describes how a comfortable two-bedroom home in one of the better parts of town was turned into a noxious drug den by her mother's amateur chemistry experiments. Ashley says the place was shrouded in darkness most of the time. The windows were covered in blankets to prevent nosy neighbors from seeing what was going on inside. Strange men came and went at all hours of the day and night. The kitchen was a constant hubbub of furtive activity.

Ashley remembers hearing her parents whispering about "the red, black, and white"—color-coded references, she later found out, to red phosphorus, black iodine, and white pseudoephedrine, all key materials used to make meth. One day, Ashley and her younger sister, Amber, came home early from school and saw their mother busy at the kitchen table, not preparing the evening meal but furiously stripping the strikers from matchboxes, getting ready to dump them in a bowl of acetone to extract the phosphorus.

"At least it was never dull," Ashley half laughs.

Ashley's mother, Charlotte, attempted to hide what she was doing from her daughters. She always made sure that Ashley and Amber were absent during the actual cooking process. "My mom's friend would take us to Wal-Mart at two o'clock in the morning just to get us out of the house," says Ashley. When Ashley and Amber returned a few hours later, their home would be filled with fumes. "The smell was awful," says Ashley. "It made me feel sick." After the dope was cooked, their mother would go upstairs and lock herself in her bedroom, where she would spend days smoking meth, emerging periodically from her shell only to go to the bathroom or for a drink of water.

"We weren't stupid," says Ashley. "We knew what was going on. By then, the police officers were coming to school and talking about meth, and we would listen to them, and we would go home and my mom would still be locked in the bedroom. Amber would go and knock on the door and shout, 'Mom, we know what you're doing in there.'"

With no mother to rely on, and unable to compete with the drug for her attention, Ashley and Amber came to depend on each other. They prepared their own food and washed their own clothes. They tidied up the pigsty that the house had become as best they could. They tried to keep the bedlam at bay by maintaining a semblance of what they imagined was a normal family life. But it was hard. Their mother and father constantly fought. One time, after hearing her father scream in pain, Ashley ran into the living room and saw him clutching his stomach as blood seeped between his fingers. Her mother had just stabbed him four times with a knife. He refused to go to the hospital because he didn't want to alert the police.

Ashley and Amber watched with dismay as their mother seemed to get progressively crazier. What started out as merely strange behavior—sitting for hours at a time at the living room table compulsively coloring in Fuzzy Posters like a frenetic five-year-old child—over time progressed into full-fledged paranoia.

"At two in the morning she'd be coming into me and my sister's room looking through the windows, thinking somebody was out there when there was nobody out there," Ashley says. "And she'd stay there for three or four hours. Other times, her and my dad used to go running and screaming through the house and hitting the ceiling with these big sticks. They thought somebody was hiding in the ceiling."

Just as alarming as the effect the drug had on their mother's behavior was the impact on her appearance as she sank further into addiction. The sisters began noticing bruises on her arms. They knew she had started shooting up because they'd discovered needles lying around the house. "Her teeth looked bad," says Ashley. "Her face was sunken in and black around the eyes. She got really skinny. She was so skinny she used to wear my clothes."

Adding to the already turbulent atmosphere in the troubled household, the police regularly paid unannounced visits looking for their mother. Charlotte was well known to the local cops. She had been arrested over twenty times, mostly on minor infractions like shoplifting, writing hot checks, and driving with a suspended license, though no drug charges were ever filed. "Please, don't take away our mom," the girls would plead with the cops when they came to the house. Officers were there so often that their parents trained a pet pit bull to growl at anyone who came onto their property wearing a uniform.

The police had heard that Charlotte was cooking meth at home, but they never managed to catch her in the act. That is, until one night at around two in the morning, when the two sisters were awakened by a crashing sound. Armed police officers had knocked down the front door with a battering ram and rushed into the living room, followed by men wearing white moon suits with respirators covering their faces and oxygen tanks on their backs. One of the policemen roughly grabbed Amber, who was sleeping on the living room couch under a blanket, thinking she was her mother. Amber screamed in terror: "I'm not my mom."

Charlotte was doing a short stint in prison for a parole violation when the police raided. Before she left, she had instructed her husband not to cook any dope while she was away, but he went ahead anyway. The remnants of the cooking process were scattered all over the kitchen when the cops burst through the door. Their father had been caught red-handed. He was arrested and led away in handcuffs.

The girls were swept up in the arms of child welfare workers and carried off to the local emergency room. "We weren't allowed to take anything out of the house," says Ashley. "They took us straight to the hospital to decontaminate us. We had to take showers and then take a whole bunch of tests and that's when they found out I tested positive for meth. They told us we had to go and buy all new clothes because they had been contaminated by the meth."

Ashley and Amber don't seem to have suffered any permanent physical damage from all those years growing up in a meth lab. Doctors have given both of them a clean bill of health. But the psychological scars left by the experience are another matter. Even though they've been reunited with their mother for nearly a year now, Ashley and Amber haven't completely forgiven her. "Me and my sister still have a lot of anger towards her for some of the stuff she did," says Ashley, now a normal fifteen-year-old with shiny, long, flaxen hair and braces on her teeth. "We never got to be kids. We had to grow up too fast. We did have birthday parties but they didn't last too long. She'd be like, 'Happy birthday, here's your cake,' and then she would go back to her room to do more meth."

Travel east along U.S. 40 from Nashville International Airport, and after about an hour's drive the ground rises sharply in a majestic fashion to reveal a vast sandstone altar covered with heavy oak forest and rutted with deep valleys. This is the Cumberland Plateau, a geological table about a thousand feet high and fifty miles wide that bisects the state from the Kentucky border in the north down to Chattanooga in the south. A rugged and outwardly peaceful place favored by hikers and hunters, its bucolic atmosphere started to change in the early 1990s, when a number of Californian meth manufacturers, attracted by the open spaces and sparse law enforcement presence, moved to the Plateau intent on creating a new market for the drug where none had previously existed. Missouri wasn't the only state to see an influx of Californian cooks during the 1990s.

Just as in Missouri, the enterprising Californians brought with them a recipe for making small batches of meth using red phosphorus, iodine, pseudoephedrine, and other materials that, unlike back home where meth-making ingredients were closely monitored, could be easily purchased at farm co-ops, auto supply stores, and pharmacies in the area. Once ensconced, they proceeded to set up culinary classes where, for a fee, they taught any of the locals who could afford the money the simple science of manufacturing meth. They also started shipping ephedrine and pseudoephedrine back to California, where it was converted into meth and sent back to Tennessee. Within a few years, rural communities across the Plateau that had never even heard of the drug were jumping with dangerous insomniacs and makeshift labs. From there meth spread southward and eastward into the rest of Tennessee. In 1996, only two meth labs were discovered in the entire state. By 2005, the figure had climbed to 1,346, the third highest number of lab seizures in the nation behind only Missouri and Iowa, an enormous increase that can be traced directly back to the Californians.

Local police have linked at least a dozen murders on the Plateau to meth. The first occurred in 1995, when a former rodeo star named Chris Tatrow kidnapped Roger Zamitt and John Harry because he suspected the duo had stolen a number of items from his trailer, including his prized collection of belt buckles he had won in rodeo events. Tatrow and some of his associates brought the two suspected burglars back to his trailer where, over a six-day period and during a massive meth binge, they tied up Zamitt and Harry and repeatedly tortured them in front of several eyewitnesses. Eventually, Tatrow dragged Zamit into the bathroom, placed a plastic bag over his head, and strangled him to death with a cord. After that, Harry was taken outside into a field, where Tatrow shot him in the side of the head.

By the end of the 1990s, the meth situation had gotten so out of hand that the feds got involved. The Drug Enforcement Administration, working in cooperation with local sheriff's departments, launched Operation Stopgap, which targeted meth cooks across the Plateau. Using information supplied by informants, the DEA drew up a target list of meth cooks in the area. The case culminated in October 2001, with the arrests of 175 suspects and the seizure of 150 methamphetamine laboratories. Operation Stopgap was a major triumph for the DEA, but meth continued to be made on the Plateau despite the best efforts of law enforcement to stamp out the problem.

Perched high atop the Cumberland Plateau sits Cookeville, population 25,000, a small and isolated community probably best known to the rest of America as the home of Tennessee Technological University, one of the top science colleges in the country. Walking along Broad Street in the downtown section, you see sturdy one- and two-story turn-of-the-century buildings housing a variety of retailers—a Christian bookshop, a store that sells uniforms, a restaurant with a patio called Crawdaddys. Someone has painted a giant mural on the side of a wall depicting the American flag rising from the smoke and flames of the Twin Towers. A nostalgic touch is provided by a neon sign from the 1950s advertising Cream City Ice Cream, which looms over the redbrick railway station, now a museum. Across the tracks stands the old Wilson's Sporting Goods plant, recently converted into a dance club-cum-sports bar called the Factory, which on the night I visited was practically empty. On the surface, Cookeville is a sleepy little burg, the sort of place that you'd expect to find in one of those airline magazine articles listing the most livable small towns in America.

But appearances can be deceptive. Behind the veil of normalcy, there's another side to Cookeville, a town that has seen more than its fair share of scandal in recent years. In a famous incident in 1998, Tennessee state senator Tommy Burks was killed execution-style with a single bullet to the head at his farm on the outskirts of Cookeville by his Republican political opponent, Byron "Low Tax" Looper, who was running against Burks for his senate seat. In 2003, Cookeville received more bad publicity after a family of tourists passing through town was mistaken for robbers, pulled over in their car by the local police, and while lying handcuffed on the ground, had to watch in horror as one of the cops blew away the family dog with a shotgun. And in August 2005, the FBI arrested two Cookeville police officers after a sting operation in which one of the officers allegedly transported what he thought was thirty kilograms of cocaine from Nashville to Chicago. In December of 2005, when I arrived in town, drug investigators had just discovered an underground pot factory hidden in a cave under a vacation home in Trousdale County, not far from Cookeville, a sophisticated facility the police estimated could produce between six and eight million dollars' worth of marijuana a year. The cave, which looked like the villain's lair in a James Bond movie, was reached from the house through a secret hydraulic door and featured offices, living quarters, and an elaborate irrigation and temperature control system. But the big problem right now in Cookeville, the one that has mobilized the whole community to take action, isn't marijuana or corrupt cops or dead pets, but meth.

Cookeville is a town on high alert. You see the signs everywhere. A skull and crossbones with the logo METH = DEATH. Nurses and doctors in the emergency room at the Cookeville Regional Medical Center complain about being inundated with quivering addicts. The local medical examiner blames meth for the majority of violent crime in the town. To tackle the problem, politicians, police officers, social workers, doctors, academics, and ordinary citizens have all banded together to launch a campaign aimed at beating back what many of them regard as the worst social ill ever to hit the area.

Tennessee Tech is at the forefront of this initiative. The university's business media center has produced a flashy, MTV-style educational DVD, complete with pounding rock music and footage of exploding meth labs, intended to warn young people and others about the dangers of the drug. In the chemistry department, a frequent target of meth cooks looking to steal ingredients, Prof. Jeffrey Boles is working on a quick-detection device to sniff out meth laboratories. Information gathered by the device can then be put into a computer to create a kind of weather map of the dispersion of toxic chemicals in the surrounding neighborhood. Boles is also developing a method of "fingerprinting" these facilities. The idea is that the meth that comes from these labs contains sufficient impurities to make it possible for law enforcement to trace the drug back to the manufacturer simply by analyzing a sample. Meanwhile, the psychology department is gathering information on children removed from meth homes to see if exposure to the drug leads to cognitive defects.

When people in Cookeville highlight the social costs that meth has had on the community, the talk inevitably turns to the effect on the town's children. "This community had come together to battle meth like nothing I've ever seen," says Betsy Dunn, a caseworker at the Tennessee Department of Children's Services. "Cookeville is a wonderful place to live. Unfortunately it's becoming poisoned by meth. It's overwhelmed the court system. It's overwhelmed the jails. It's overwhelmed the child services system. Meth is the worst form of child abuse I've ever seen."

In July 2006, when Putnam County detectives conducted a search of Little Learners, a day care center located down a quiet, tree-lined cul-de-sac in Cookeville, what they discovered there left them shaking their heads in disbelief. Inside the sprawling wooden bungalow, they found half a dozen children lying fast asleep on the floor, seemingly oblivious to the offensive odor permeating the place. Tiptoeing around the kids, the detectives entered an adjoining room, where they came across plastic tubing and propane tanks, as well as supplies of pseudoephedrine and iodine—all the makings of a working meth lab. Swab tests done at the site quickly confirmed that chemical residue was present in the carpet, on the curtains, in the kitchen, and on some of the toys the children played with. Panicked parents rushed their young ones to the doctor to have them tested.

After the owner of the center and her boyfriend were arrested and charged with manufacturing methamphetamine and reckless endangerment, Putnam County sheriff David Andrews spoke for most of the community when he told the local media, "I just cannot imagine anybody having a meth lab around children, much less a day care."

There are a myriad of ways in which meth can put children at risk, especially if the parents are manufacturing the drug in the family home. Since the year 2000, about fifteen thousand children nationwide have been found by law enforcement officers living in meth labs, according to the El Paso Intelligence Center (EPIC), which maintains a national database on clandestine laboratory seizures. Of those fifteen thousand, about a quarter of them were exposed to toxic chemicals, and ninety-six suffered injuries. Roughly one in ten of the kids removed from these labs test positive for methamphetamine. Eight children have died.

Of all the issues swirling around meth use and abuse in America, the damage the drug does to children is the most emotive and controversial. In the long term, alcohol probably causes far more hurt than meth on the home front. The National Survey on Drug Use and Health estimates over 4 million children live with alcoholic parents, whereas, according to the same survey, there are only six hundred thousand regular users of meth in the entire country. But drunks don't brew their own booze in their children's bedrooms. Even those who favor a more tolerant approach to drug policy naturally recoil at the sight of parents so selfish they choose meth over the welfare of their own offspring. It's easy to see why emotions run so high when you hear some of the horror stories. Meth manufactured next to cribs containing sleeping children. Toddlers badly scalded by boiling chemicals. Parents who wear gas masks while making the drug but leave their children unprotected. In one particularly notorious incident in Southern California in 1996, a meth lab exploded in a trailer home and the mother fled the scene in a panic, leaving her three boys—aged one, two, and three—to be burned alive. The libertarian argument that drug use is a personal choice, essentially a victimless crime, and that the state has no business deciding what substance the individual puts into his or her body is contradicted by the real harm that meth does to the most defenseless among us.

Even among heavy drug users, the topic excites strong passions. "Anybody who *does* drugs in front of their children should be shot," said one tweaker between hits on a glass pipe. "Anybody who *cooks* drugs in front of their children should be shot and buried, then dug up and shot again."

Terrible things can happen when parents take meth. Not always. Not inevitably. But often enough to warrant public concern. Under the influence of the drug, users can become volatile and paranoid, incapable of maintaining the sort of stable home environment necessary for a kid to develop. Crashing parents often sleep for days following a binge, leaving their children unattended. In one incident in Utah, a mother fell into such a deep slumber, she didn't notice she had accidentally rolled over and smothered her child to death, until she woke up the next day. In another incident, this one in Omaha, Nebraska, a mother was so zonked out she didn't hear the cries of her newborn baby as it was being savagely attacked by a pet pit bull.

Police and child welfare workers frequently report stumbling across meth homes where the parents are so preoccupied with their addiction that they ignore their kids, leaving them living in Dickensian squalor as if they were abandoned animals their owners had grown bored with. Kids go hungry, since nutrition is not a big concern when a parent is high on meth. One of the first things police do when they raid a home meth lab is to look in the fridge. Often, there's no food, just jars of toxic chemicals. Crying babies are discovered wearing soiled diapers that haven't been changed in days. The children often lack basic medical care and some of them haven't seen a doctor since they left the womb. A two-year-old girl was discovered at a meth lab in Sacramento, California, with open sores on her face. Cops initially thought she had been burned. It turned out the weeping wounds were untreated cockroach bites.

These are hardly the only risks. Children can ingest the drug by mistake. Kitchen chemists use ordinary household items like spoons, bowls, and plates to mix the ingredients and then allow their kids to eat from the same crockery. That's how the drug found its way into Ashley's system. An additional peril is parents leaving needles lying around the house. At another meth lab bust in Sacramento, five children, ranging in ages from one to seven, were removed and all of them tested positive for hepatitis C. They'd contracted the disease after accidentally sticking themselves with discarded syringes left in the area where they played. Another danger is that parents sometimes leave hazardous chemicals employed in the cooking process stored in unmarked jars lying around the home. In 2002, an infant in Jasper County, Missouri, died after drinking camping fuel, a commonly used solvent employed in the extraction of methamphetamine.

Little is known about the long-term health effects on children exposed to meth-making chemicals. But a 2003 study conducted by John Martyny, an associate professor of medicine at the National Jewish Medical and Research Center in Denver and a leading expert on meth lab contamination, found that high levels of toxic chemicals released during the cooking process spread throughout the homes where the drug is being made. "The methamphetamine is deposited everywhere, from walls and carpets to microwaves, tabletops, and clothing," said Martyny in the wake of the report. "Children living in those labs might as well be taking the drug directly." Toddlers who spent a lot of time crawling on the floor and putting objects in their mouths may be particularly at risk. As part of the study, Martyny examined the results of a controlled cook conducted in a motel room in which a child's teddy bear was placed about twelve inches from the area where the drug was being manufactured. Once the cook was complete, Martyny measured the level of chemicals in the bear's fur and found that a child could be "exposed to significant concentrations of methamphetamine—particularly if the toy is placed in the mouth."

Some parents even go so far as to enlist their children in the manufacturing process. It's not unheard of for kids to be discovered at meth labs popping pseudoephedrine pills from blister packs or tearing up match boxes. "Last month, one of the Children's Division workers removed a little boy whose fingers were black from stripping the lithium out of the batteries," says Melissa Haddow, executive director of the Community Partnership of the Ozarks in Springfield, Missouri. Haddow worries that beyond any physical harm, the biggest damage done to these children may be psychological. "It's well established that the children who grow up in methamphetamine homes have significant attachment disorders," she says. "The police will storm a house in hazmat suits with guns drawn, and the young children are so used to being ignored they don't even look up. These children are either terribly withdrawn or very aggressive, and they're going to grow up and follow the same path as their parents if we don't do something. It's a drug that doesn't just affect the user but has an incredible effect on the entire family unit."

Legislators in at least six states have responded to the outcry about the damage that meth does to kids by passing tough new laws that define the use or production of methamphetamine when children are nearby as child abuse, irrespective of any physical or mental damage the children in question might have suffered. In South Dakota, a state where an estimated 7 percent of children in foster care are there because of meth, parents can now be arrested and charged with child abuse, and their young taken away, if they "knowingly expose the child to an environment that is being used for the manufacture, use, or distribution of methamphetamines." In Michigan, Governor Jennifer Granholm said after signing similar legislation, "For the first time, we can now charge those who expose children to the dangers of methamphetamine production with child abuse—because that's what it is."

Charlotte Sanders is something of a local celebrity these days. The story of how this ordinary middle-class housewife lost her two daughters as a result of her meth addiction but ultimately regained custody of them after beating the drug with the power of prayer has attracted the attention of CNN, ABC News, and *The Washington Times*. She's been featured in antimeth adverts and has testified before a congressional committee investigating the link between meth and child abuse. Tonight, she's lecturing to a small group of recovering addicts at the First United Pentecostal Church on North Dixie Avenue in Cookeville. To illustrate the toll meth took on her physically, she flashes up on a screen her old police mug shots, souvenirs of her decade-long love affair with the drug. The roly-poly, ruddy-cheeked Christian mom in a sensible red sweater bears little resemblance to the ratty-haired, stick-thin blonde with the screw-you sneer and the smudged lipstick depicted in the photos.

"I knew tweakers who were so desperate that when they ran out of dope they would eat their own scabs and boogers, or the gunk in their eyes, or drink their own urine because they thought there was meth in it," she says.

Charlotte Sanders took her first hit of meth just after the birth of her second daughter, Amber. She was twenty-three, and she was at a wedding reception when someone offered her a toke on a pipe.

She'd done drugs before—some coke and marijuana, as well as pre-scription Xanax tablets. But this was different. The brilliant flash of electric energy she felt coursing through her body was like nothing she'd ever experienced before. "I stayed up for four days straight," she says. "I got down on my hands and knees and cleaned my kitchen floor with a toothbrush. I was ironing my curtains. I had never ironed a curtain in my entire life. I felt like a supermom. I had no idea the drug was so addictive."

Charlotte doesn't fit the stereotype of the meth-using mom. She didn't grow up in a trailer park. She wasn't poor. She wasn't from a broken home. Far from it—she lived with both of her parents in a luxury four-bedroom, three-bathroom house overlooking a private golf course. Her father was the town's biggest landlord and he owned a successful car dealership. Neither her mother nor her father had any history of substance abuse. "I came from a well-to-do family," she says. "We weren't raised with drugs and alcohol. We weren't exposed to that type of thing."

At school, Charlotte was an average student. "I wasn't no scholar, that's for sure," she laughs. But she did excel at sports, especially basketball, where she earned the title all-American, all-State. In her high school years, she ran with a rich-kid crowd that hung out at the country club and frequently got drunk. They were the children of Cookeville's ruling class. Some of the crowd snorted coke. And if any of them ever got into trouble, as they frequently did, their parents were always there to bail them out.

"There were no consequences for our bad behavior," Charlotte recalls. "Our parents were attorneys, doctors, judges, preachers. If one of my friends was caught with drugs, it was handled discreetly. You'd be sent out of state to a private boarding school or an expen-sive drug treatment center. You never saw them go to jail, you never saw them arrested, and you never saw their parents publicly embar-rassed. It was all covered up."

Charlotte got married straight out of high school to a construction worker named Charles, much to her father's consternation. She was eighteen, he was twenty-three. The dad wanted his daughter to marry someone from the same social class. But she was going through a rebellious phase and was attracted to bad boys. "I liked Charles because my dad hated him," says Charlotte. "He was a manly man, tattooed, very good-looking, with these huge arms he would wrap me up in. He was the exact opposite of the preppy boys I knew with their penny loafers and polo shirts with the collars turned up."

By the age of twenty, Charlotte had given birth to her first child, Ashley, and was content to settle down into a quiet existence as a mother, wife, and homemaker. Then meth took over her life. At this point in the narrative, you might expect that the reason she got into trouble was because of her working-class husband. Meth has long been regarded as a blue-collar drug. But *she* was the one who introduced *him* to meth. "People think meth is a poor man's drug," she says. "Well, let me tell you, it isn't anymore."

Meth was once known as a drug mainly for low-income males, but today, in some parts of the country, nearly as many women take meth as men. In Montana, for instance, the state health department reported that in 2004 women accounted for 49 percent of all the meth users in the state, up from 40 percent two years before. In San Diego, nearly half of the women arrested, and *more than* half in Honolulu, test positive for the drug. Nationwide, women make up about a third of the total drug-using population, but with meth the figure is more evenly split between the sexes. The 2004 National Survey On Drug Use and Health reports that 0.5 percent of female respondents to the survey have used meth at least once a year, compared to 0.7 percent for men. According to Prof. Richard Rawson, a well-known drug treatment expert at the University of California, Los Angeles, the typical gender ratio for those entering rehab for heroin addiction is three to one in favor of the males and two to one for cocaine. With methamphetamine, nearly as many women enter these programs as men.

Meth is said to have a particular appeal to women on account of the drug's appetite-suppressing properties. People forget that methamphetamine was initially marketed by the medical establishment in the 1950s as a women's drug, an all-purpose cure-all for the anomie afflicting depressed housewives at the time. Medicines containing methamphetamine and amphetamine were routinely prescribed to help women lose weight, beat the blues, or obtain an extra boost to finish the housework. Advertisements for meth products in the medical journals of the period featured illustrations of wasp-waisted Suzie Homemakers cooking, cleaning, and vacuuming, with contented smiles on their faces. Doctors even prescribed methamphetamine products to pregnant women. There's a common perception today that women are attracted to meth mainly as a diet aide—the Jenny Crank diet, as it's jokingly called. In a culture that brainwashes women into believing that thinness is synonymous with attractiveness, women are driven to use the drug to fulfill societal expectations of beauty, or so the argument goes.

Charlotte thinks this idea is overstated. Maybe low-dose users take the drug for this purpose, she allows. But there are much easier ways to slim down than shooting syringe after syringe of hillbilly crank into your veins. "No woman I know got into meth to lose weight," she says. "We did it for the same reason the men did it. We liked getting high."

Though Charlotte didn't know it at the time, the first hit of meth she took at the wedding reception came directly from the home laboratory of one Glenn Ray Alcorn, the Johnny Appleseed of meth in Cookeville. Alcorn—a mean-looking man, about five foot ten, with broad shoulders, who sported leather chaps and wore his hair pulled back in a ponytail—was one of the Californian cooks who turned up unannounced on the Cumberland Plateau during the early 1990s.

After arriving in Cookeville around 1990, Alcorn set up a cooking school, and charged up to $10,000 a student—plus a cut of any future profits—to teach students how to manufacture the drug. Alcorn was known to be extremely paranoid. Until he was arrested in 1998 with a pound of meth and enough weaponry to start a small civil war, Alcorn lived in a fortified single-wide trailer on the outskirts of town. Doberman pinschers patrolled the property. He placed trip wires at the entrance to the trailer and installed surveillance cameras in the surrounding trees to alert him if anybody came onto the lot.

Charlotte grew friendly with Alcorn and, after she could no longer afford to support her habit, started selling drugs for him. She became one of the only female cooks in the area after she learned to make the drug by watching Alcorn in action and by reading Uncle Fester's *Secrets of Methamphetamine Manufacture*. "A lot of people around here learned to cook using that book," she says, before adding, "I'm sorry to say I was a really good cook. The stuff I made was very pretty, very clear and crystal-looking." Not like the color-tinted meth common in the area, a sign that the drug hadn't been properly synthesized.

Charlotte explains that the effect of meth on the user varies greatly depending on the acidity—the pH level—of the final product. The more hydrochloric acid added to the mix, the more intense the high. "If you pH it to six point zero, six point five, they call that the love drug because it makes you want to have sex. PH it a little higher and it makes you want to stay up and talk all night. My thing was to see how high I could get the pH level, nine point five, ten point zero. I liked it hot. I liked it teeth clenching. My jaw would hurt for days afterwards."

By this stage, the authorities had received word that Charlotte was neglecting her two daughters. Teachers noticed that Amber and Ashley were constantly late for school and were falling behind in classes. The school suspected something was wrong. "The teachers could smell the meth on our clothes," says Amber. "They asked us if anything was going on at home. But we never told on her."

"They were really protective," says Charlotte. "They would always cover for me when teachers would ask them questions about their home life. They would always have excuses for why they were late. They didn't want to be taken away and put in foster care."

The school contacted the Tennessee Department of Children's Services. A social worker came to visit the home and warned Charlotte that if she was caught using or making meth, her daughters would be taken away from her. Charlotte denied everything. Amber and Ashley were eventually removed from Charlotte's custody and went to live with their grandparents after the police raided the house, but even then Charlotte continued to use. Forced into treatment, she went through thirteen different programs but none of them worked. She still loved her children, but she just couldn't break the drug's grip. In the end, it wasn't the numerous 12-step meetings she attended that got her to quit meth for good but a religious epiphany.

Charlotte was in prison, serving a ninety-day sentence on yet another parole violation, when she suffered a seizure. Lying on her cell bed, she thought she was about to die. Her cell mate pleaded with the prison guards for medical assistance but they ignored her. Never a particularly religious person, Charlotte nonetheless started to pray, "Please God, help me. I'm a drug addict and I'm really sick." That night, she asked some of her fellow inmates to carry her to a service in the prison chapel, where she collapsed on the floor. As the members of the congregation prayed over her prostrate body, she claims she felt something stirring deep inside of her. "It's hard to explain," she says. "But at that moment, I knew I would never take meth again."

After getting out of prison, she divorced her husband and began attending the First United Pentecostal Church, where she tried to assist others addicted to the drug by teaching a class there in the hope that her story would inspire them to kick the habit. It took three years, but eventually a sober Charlotte won back custody of her children. "For a long time afterwards, they'd start going off on me, calling me a drug addict and a meth head," she says. "I had to sit them down and tell them, 'You've got to stop, this is not going to happen anymore.' I told them, 'God has forgiven me, you have to, too.' I did what I did but that's in the past. All I can do now is be a good mother and try to help others to get off this drug."

Charlotte continues to suffer from seizures once or twice a week, which she blames on her years of meth abuse. She's not allowed to drive a car and she can never be alone in case she collapses and needs help. Even now, after three years without the drug, she still sometimes thinks about how she felt when she used to get high. "Whenever I go to the doctor and he puts a needle in my arm to take blood, I get the heebie-jeebies just waiting on the rush," she says.

Frequently, Betsy Dunn gets a phone call at three in the morning. She knows before she picks up the receiver who is on the other end of the line and why they're calling: "Betsy, we've discovered another child at a meth lab." Dunn, a case manager at the Tennessee Department of Children's Services, wipes the sleep from her eyes and drags herself out of bed, puts on her leather bomber jacket, the one with METH = DEATH: NOT IN OUR COMMUNITY emblazoned on the back, and then heads out in her SUV to the scene of the latest incident. Pulling into the driveway, she can often smell the chemicals coming from the home. Following an established protocol laid down by the state, she never enters the house for her own safety but waits until the children are brought outside by the police. Dunn then checks to see if the children have any obvious injuries, such as burns or cuts, that need on-site attention, and then she accompanies them to the ER at the Cookeville Medical Center. Wearing latex gloves, she strips the children of their clothing and then leads them to a special decontamination room, a tiled area with a showerhead and a floor drain, where they are thoroughly washed. Then the children are dressed in paper gowns and taken to another room, where they undergo a series of tests including urinalysis, a respiratory check, and blood samples. While they're waiting to be prodded and poked by doctors, Dunn asks them when was the last time they ate, and then she conducts a preliminary interview with the children to find out just how much they know about what is going on.

"Imagine how traumatic it is," she says. "Someone showing up at your home while you're watching television one night, and somebody says you need to come with me and you're seeing your parents arrested and, oh yeah, you can't take anything with you, you can't take that blanket you need to sleep at night, you can't take that teddy bear, you can't take that pillow. Nothing goes with you except the clothes on your back, and you're going to subsequently lose those clothes as well. So they lose everything that is familiar to them, including their parents. And then they go to the emergency room. I hate the emergency room and I'm an adult. So you talk to these children and then they tell you about the 'bad stuff' that Mommy and Daddy are doing. I've come across eight- or nine-year-old children who are able to describe to me how to make methamphetamine. They talk about 'cooking the white stuff.' I hear children talking about their mommies 'making rock candy on the stove.' I can remember a case I worked last June, a little girl I removed, her and her two brothers, when I explained to her she needed to come with me, she asked was it because of 'that yucky smell that makes me feel sick.' Even at that age, the children know that something is not right. I've had children tell me that a family outing meant going to this store to get this item, and going to another store to get that item. And they would tell me a list of ingredients used to make meth. Then they go through a battery of tests and they have blood drawn. The most traumatic thing for a child is to get a shot. So what I do, I get stuck first. I do that because if that makes it easier for the child, I'm going to go first. I've had my blood drawn so many times I can't begin to tell you. And usually the children will hold my hand while I'm doing it. And then we switch and I hold their hand while they get stuck."

Dunn estimates in the last six years she's removed roughly a hundred children from meth homes in and around Cookeville, half of them found in working labs. She says that about one-fifth of the child abuse complaints she receives at her office involve methamphetamine use or production.

"It happens in the best of homes and it happens in the worst of homes," she says. "I've removed children from trailer parks. And I've removed children from lavish houses in upper-class neighborhoods. Meth affects all different walks of life."

Dunn is the social worker who took away Ashley and Amber. "I think the world of Charlotte," she says. "I'm so proud of her. She's a totally different person than when she was on drugs."

I met Dunn for the first time on a chilly December morning in the lobby of the Child Protection Services building, a warehouselike structure on the edge of Cookeville. Dunn, an animated, good-looking blond woman who reminded me a bit of Erin Brockovich, was hugging one of her clients, a young woman in her early twenties wearing a toboggan hat. Dunn had placed two of her children in foster care after police had discovered her and her boyfriend cooking meth in their home.

"Honey, I didn't recognize you with that hat," says Dunn. "How are you doing? You still clean?"

The woman says she is.

"I'm so proud of you," says Dunn. "Keep up the good work."

"Thank you for saving my life, Betsy," says the woman. "And thank you for saving my kids. I'll never forget what you did for me."

"It's moments like that that make this job worthwhile," says Dunn, as she drives away from her office, heading across town to the projects. Two months later, the woman Dunn hugged in the lobby would be dead, the result of a suspected meth overdose. But today Dunn is glowing with happiness that one of her clients is seemingly doing so well.

Dunn wants to show me the place where she encountered her

first-ever meth lab. Cookeville's version of the projects is not like the big city. There are no tower blocks. A couple of dozen grim-looking one-story brick homes with concrete porches cling to the side of a scrubby hill. A police substation guards the entrance. It was here in late 1999 that Dunn entered a home after she got a tip about a child whose parents were doing a lot of drugs.

"I didn't know what drugs the parents were taking," she says. "So I was walking around inside this home picking up stuff. There were turkey basters, Visionware, Red Devil lye, a propane torch, and there were these chemicals in mason jars. 'What is this?' I asked the policemen, but they didn't know what it was either. After about twenty minutes, I developed this really terrible headache and started coughing. And my coworker broke out in a rash from head to toe. It wasn't until the next day we found out it was a meth lab. I had no idea people were cooking meth in Cookeville. I'd heard of meth, but I thought it was something that just happened in California."

The most heartbreaking case that Dunn ever encountered involved a seventeen-year-old mentally challenged boy she found living in a meth lab. "He had just undergone a liver transplant," she recalls. "[He] was a very intelligent young man—with limitations, of course. I sat in the emergency room with him for five hours and watched him eat four trays of food. The child had only had a hot dog the day before. He was able to tell me about the bad stuff his parents were doing. He told me how they made the meth and how they scraped the white stuff into bags and put it up their noses."

"We discovered we had the same birthday," she continues. "He gave me a Winnie the Pooh bear which I will cherish for the rest of my life."

Dunn's voice starts to crack and tears well up in her eyes. "I'm sorry," she says. "Just give me a moment. This is very difficult for me to talk about. All he ever needed was somebody just to pay attention to him. Thankfully, he is now in a wonderful foster home and he's doing really well."

Some critics contend that social workers are too eager to take away children from drug-abusing parents, that by putting these kids in foster care you can end up harming them more than the drug does. It's better for the child to stay with the mother while she undergoes treatment, says Brown University's Dr. Barry Lester, who urges the development nationwide of Family Treatment Drug Courts, like the ones they have in Rhode Island, which seek to preserve the family unit while at the same time helping the parents quit drugs. "The last thing I want to do is remove a child from their parents," says Dunn. "But if a child's safety is at risk, I'll do it every time. Sometimes we have no choice. If we find a child in a meth lab, then that's a no-brainer. That child is leaving the house. But we don't automatically remove a child if we find the parents using meth. It all depends on the type of environment. The child's safety is paramount. If a mother makes a good-faith effort to clean up and she is willing to work with Child Services and it's been assessed that the child is living in a safe environment, then we won't take the child. But some of the parents just walk away from their children. They care so little about them they can't even be bothered to turn up for child custody hearings. I've had parents say to me, 'Take my children. I can give up my children, I just can't give up the drug.' In a situation like that, it's in the child's best interests not to be reunited with their parents."

I ask Dunn what sort of reaction she gets from parents whose children she has taken away from them. A lot of them must hate her. "A lot of people do hate me," she says. "It pisses people off. They think it's none of our business. Well, it *is* our business. When children are being abused and neglected, it's everybody's business."

The good news is that recently Dunn has seen a drop-off in the number of children being removed from meth labs in the area. According to her, in 2005, 93 children were taken into the custody of Child Services in the Cumberland Plateau region either because their parents were using or manufacturing the drug, compared to 114 the year before and 179 the year before that.

But you won't find Dunn jumping for joy at these numbers. "Meth is not going away," she says. "It's just taking a bit of a nap. I'm not a pessimist; I'm a realist. But meth is here to stay. I wish I could say otherwise."

After bidding farewell to Cookeville, I decide to give Dr. Barry Lester a call. Lester is the director of the Brown Center for the Study of Children at Risk at Brown University in Rhode Island. The picture posted on the college Web site of a bearded, grandfatherly figure with a jolly smile makes him look like a department store Santa Claus out of season. In reality, he's one of the country's foremost authorities on child development. At the moment, he's conducting the first-ever large-scale, long-term, multisite study examining the effects of prenatal methamphetamine exposure on children. I wanted to talk to Dr. Lester about a question that had been puzzling me for a while.

In the last couple of years, the news media has been full of sensational stories about the devastating effects meth can have on newborn babies. So-called meth babies have become a hot-button topic. National Public Radio reported that in one Minnesota county, a baby is born addicted to meth every week. A CNN correspondent gravely intoned over footage of a fragile, jittery newborn: "This is what a meth baby looks like, premature, hooked on meth, and suffering the pangs of withdrawal." CBS News wondered whether America was seeing the creation of a generation of meth babies.

This was mild compared to an article that ran in *The Minneapolis Star Tribune*, in which a nurse was quoted about the rumors she'd heard of "meth babies" being "born with missing and misplaced body parts. She [the nurse] heard of a meth baby born with an arm growing out of the neck and another who was missing a femur." Not to be outdone, neonatalogist Dr. Michael Sherman, a professor of pediatrics at the University of Southern Illinois, told the press that a pregnant woman using meth was six times more likely to give birth to a damaged baby. "There might be skeletal abnormalities, where they might have club foot, or developmental abnormalities or missing parts of their arms or legs as a consequence of this abuse," he said.

Across the country, prosecutors are trying to break new legal ground by launching test cases against women who take meth while they're pregnant. They've met with varying degrees of success, largely because it's unclear whether a fetus actually constitutes a person under existing law. Meth-using moms have been accused of everything from child endangerment to manslaughter, even murder, and in one case in Alabama, something called "child torture," after a mother gave birth to a baby that tested positive for the drug. One of the first such cases to attract national media attention was that of Tayshea Aiwohi. In 2004 she was convicted in Honolulu of manslaughter in the death of her son, Treyson, who was born four weeks premature and died at home two days after being born. Prosecutors claimed the mother took so much meth during her pregnancy that she ended up poisoning the child in utero. Hawaii's Supreme Court overturned the conviction the following year, reasoning that when she smoked the drug, the baby was not as yet born and therefore wasn't covered under state law, a decision that outraged antiabortion activists. In August 2006, another woman, twenty-six-year-old Stacey Sturdevomt of Missouri, who smoked meth once a month and smoked marijuana to ease her labor pains, was sentenced to five years in prison.

But the case that really caught my eye was one involving a woman named Amy Prien from Riverside, California, a thirty-year-old mother of four until her youngest, Jacob, died in January 2002, three months after he was born. Initially the cause of death was listed by the coroner as sudden infant death syndrome. But then the toxicology reports came back. Jacob had actually died of heart failure from acute methamphetamine intoxication. When detectives did not believe her explanation as to how the meth got in the child's system, Prien was arrested and charged with second-degree murder. What was unusual about this case is that the prosecution claimed the murder weapon was the mother's own breast milk. Evidence presented at the first trial in 2003 suggested that Prien smoked meth throughout her pregnancy and continued to do so afterward while she was breast-feeding. The prosecution said she had put her son in danger not only by exposing him to meth, but when she discovered the baby wasn't breathing she delayed calling 911 until she had concealed her drug supply. Prien was found guilty, but the verdict was overturned on appeal. At a second trial in June 2006, the jury deadlocked. Ultimately, she pled guilty to a lesser charge of involuntary manslaughter and was sentenced to serve ten years in prison for child endangerment. Clearly, Prien is not going to win any Mother of the Year awards. But is it really possible to transmit meth through breast milk? And if it is, is it possible to transmit enough of the drug to kill an infant?

"Methamphetamine can be transmitted through breast milk, that's true, but exactly what gets transmitted and how much is not really known," said Dr. Lester. "There's not a lot of information on this. But it seems very unlikely that enough gets transmitted to cause the death of a child. It sounds to me like another example of this attempt to demonize drug-using women. It's a repeat of the hysteria surrounding cocaine-using mothers during the nineteen eighties."

Remember crack babies. Remember the public alarm at the possibility that a generation of throwaway children was being born deformed both physically and emotionally—"a biological underclass," in columnist Charles Krauthammer's memorable phrase, a species of subhuman mini-Morlocks condemned to a life of violence, crime, and poverty because of their mothers' drug use. It certainly made for a dramatic story. The problem with "crack babies" was that they were more myth than reality, a classic case of junk-science-meets-pack-journalism.

The crack baby scare got rolling with a 1985 article in *The New England Journal of Medicine* by the prominent pediatrician Ira Chasnoff.

Chasnoff studied the newborn babies of twenty-three cocaine-using mothers and reported serious birth defects in their offspring. Even though Chasnoff warned that his study was limited and more research was needed, CBS jumped on the report and was reputedly the first news outlet to use the term "crack baby." In one of the network's early segments on the phenomenon, CBS quoted a social worker who predicted that a crack baby she was taking care of would grow up to be a "twenty-one-year-old with an IQ of fifty, barely able to dress herself." Practically overnight, crack babies became a media sensation. Before long, every journalism outfit in town was competing with each other for photos and footage of this shocking new trend. Crack babies became a sought-after commodity, as reporters scoured hospitals looking for trembling infants. If they couldn't find an actual crack baby, then any premature baby would do. Pictures of crying children were broadcast, regardless of whether their mother had actually smoked cocaine or not.

In 1991, after the crack baby hysteria had subsided somewhat, the National Institute on Drug Abuse decided to fund the first-ever long-term research project to once and for all determine the truth behind the scare stories. Dr. Lester was picked to head the study. Fifteen hundred babies in four different cities (Providence, Memphis, Detroit, and Miami) were examined. What Lester discovered surprised him. Crack-using mothers ran the risk of giving birth to babies that were a bit premature or slightly underweight, but there was none of the gruesome physical deformities that had been predicted. "What we found was that the differences between cocaine-using mothers and mothers who didn't use cocaine were fairly mild, not severe, and relatively subtle," he says. "There was no difference in the effects of cocaine on the babies than the effect of mothers smoking cigarettes."

According to Lester's findings, heavy alcohol consumption, which many of the crack-using moms indulged in to help them come down from binges, was considerably more harmful to the fetus than cocaine alone. The negative effects observed in crack babies were more the result of polydrug use than cocaine by itself.

"The mantra of the nineteen eighties was that these kids were going to be forever lost to society," says Lester. "That just wasn't true. They had problems but the problems could be corrected. They were not lost. And the same seems to be true of methamphetamine. We're in the realm of the treatable, not train wrecks."

Dr. Lester's current methamphetamine project is still in its early stages. Four hundred babies at five different locations—Iowa, Oklahoma, California, Hawaii, and, as a point of international comparison, Auckland, New Zealand—are being tracked. At the moment, the children have only reached the age of two, so Lester is loathe to draw any definitive conclusions about the long-term effects of prenatal meth exposure, but from what he's seen so far, "our preliminary findings suggest the effects of methamphetamine are similar to cocaine. We find that some children of women who use meth have difficulty establishing bonding relationships, which hurts their emotional lives. But how much of this is because of the meth and how much is because some of these children are bouncing around from foster care to foster care is hard to untangle. Poor health care, multiple foster homes, poor parenting skills, poverty; all these factors can be just as devastating as the drug itself. Just as with cocaine, the environment exacerbates the effect of the drug."

How could this be? Surely, a drug as powerful as crystal meth can't be good for a baby in the womb. And it's not as if the media is making up these stories out of thin air. There are plenty of researchers who think that meth causes birth defects. Witness the 2005 University of Toronto study done on pregnant mice that was extrapolated to suggest just one hit of meth was enough to cause serious long-term damage to unborn children.

Speaking generally about meth research, Lester says, "A lot of doctors and researchers overinterpret their findings. You've got to understand, a lot of clinical people, they see babies with problems, and they look at the chart and they see the mother is using meth and they say, 'Oh my God, it must be the meth.' "

None of this is to say that mothers using meth while they're pregnant is a good idea. But unlike heavy alcohol use, which can lead to birth defects called fetal alcohol syndrome, and unlike heroin, which can cause something similar to addiction in newborns, there is no fetal meth syndrome, according to Dr. Lester. "It's not the case that we don't need to be worried about these babies," he says. "We do. It's possible that there are long-term effects we don't know about yet. But if I went into a nursery, I couldn't pick out a meth baby, and neither could anybody else."

Lester fears that history is repeating itself with the current panic about pregnant moms who use meth. Many of the same false claims made about crack cocaine in the 1980s are now being recycled to describe meth babies. That's why in July 2005, he and ninety other eminent doctors and researchers in the fields of drug treatment and pediatrics (including Ira Chasnoff, whose 1985 study sparked the whole crack baby scare) issued an open letter to the media criticizing journalists' use of the phrases "meth babies" and "ice babies" as "stigmatizing terms" that "lack scientific validity and should not be used." The letter went on to protest that being labeled a meth baby could end up hurting the child more than the drug itself: "We are deeply disappointed that American and international media as well as some policymakers continue to use stigmatizing terms and unfounded assumptions that not only lack any scientific basis but also endanger and disenfranchise the children to whom these labels and claims are applied. Similarly, we are concerned that policies based on false assumptions will result in punitive civil and child welfare interventions that are harmful to women, children and families rather than in the ongoing research and improvement and provision of treatment services that are so clearly needed."

"There are a lot of people out there who are angry at these women and they want them punished," says Lester. "I urge people to keep a cool head and let's not prejudge. What we need to do is get these women into treatment, not jail them."

Still, even if meth babies are a myth, meth orphans aren't. Just ask Ashley and Amber. In the end, the panic about meth babies may be, as University of Chicago professor Harold Pollock once said of the crack baby scare "a pediatric problem misdiagnosed as an obstetric problem." It seems probable that the real injury that meth does to kids occurs not in the womb but after they've left the hospital.

EPIDEMIC? WHAT EPIDEMIC?

nce or twice every decade, we seem to experience a new "drug epidemic." A substance that has usually been around for some time is declared a contemporary plague. Claims are made in the newspapers about the drug's addictiveness and prevalence. Horrific tales of ruin straight out of a Victorian penny dreadful are offered up as evidence that this is the worst drug ever, a destructive high like no other, at least since the last "worst drug ever." In response, self-righteous politicians, puffed up like blowfish, propose even harsher prison terms than the already draconian ones on the books. A frightened citizenry, fired up by the hysterical media accounts, goes along with the crackdown, fearful for the safety of their loved ones, whom they imagine are about to be swept away by a blizzard of white powder. And each and every time the claims are shown to be inflated. Crack cocaine didn't harm a whole generation of inner-city black babies. Ecstasy didn't cause widespread brain damage among electronic music fans. Heroin never became America's drug of choice. Somehow, despite all the apocalyptic predictions of impending doom, the republic survived. Yet, in an act of historical mass amnesia, every seven years or so, the cycle begins anew.

The latest chemical bogeyman to get the sky-is-falling treatment is crystal meth. Scare stories about intoxicating substances have been a staple of America newspapers since the temperance crusades of the nineteenth century. Throughout 2005 and 2006, hundreds if not thousands of media reports about methamphetamine have painted a portrait of a diabolical new substance—the "one-hit-and-you're-hooked" drug—spreading across the nation like wildfire, an evil scourge that enslaves users and threatens every neighborhood in America. Amidst this orgy of publicity, a *Newsweek* cover story stood out. "America's Most Dangerous Drug," blared the headline, even though the accompanying article failed to cite a single statistic to back up that dubious claim. Even the normally sober and reliable PBS show *Frontline* contributed to the fear-mongering when the program stated that there were 1.5 million meth addicts in America. Actually, the number is 1.4 million, and the figure represents not the number of addicts but the number of people the federal government estimates have taken meth at least once in the previous twelve months. A huge difference.

Meanwhile, politicians and law enforcement officials issue dire warnings, comparing the drug's impact to the scourge of crack cocaine in the 1980s. A conference of attorney generals called meth "the biggest illegal drug threat in America today." In 2005, then Nebraska congressman Tom Osborne said, "Meth is the biggest threat to the United States, maybe even including Al Qaeda." A CNN/Gallup poll ranked crystal meth as the second biggest fear in rural America, ahead of terrorism and behind only child molestation.

Brian Schweitzer, the governor of Montana, told *The New York Times* about the meth situation in his state: "It's destroying families. It's destroying schools. It's destroying our budgets for corrections, social services, health care. We're losing a generation of productive people. My God, at the rate we're going, we're going to have more people in jail than out of jail in twenty years."

A different article about meth in the *Times* quoted a New York State police captain: "Meth makes crack look like child's play, both in terms of what it does to the body and how hard it is to get off."

While some of this concern is legitimate, some is overblown. One of the elements missing from all the meth media accounts is any sense that drug trends are self-limiting phenomena. As sociologist Harry G. Levine says, "Most people don't like most drugs." The media in their rush to demonize meth tends to confuse potency with addictiveness. There's no doubt that methamphetamine is a very powerful drug. But that doesn't necessarily mean it's more addictive. Potency oftentimes acts as a barrier to addiction. Except for the hardcore few, most drug users are looking to get a little toasted, not permanently blasted out of their brains.

"The number of people who are going to be interested in injecting a syringe full of crystal meth into their veins for any length of time is extremely limited," says sociology professor Craig Reinarman, coeditor with Harry G. Levine of the seminal collection *Crack in America: Demon Drugs and Social Justice*, which debunked many of the media myths surrounding crack cocaine. "That's a very intense form of drug use. The fact of the matter is that if you look at the rate of discontinuation, for meth, that figure is over 90 percent, and the same was true of crack cocaine. Most of the people who use meth don't stay with it for very long or continue to use it very often. The more intense and overpowering a drug is, then the more that's true."

As for the claim that meth is deadlier than other hard drugs, that also strains credulity. "Meth Is Death," a Web site sponsored by the Tennessee District Attorney, claims that "the life expectancy of a habitual meth user is only five years." This old myth was first circulated by the underground press during the "Speed Kills" campaign in the 1960s. The Web site, a notorious repository of fake facts about meth that end up being quoted by gullible journalists and politicians, also says that "one in seven high school students will try meth," "only 5% of meth addicts are able to kick it and stay away," and "99% of meth users are hooked after the first try." Author Jacob Sullum, a frequent critic of drug war hysteria, added up these numbers and wrote in a column on *Reason* magazine's Web site: "Do the math (which the Tennessee District Attorneys General Conference clearly didn't), and you will see that 13.4 percent of Americans die as a result of methamphetamine abuse within five years of graduating from high school. According to the Census Bureau, there are more than 20 million 15-to-19-year-olds in the United States, so we are talking about hundreds of thousands of deaths a year, and that's not even counting people who start using meth *after* high school."

While deaths due to methamphetamine did rise in a dramatic fashion during the 1990s, cocaine still remains the number one killer when it comes to fatal overdoses, though you wouldn't know this from all the media coverage. The Drug Abuse Warning Network (DAWN) collects data from medical examiners and hospital emergency rooms in 121 cities around the country. The 2004 survey says that cocaine, either taken alone or in combination with other drugs, accounted for 39 percent of all drug deaths in 2003. Kansas City, Missouri, which is smack in the heart of a state thought to have one of the worst meth problems in the country, reported 42 cocaine-related deaths, compared to 12 amphetamine and methamphetamine-related deaths. (Amphetamine and methamphetamine are grouped together for the purposes of the survey.) In the New York area, nine people died of methamphetamine and amphetamine, compared to 527 due to cocaine. Even in Phoenix, Arizona, which posted more meth-related deaths than any other city in America, cocaine fatalities still outstripped amphetamine by 144 to 122. Only in San Diego, a major transshipment point for meth coming into the United States from Mexico, do amphetamine-related deaths outnumber those due to cocaine. While San Diego wasn't included in the latest survey, in 2002 there were 81 meth deaths and 50 amphetamine deaths, compared to 36 cocaine deaths.

Granted, this data is somewhat skewed since DAWN, while extensive, only covers urban areas. Meth is as much a rural phenomenon as an urban one, and as a consequence some meth deaths are most likely going unnoticed. There are no comprehensive national numbers for meth-related fatalities. But it seems highly improbable that thousands of tweakers are dying every week, as the "Meth Is Death" Web site appears to claim.

What about the pharmacological properties of methamphetamine? Isn't the drug itself inherently dangerous? We like to blame the chemical for all the bad things that flow from drug abuse. We buy into this idea that some intrinsic property of the substance is the cause of all the trouble, rather than the screwed-up human beings taking the drug. But the reality is more complicated—the same drug used in different ways can have widely varied effects. And it's not as if we don't know what methamphetamine does when taken by large numbers of people. For over thirty years, millions of Americans ingested billions of legal amphetamine and methamphetamine pills, and most of them suffered no lasting ill effects. And if methamphetamine is so inherently dangerous, why do we still give dextroamphetamine to children and fighter pilots?

"You can die from too much caffeine," says Prof. John P. Morgan of the City University of New York Medical School. "It's the dose that makes the poison."

According to Centers for Disease Control, more than 400,000 people die each year in the United States from tobacco use, 120,000 from alcohol. Meth doesn't even come close.

Some critics charge that the current hysteria about meth is part of a concerted campaign on behalf of local police and welfare agencies to advance their own political agendas. Federal funding is what is at stake here. Agencies stand to gain from these scare stories because they pressure politicians into allocating more money for treatment and enforcement. The bigger the hype, the bigger the budget.

Much media attention was given to a July 2006 report issued by the National Association of Counties (NACO) entitled "The Methamphetamine Epidemic: The Criminal Effect of Meth on Communities," which claimed that of 500 law enforcement agencies surveyed in 44 states, 48 percent of them cited methamphetamine as their number one drug problem, compared to 22 percent for cocaine, the same percentage for marijuana, and 3 percent for heroin. *USA Today*, *The New York Times*, CBS News, ABC News, MSNBC, Fox News Channel, the Associated Press, *The Washington Post*, and scores of other media outlets uncritically trumpeted the organization's findings. The survey didn't ask the law enforcement agencies that participated to supply hard data about meth-related crimes, but simply asked their opinion as to what drug caused the most crime in their jurisdiction. Given the survey was subtitled "The Criminal Effect of Meth on Communities," the answer that was expected is obvious.

The key question is by how much has methamphetamine helped to spur crime. The survey states that in the previous twelve months 55 percent of counties reported that robberies and burglaries had increased because of meth, 48 percent said domestic violence had increased, and 41 percent said assaults had increased. The survey did not state by what margin these crimes grew. One of the few skeptical voices in the mainstream media came from the McClatchy-Tribune wire service, which noted: "While conducted scientifically, the survey is also a political document intended to rally support for additional federal spending. In some cases, the statistics are skewed to make a point. County officials, for instance, noted that "100 percent" of counties in California and Arizona reported that meth is the No. 1 drug problem. Buried in the back of the report is the fact that only three counties in California and one county in Arizona were part of the survey."

U.S. Department of Justice statistics paint a different picture from the one presented in the National Association of Counties report. The DOJ's latest report, "Survey of Inmates in State and Federal Correctional Facilities," which was released in October 2006, surveyed 14,500 state prisoners and 3,700 federal prisoners for the year 2004. The study found that 11 percent of state inmates purportedly used meth in the month prior to their crime (6 percent at the time of the offense), compared to 21 percent for cocaine (12 percent at the time of the offense) and 40 percent for marijuana (15 percent at the time of the offense).

The numbers culled from the federal system follow a similar pattern: 10.1 percent of federal inmates surveyed reported meth use in the month before their crime (7.2 percent at the time of the offense) compared to 18 percent for cocaine (7.4 percent at the time of the offense) and 36.2 percent for marijuana (14 percent at the time of the offense).

While methamphetamine use among prisoners has increased by more than half since 1997, cocaine and marijuana still remain considerably more popular among criminals, as they are among the general public. (An interesting aside, given the drug's reputation as a spur to aggression, is that the survey also reported that only 6 percent of violent offenders were methamphetamine users, who were twice as likely to be behind bars for property crimes and three times as likely to be incarcerated for nonviolent drug offenses.)

Six months earlier, NACO had put out another survey ("The Effects of Meth Abuse on Hospital Emergency Rooms") in which they oversampled the rural areas where meth is most present. This study claimed that 73 percent of the two hundred hospitals surveyed reported that the number of meth-related visits had increased in the last five years, and nearly half of the hospitals said meth was the cause of more ER visits than any other drug. Again, the federal numbers disagreed. In 2005, the Drug Abuse Warning Network reported nearly 18,000 meth-related hospital emergency room visits, only a fraction more than the number a decade ago. Compare this to the first half of the 1990s, when meth ER visits nearly tripled. Overall, methamphetamine and amphetamine combined together ranked behind alcohol, cocaine, marijuana, and heroin in emergency room mentions, accounting for only about 7 percent of total visits, according to the DAWN statistics.

What about the common wisdom that meth is a rapidly rising national epidemic? I guess it depends how you define "epidemic," a word now used so expansively it's almost meaningless. Obesity. Gambling. Child abuse. It seems like everything is an epidemic. The American Heritage Dictionary defines "epidemic" as "an outbreak of a contagious disease that spreads rapidly and widely." So you would think a minimum qualification for characterizing something in such a way would be that the popularity of the phenomena in question is on the rise. Apparently, that's not the case with meth. The use of the word "epidemic" clearly implies a dramatic increase. And while meth did spike in popularity during the 1990s, since 2000 use of the drug has remained pretty much flat on the national level, according to every major survey, even declining slightly in some categories. The drug is now more widely available than ever, thanks to the increased output of the Mexican superlabs, which supply most of the meth consumed in this country. But that doesn't appear to have translated into more users.

The University of Michigan's Monitoring the Future survey, an ongoing study of the drug habits of students in private and public schools, reveals that the percentage of twelfth-graders who report having used meth at least once in their lives has dropped from 6.2 percent in 2004 to 4.5 percent in 2005. Since 1999, when the survey first started tabulating methamphetamine separate from general amphetamine use, the number of twelfth graders who claim to have taken the drug at least once has either declined or remained steady nearly every year. A more recent survey of teen drug use, this one released in June 2006 by the Centers for Disease Control and Prevention, backs up the Monitoring the Future numbers. The Youth Risk Behavior Survey interviewed fourteen thousand youngsters and found that the proportion of them who report ever having taken methamphetamine has declined by more than a third since 2001, from nearly 10 percent to a little more than 6 percent, part of an across-the-board drop in teenage drug use in general.

Similarly, the latest National Survey on Drug Use and Health, which was released in September 2006, reports that in 2005, 10.4 million Americans aged twelve and older (4.3 percent of the population in that age group) had ever used methamphetamine compared to 11.7 million (4.9 percent) in 2004, 12.3 million (5.2 percent) in 2003, and 12.4 million (5.3 percent) in 2002. Past-year and past-month use also showed little change. The number of people using meth at least once in the previous twelve months (1.3 million) was down slightly from the year before (1.4 million) and was almost exactly the same as the year before that. The survey estimates the population of regular users at approximately 512,000, a slim decrease from 583,000 in 2004, 607,000 in 2003, and 597,000 in 2002. The most surprising statistic contained in the report was the number of people who tried methamphetamine for the first time in 2005: 192,000, a significant drop from 318,000 the previous year and the lowest tally recorded since 1968.

Because drug surveys are by their nature lagging indicators, and since asking consumers to honestly detail the frequency of their drug use is a bit like asking them how often they masturbate, in theory methamphetamine use might have grown in recent years, but it hasn't shown up in the numbers. According to a threat assessment issued in 2005 by the National Drug Intelligence Center: "National-level data do not indicate a clear trend—either increasing or decreasing—with respect to rates of methamphetamine use."

The one set of legitimate statistics that has shown a marked increase in recent years is the number of people seeking help for methamphetamine addiction at publicly funded treatment facilities. Reporters often cite this dramatic rise as proof that America's meth problem is growing at an alarming rate. Admissions have increased fivefold nationwide since the early 1990s, doubling since 1999. California treated three times as many people in 2004 for meth addiction than for cocaine and twice as many than for heroin, according to the Department of Health and Human Services' Treatment Episode Data Set. In Oregon, eight times as many people were admitted for meth compared to cocaine, and three times as many compared to heroin. Even so, on the national level, methamphetamine is far from being the number one reason why addicts seek treatment. About two-fifths of the people who enter treatment are there primarily for alcohol. Meth accounts for about 7 percent of all treatment admissions, compared to 13.7 percent for cocaine, 14.2 percent for heroin, and 15.9 percent for marijuana.

Leaving aside the role that court-mandated treatment programs has played in boosting these numbers, isn't a more plausible interpretation of this data not that meth is gaining in popularity, but that a growing number of tweakers who began using in the 1990s, when meth was on the rise, have now decided to quit? This makes sense if you believe estimates from drug treatment experts who say that it takes on average seven years from first discovering the drug for the typical meth addict to seek medical help.

New York mayor Fiorello La Guardia once quipped: "Statistics are like alienists; they will testify for either side." But based on the numbers, the claim that meth is a rapidly escalating national epidemic fails to hold up.

All of this is not to say that crystal meth doesn't pose a significant problem in contemporary America, one serious enough that it needs no exaggeration. Meth can and does shatter lives. The damage done by the drug is all too real and often out of proportion to the actual number of users. A dozen tweakers are going to cause far more problems for small-town police officers than a dozen potheads. And meth's effects go way beyond the wreckage of individual lives, creating a ripple effect in the wider community, having an impact on people who would never dream of taking an illegal substance. In some parts of the country, the effect has been devastating, yet other parts have been left relatively untouched by the drug. Mark Kleiman, a professor of public policy at the University of California, Los Angeles, is critical of those who claim America's meth problem is all the product of media hype; he points out that just because the media exaggerates an issue doesn't mean it's not a real problem. Even the most ridiculous drug scare story usually contains an element of truth. But like past media panics—Satanic child abuse, date rape on campus, flesh-eating bacteria—meth too will pass.

The medicalization of our drug discourse is now so ingrained, we're now used to thinking about illicit substances in terms of "epidemics" and "diseases." We've had it hammered into our heads that drug use is a type of contagion, and it's sometimes hard to see the truth that first and foremost crystal meth is a cultural trend, albeit one that impacts both personal health and public policy. Most recreational drug trends follow a similar pattern. Typically, the drug is first adopted at the subcultural level by some group usually on the fringes of society. A small coterie of trendsetters (jazz musicians for heroin, outlaw bikers for meth, ravers for Ecstasy, hippies for pot and LSD) embrace the drug as their own, using it not just to get high but as a badge of group identity. Attracted not just by the chemical itself, but by the lifestyle that comes with it, more and more young people take the drug for the first time and in this way the substance spreads into the middle classes. From here, alarm bells begin to ring among law enforcement agencies and the first media scare stories start to appear, which helps to publicize the new trend. From there the popularity of the drug often skyrockets, as it did for meth in the first half of the 1990s. (The media ignore their own role in helping create a market for illegal drugs, ignore the way usage is accelerated by journalistic hype. What fun-seeking, rebellious teenager wouldn't want to give meth a try at least once after reading the predictable claims about the drug being "better than sex" or "like twenty orgasms"?)

Then comes a leveling-off phase. The particular substance doesn't grow in attractiveness but neither does it drop in popularity much, which is followed a few years later by the inevitable decline. Witness the fall-off in Ecstasy use after the rave scene collapsed. This doesn't mean that the drug in question entirely disappears. There are still many inner-city neighborhoods in America where crack cocaine remains king, just as there are still ravegoers out there waving glow sticks and eating Ecstasy. But the panic passes as the substance recedes from the public consciousness, inevitably replaced a few years later by the latest drug du jour. While law enforcement crackdowns and public education campaigns do have some effect, ultimately what decides when a drug trend starts to falter is when a critical mass of users decide enough is enough and either quit getting high altogether or switch to another substance.

The first job I took after coming to America in the late 1980s was promoting hip-hop nights at an East Village nightclub called The World. I remember the acrid smell of crack cocaine wafting throughout the club and how at the end of each night, the busboys would have to sweep up all the plastic vials left behind on the dance floor. Then, after a few months, something changed. Instead of crack, the air was now filled with a more fragrant odor. The customers were sucking on hollowed out cigars filled with marijuana called blunts. What the hell was going on? Homeboys didn't smoke pot; hippies did. What had occurred was one of those dramatic shifts in taste that often characterize drug trends. Crack had been around long enough that drug users had seen with their own eyes the ill effects that heavy consumption had wrought on family, friends, and in their neighborhoods. Crack suffered a backlash, especially among younger drug takers who witnessed firsthand the devastating impact that the drug had on their older brethren. "Crack whore" and "crackhead" became terms of abuse. In short, smoking crack had fallen out of fashion.

Drug researcher Andrew Golub, who lectures in sociology at the University of Vermont, defines four different stages in the development of a drug trend—incubation, expansion, plateau, and decline. At the moment, methamphetamine seems to be stuck on the plateau stage of development, as it has been for about five years. As it gains ground in some parts of the country, in other parts it slips. If it is attracting new users, then that is counterbalanced by others quitting the drug.

The sense I get from talking to tweakers and perusing the statistics is that this current wave of methamphetamine abuse has already peaked in this country, at the same time as understanding of the drug's downside is on the rise. Some of the people I interviewed had already made the switch to other substances. Especially in rural areas, a lot of former meth junkies are going the Rush Limbaugh route and abusing prescription drugs, particularly OxyContin and Avinza (morphine sulfate), which might seem odd since meth and morphine have such wildly different effects. But if you look at drug trends in a broader context, you often see a vogue for stimulating substances followed by a trend for downers. In the 1960s intravenous heroin junkies became speed freaks and then, after methedrine was banned in 1970, switched back to heroin. After so many years being up all the time, users want to mellow out for a while.

"A lot of the meth needle junkies in this area, they can't get the home-brewed stuff anymore," says one former Tennessee meth cook who goes under the pseudonym The Hillbilly Chemist. "They don't get the same rush from Mexican ice, so they shoot up Avinza instead."

Drug abuse comes in cycles. Sooner or later, the fashion for meth, like previous drug "epidemics," will begin to wane, if it hasn't already. Meth won't disappear overnight as a law enforcement and public health issue, and the drug may well continue to be a common bugbear in certain parts of the country for years to come. "As long as people need to work long hours in tedious, physically demanding jobs and as long as people want to lose weight, the attraction of methamphetamine is likely to remain," writes Richard Rawson, the assistant director of the Integrated Substance Abuse Program at the University of California, Los Angeles, noting the drug's enduring decades-long application as a diet aide and an energy booster. But it's quite possible that ten, fifteen years from now, we'll look back, as we do with crack cocaine in the 1980s, and wonder whether all the hype and hysteria was really warranted.

"Why we demonize drugs is because we're in denial about their utility," says Andrew Golub. Without minimizing the dangers of abuse, he points out that "methamphetamine is a very useful drug. It makes you alert, it allows you to work hard, it stops you from falling sleep, and it helps you to lose weight. Methamphetamine use will probably persist at an endemic level for years to come, but it's unlikely to turn into an epidemic. Meth use has been out there for decades and it will continue to be."

Same as it ever was.

BIBLIOGRAPHY

Alligood, Leon. "Cookeville Pair Jailed on Meth Charges." *The Tennessean*, July 18, 2006.

———. "Nightmare Called Meth Leaves Small Towns Reeling." *USA Today*, August 26, 2001.

Allison, Wes. "Methamphetamine: The Social Toll on Rural America." *St. Petersburg Times*, November 9, 2003.

"Amphetamine Kicks." *Time* magazine, February 2, 1959.

Astorga, Luís. "Drug Trafficking in Mexico: A First General Assessment." UNESCO (www.unesco.org/shs/most), 1994–2003.

Atrens, Dale. "Drug Addiction as Demonic Possession." *Overland*, vol. 158 (autumn 2000).

Barayuga, Debra. "Ice Addict Cleared of Killing Newborn." *Honolulu Star-Bulletin*, November 30, 2005.

Barnett, Erin Hoover. "Child of the Epidemic." *The Oregonian*, October 7, 2004.

Bell, Robert R., President of Tennessee Technological University. Testimony before the Committee on Science, U.S. House of Representatives, March 3, 2005.

"Benny Is My Co-Pilot." *Time* magazine, June 11, 1956.

Bialik, Carl. "A Bad Meth Stat Lingers On." *The Wall Street Journal*, March 11, 2006.

Biberica, Felicia. "Kids Can Be Incidental Victims of Meth Labs." ABC News, December 12, 2004.

Box, Steve. *The Leviathan: The Nation Testifies*. Smiths Grove, Kentucky: Above All Ministries, 2003.

———. *Meth=Sorcery: Know the Truth*. Smiths Grove, Kentucky: Above All Ministries, 2000.

Brecher, Edward M. *Licit and Illicit Drugs*. London: Little, Brown, 1972.

Brown, David. "AIDS Case in New York May Not Be Harbinger of Supervirus." *The Washington Post*, February 19, 2005.

———. "Why the U.S. Has Not Stemmed HIV." *The Washington Post*, August 13, 2006.

Burgess, Stanley. "Perspectives on the Sacred: Religion in the Ozarks." *OzarksWatch*, vol. 2 (fall), 1988.

California Society of Addiction Medicine (CSAM). "Recommendations to Improve California's Response to Methamphetamine." 2005.

Case, Patricia. "The History of Methamphetamine: An Epidemic in Context." PowerPoint presentation, the First National Conference on Methamphetamine, HIV, and Hepatitis, August 19, 2005.

Centers for Disease Control and Prevention (CDC). "Anhydrous Ammonia Thefts and Releases Associated with Illicit Methamphetamine Production: 16 States, January 2000–June 2004." *Morbidity and Mortality Weekly Report*, April 15, 2005.

———. "HIV/AIDS Among Men Who Have Sex with Men," July 2006.

———. "Increased Mortality and Morbidity Associated with Abuse of Methamphetamine: United States, 1991–1994," *Morbidity and Mortality Weekly Report*, December 1, 1995.

———. "Methamphetamine Use and HIV Risk Behaviors Among Heterosexual Men: Preliminary Results from Five Northern California Counties, December 2001–November 2003," *Morbidity and Mortality Weekly Report*, March 17, 2006.

———. "Public Health Consequences Among First Responders to Emergency Events Associated with Illicit Methamphetamine Laboratories: Selected States, 1996–1999," *Morbidity and Mortality Weekly Report*, November 17, 2000.

———. "Youth Risk Behavior Surveillance: United States 2005," *Morbidity and Mortality Weekly Report*, June 9, 2006.

Chapman, Stephen. "Latest Drug Crisis: Crying Meth." *Tracy Press*, August 9, 2005.

Chun, Rene. "The Most Dangerous Man in America." *George*, January 2000.

Clemons, Laura. "Paradise Lost." *Tennessee Tech Visions*, fall 2004.

Community Epidemiology Work Group. "Epidemiological Trends in Drug Abuse." U.S. Department of Health and Human Services, January 2005.

Cosgrave, Bronwyn. "High and Mighty." *The Guardian*, November 26, 2004.

Crary, David. "Gays Mobilize Against Meth Addiction." Associated Press, April 4, 2005.

Cunningham, James K., and Lon-Mu Liu. "Impacts of Federal Ephedrine and Pseudoephedrine Regulations on Methamphetamine-Related Hospital Admissions." *Addiction* 98 (9), 2003.

Davies, John Booth. *The Myth of Addiction.* Amsterdam, Netherlands: Routledge, 1992.

Denton, Mary Jo. "Children Found Near 'Full Meth Lab.' " *Cookeville Herald-Citizen,* July 17, 2006.

Diabolique. "Monsters, Inc." *Genre,* May 2004.

Dillon, Sam. "Mexican Drug Dealer Pushes Speed, Helping Set Off an Epidemic in U.S." *The New York Times,* December 27, 1995.

Dobkin, Carlos, and Nancy Nicosia. "The War on Drugs: Methamphetamine, Public Health, and Crime" (draft), August 11, 2005.

Drug Abuse Treatment Outcome Studies (DATOS), overview of national treatment outcome studies 1991–1993, PowerPoint presentation.

Drug Abuse Treatment Outcome Study (DATOS), National Institute on Drug Abuse, 1997.

Drug War Chronicle. "The Methamphetamine Epidemic: Less Than Meets the Eye." Stopthedrugwar.org, August 5, 2005.

Dunn, Betsy. Tennessee Department of Children's Services, testimony before the U.S. House of Representatives, Government Reform Committee, July 26, 2005.

Eck, John E., and Jeffrey C. Gersh. "Drug Trafficking as a Cottage Industry." *Crime Prevention Studies* 11: 241–71.

Eckert, Eric. "Recovering Family Ministers to Meth Addicts." *Springfield News-Leader,* April 11, 2004.

———. "38 Charged in Meth-Linked Probe." *Springfield News-Leader,* April 2, 2004.

Egan, Timothy. "Pastoral Poverty: The Seeds of Decline." *The New York Times,* December 8, 2002.

Embree, David. "The Ozarks: Buckle of the Bible Belt or Haven for Religious Diversity." *OzarksWatch,* 1999.

Eskridge, Chris. "Mexican Cartels and Their Integration into Mexican Socio-Political Structure." *Corruption on the Border* newsletter, 1999.

Fallik, Dawn. "Meth Makers Prey on Ammonia Tanks." *St. Louis Post-Dispatch,* October 28, 2000.

Farren, Mick. "Faster, Speedfreak! Cook! Cook!" *Los Angeles City Beat,* August 18, 2005.

France, David. "The Invention of Patient Zero." *New York* magazine, April 2, 2005.

Franey, Christine, and Mike Ashton. "The Grand Design Lessons from DATOS." *Drug & Alcohol Findings* 7 (2002).

Frank, R. S. "The Clandestine Drug Laboratory Situation in the United States." *Journal of Forensic Sciences* 28, no. 1 (1983): 18–31.

Frontline. "The Meth Epidemic." PBS, February 14, 2006.

Gold, Scott. "Breast Milk Cited in Meth Fatality." *Los Angeles Times,* January 20, 2003.

Golub, Andrew, et al. "Projecting and Monitoring the Life Course of the Marijuana/Blunts Generation." *Journal of Drug Issues* 33, no. 2 (2004): 361–88.

———. "Subcultural Evolution and Illicit Drug Use." *Addiction Research and Theory* 13, no. 3 (June 2005): 217–29.

——— and Bruce D. Johnson. "Crack's Decline: Some Surprises across U.S. Cities," National Institute of Justice, July 1997.

Granfield, Robert, and William Cloud. *Coming Clean: Overcoming Drug Addiction Without Treatment*. New York: New York University Press, 1999.

Green, Sherry. "Preventing Illegal Diversion of Chemicals: A Model Statute." U.S. Department of Justice, November 1993.

Greider, Katherine. "Crackpot Ideas." *Mother Jones*, July/August 1995.

Grinspoon, Lester, and Peter Hedblom. *The Speed Culture: Amphetamine Use and Abuse in America*. Cambridge, Massachusetts: Harvard University Press, 1975.

Guerrero, Mauricio. "Los Amezcuas, Reyes de las Metanfetaminas." *Contenido,* June 1, 2000.

Gunn, J. W., et al. "Clandestine Drug Laboratories." *Journal of Forensic Sciences* 15, no. 1 (1970): 51–64.

Haight, Michael Ann. "Drug Trends in San Diego." PowerPoint presentation at Substance Abuse Research Consortium semiannual meeting, September 13–14, 2005.

Hair, Margaret. "Methamphetamine Problem Spreading, Survey Finds." McClatchy-Tribune News Service, July 18, 2006.

Haislip, Gene R. "Commerce in Drugs and Chemicals and the Detection of Clandestine Laboratories," United Nations Office on Drugs and Crime, 1984.

———."Methamphetamine Precursor Control in the 1990s," Drug Enforcement Administration, January 1996.

Halkitis, P. N. "An Exploratory Study of Contextual and Situational Factors Related to Methamphetamine Use Among Gay and Bisexual Men in New York City." *Journal of Drug Issues* 33, no. 2 (spring 2003): 413–32.

————— et al. "A Double Epidemic: Crystal Methamphetamine Drug Use in Relation to HIV Transmission Among Gay Men." *Journal of Homosexuality* 41, no. 2 (2001): 7–35.

————— and Paul Galatowitsch. "All That Glitters: The Ups and Downs of Methamphetamine." Thebody.com, October 2002.

Hammer, Mark R. "A Key to Methamphetamine-Related Literature." New York State Department of Health, 2006.

Harman, Danna. "Mexicans Take Over Drug Trade to U.S." *The Christian Science Monitor,* August 16, 2005.

Harris, Brad. "Risky Business: Managing Methamphetamine Cleanups." Missouri Department of Natural Resources, spring 2001.

Harris, John. "Quaaludes: The Strange Tale of the World's Most Unpleasant Recreational Drug." *Q,* January 2001.

Hathaway, Mathew. "Agents Say Meth Labs Pose Danger in Forest." *St. Louis Post-Dispatch,* June 30, 2002.

————. "Meth Makers Find Ammonia Ripe for Stealing." *St. Louis Post-Dispatch,* April 18, 2004.

————. "Mexican Gangs May Be Moving into Meth." *St. Louis Post-Dispatch,* March 1, 2006.

————. "Police in Meth Belt Scramble to Keep Up." *St. Louis Post-Dispatch,* January 25, 2004.

Heischober, Bruce, and Marissa A. Miller. "Methamphetamine Abuse in California." *Methamphetamine Abuse Epidemiologic Issues and Implications,* National Institute on Drug Abuse, 1991.

Hogshire, Jim. "Biochemical Warfare." *Icon* (no date).

Holley, Mary. *Crystal Meth: They Call It Ice.* Mustang, Oklahoma: Tate Publishing, 2005.

Hucklenbroich, Frankie. *Crystal Diary: A Novel.* Ann Arbor, Michigan: Firebrand Books, 1997.

Hunt, Dana, et al. "Methamphetamine Use: Lessons Learned." Abt Associates, U.S. Department of Justice, March 2005.

Huus, Kari. "Mexican Meth Fills Gap in U.S. Meth Epidemic." MSNBC, September 18, 2006.

"Illegal Drug Factories Finding Haven in Rural Areas of State." *St. Louis Post-Dispatch,* June 12, 1989.

Jacobs, Andrew. "Battling HIV Where Sex Meets Crystal Meth." *The New York Times,* February 21, 2006.

———. "The Beast in the Bathhouse," *The New York Times,* January 12, 2004.

Janofsky, Michael. "Bookstore Battles Cops' Request for Sales Records," *The New York Times,* November 26, 2000.

Jefferson, David. "Meth: America's Most Dangerous Drug." *Newsweek,* August 8, 2005.

Jenkins, Philip. *Synthetic Panics.* New York: New York University Press, 1999.

Johnson, Dirk. *Meth: The Home-Cooked Menace.* Center City, Minnesota: Hazelden, 2005.

Joseph, Miriam, and Julian Durlacher. *Speed: Its History and Lore.* London: Carlton Books, 2000.

King, Ryan S. "The Next Big Thing? Methamphetamine in the United States." The Sentencing Project, June 2006.

Kleiman, Mark. "Debunking the Debunking: The Meth Problem Is Real." *The Huffington Post* (www.huffingtonpost.com), June 15, 2006.

———. "The Methamphetamine Epidemic: Even Real Problems Get Hyped." The Reality-Based Community (www.samefacts.com), August 28, 2005.

Kobayashi, Ken. "Meth Mother's Conviction Overturned." *The Honolulu Advertiser,* November 30, 2005.

Konigsberg, Eric. "The Man and the Meth." *Philadelphia* magazine, May 1996.

Lambe, Joe. "Catching a 'Giant Monster' of Meth." *The Kansas City Star,* March 29, 1999.

Lavigne, Yves. *Hells Angels: Into the Abyss.* New York: HarperCollins, 1996.

Lee, Steven J. *Overcoming Crystal Meth Addiction: An Essential Guide to Getting Clean.* New York: Marlowe & Company, 2006.

Lester, Barry. "One Hit of Meth Enough to Cause 'News Defects.'" Join Together (www.jointogether.org), August 17, 2005.

Maier, James. "Speed Demon." *Salon,* March 21, 2005.

Marosi, Richard. "U.S. Crackdown Sends Meth Labs South of Border." *Los Angeles Times,* November 26, 2006.

Martyny, John. National Jewish Research Results: Clandestine Methamphetamine Laboratories, 2005.

McCoy, Max. "Ice: A Spiritual Journey." *The Joplin Globe* (Missouri), January 31, 2006.

———. "Local or Imported, Meth Still Top Issue." *The Joplin Globe* (Missouri), January 29, 2006.

McLemore, Bill. *Meth: What's Your Destination?* Springfield, Missouri: Bill McLemore Ministries, 2006.

Menner, Laura Bauer. "Ammonia Thefts Latest Battle in Meth War." *The Springfield News-Leader,* January 18, 1999.

———. "Demystifying the Drug That Holds Thousands of Ozarkers Captive." *The Springfield News-Leader,* July 8, 2001.

———. "Explosion Linked to Drug-Making Chemicals Claims a Son—and Inspires a Crusade." *The Springfield News-Leader,* December 9, 2001.

———. "Meth's Chaotic Toll." *The Springfield News-Leader,* July 8, 2001.

———. "Ozarks Farmers Guard Volatile Ammonia." *The Springfield News-Leader,* December 2, 2001.

Meth: A County in Crisis. A&E Television Networks movie on DVD, 2005.

Mieszkowski, Katharine. "AIDS Scare Is Overblown." *Salon,* February 17, 2005.

Miller, Marissa, and Nicholas J. Kozel (editors). "Methamphetamine Abuse: Epidemiological Issues and Implications." National Institute on Drug Abuse, 1991.

Monastero, Frank. "Regulations for the Regulation of Selected Chemicals and Controlled Substance Analogs." President's Commission on Organized Crime, 1986.

"Monitoring the Future: National Results on Adolescent Drug Use." National Institute on Drug Abuse, 2005.

Moore, Molly, and Douglas Farah. "Case of 'Kings of Meth' Puts U.S.-Mexico Relations to the Test." *The Washington Post,* October 24, 1988.

Morgan, John P. "History of Methamphetamine." PowerPoint presentation, the First National Conference on Methamphetamine, HIV, and Hepatitis, August 20, 2005.

Morgan, Patricia. "Ice and Other Methamphetamine Use: An Exploratory Study." National Institute on Drug Abuse, 1994.

Mosedale, Mike. "Meth Myths, Meth Realities." *City Pages* (Minneapolis/St. Paul, Minnesota), May 14, 2003.

Moushey, Bill. "Federal Sting Often Put More Drugs on the Streets." *Pittsburgh Post-Gazette,* November 23, 1998.

Mundy, B. J. "Basic Meth Investigations—Tennessee." PowerPoint presentation, U.S. Drug Enforcement Administration, 2005.

National Association of Counties (NACO). "The Meth Epidemic in America." July 2005.

————. "The Meth Epidemic in America II." January 2006.

————. "The Meth Epidemic in America: The Criminal Effect of Meth on Communities." July 2006.

National Clandestine Laboratory Database. "Total of All Meth Clandestine Laboratory Incidents" (maps). U.S. Drug Enforcement Administration (www.dea.gov).

National Drug Intelligence Center. "National Drug Threat Assessment." 2005–2007.

National Household Survey on Drug Abuse (NHSDA). "Children Living with Substance-Abusing or Substance-Dependent Parents." *The NHSDA Report,* June 2, 2003.

National Survey on Drug Use and Health (NSDUH). Substance Abuse and Mental Health Services Administration (SAMHSA), 2002–2005.

Office of National Drug Control Policy. "The Price and Purity of Illicit Drugs: 1981 Through the Second Quarter of 2003." November 2004.

Olsson, Karen. "Every Man a Kingpin: Scenes from Rural America's Drug Wars." *The Texas Observer,* May 11, 2001.

Ornstein, Charles. "Quitting Meth Pays Off." *Los Angeles Times,* November 14, 2005.

Overstreet, Sarah. "Minister Who Kicked Meth Habit Now Leads Area Support Group." *The Springfield News-Leader,* June 9, 2002.

Owen, Frank. "No Man Is a Crystal Meth User unto Himself." *The New York Times,* August 29, 2004.

Pennell, Susan, et al. "Meth Matters: Report on Methamphetamine Users in Five Western Cities." National Institute of Justice, April 1999.

"Pep Pill Poisoning." *Time* magazine, May 10, 1937.

Pollack, Harold. "When Pregnant Women Use Crack." *Drug Policy Analysis Bulletin,* February 2000.

Potter, Mark. "Meth Labs: A Toxic Threat to Rural America." NBC Nightly News, March 10, 2004.

Press, Eyal. "Lead Us Not into Temptation." *The American Prospect,* April 9, 2001.

Proceedings of the Border Epidemiology Work Group (BEWG). National Institute on Drug Abuse, September 2004.

Pugmire, Lance. "Trask Warns Meth Users." *Los Angeles Times,* July 1, 2003.

Pyle, Emily. "A Day in the Life of a Christian Treatment Center." *The Austin Chronicle,* December 15, 2000.

Quitkin, Megan. "Crystal Mess." *Business & AIDS,* fall 2005.

Rawson, Richard A., et al. "A Multi-Site Comparison of Psychosocial Approaches for the Treatment of Methamphetamine Dependence." *Addiction* 99, no. 6 (2004): 708–17.

———. "Will the Methamphetamine Problem Go Away?" *Journal of Addictive Diseases* 21, no. 1 (2002).

Reinarman, Craig, and Harry J. Levine (editors). *Crack in America: Demon Drugs and Social Justice.* Berkeley, California: University of California Press, 1997.

Reuter, Peter. "The Limits of Drug Control." The American Foreign Service Association (www.afsa.org), January 2002.

——— and Harold Pollack. "How Much Can Treatment Reduce National Drug Problems?" *Addiction* 101, no. 3 (March 2006): 341.

——— and Jonathan P. Caulkins. "Does Precursor Regulation Make a Difference?" *Addiction* 98, no. 9 (September 2003): 1177–79.

Sanello, Frank. *Tweakers: How Crystal Meth Is Ravaging Gay America.* New York: Alyson Books, 2005.

Sauerwein, Kristina. "Missouri Officials Fight Explosion of Meth Crime." *St. Louis Post-Dispatch,* March 1998.

Self, Will. "Thomas Szasz: Shrinking from Psychiatry," *Junk Mail.* New York: Grove Press, 2006.

Serrano, Richard A. "DEA Seizes Business Called 'Granddaddy' to U.S. Meth Labs." *Los Angeles Times,* August 20, 1988.

———. "Operation Crankcase: 'Chuck' Stood Guard in Lab Sting." *Los Angeles Times,* March 21, 1989.

Serwer, Andrew E. "The Hells Angels' Devilish Business." *Fortune,* November 30, 1992.

Sevick, James R. "Precursor and Essential Chemicals in Illicit Drug Production: Approaches to Enforcement." National Institute of Justice, October 1993.

Shafer, Jack. "Crack Then, Meth Now." *Slate* (www.slate.com), August 23, 2005.

———. "How Not to Report About Meth." *Slate* (www.slate.com), March 21, 2006.

———. "How to Find a Meth Dealer." *Slate* (www.slate.com), July 31, 2006.

———. "Methamphetamine Propaganda." *Slate* (www.slate.com), March 3, 2006.

———. "The Meth Capital of the World." *Slate* (www.slate.com), August 4, 2005.

———. "Meth Madness at *Newsweek*." *Slate* (www.slate.com), August 3, 2005.

———. "A Meth Test for the Press." *Slate* (www.slate.com), June 14, 2006.

———. "Pfft Goes the Methedemic." *Slate* (www.slate.com), July 21, 2006.

———. "This Is Your County on Meth." *Slate* (www.slate.com), January 19, 2006.

Shan, Yogi. "Alt. Drugs Clandestine Chemistry Primer and FAQ." Erowid (www.erowid.org), 1995.

Shernoff, Michael. "Crystal's Sexual Persuasion." *The Gay and Lesbian Review Worldwide,* July/August 2005.

Shirk, Martha. "The Meth Epidemic: Hype Vs. Reality." *Youth Today,* winter/spring 2006.

Shone, Mark. "The Epidemic on Aisle 6." *Legal Affairs,* November/December 2004.

Smith, David E., and John Luce. *Love Needs Care.* London: Little, Brown, 1971.

Smith, Raymond, and Aldrin Brown. "Inland Drug Empire." *The Press-Enterprise,* January 23, 2000.

Smith, Roger C. "The Marketplace of Speed: Violence and Compulsive Methamphetamine Abuse." Unpublished, 1969.

Sniffen, Michael J. "Drug Agents Break up Major Methamphetamine Ring Operating in U.S." Associated Press, December 5, 1997.

Specter, Michael. "Higher Risk." *The New Yorker,* May 23, 2005.

"Speed Demons." *Time* magazine, April 2. 1984.

Strausbaugh, John, and Donald Blaise. *The Drug User: Documents 1940–1960.* New York: Blast Books, 1991.

Strike. *Sources.* San Antonio, Texas: Panda Ink, 1998.

———. *Total Synthesis II.* San Antonio, Texas: Panda Ink, 1998.

Sullum, Jacob. "Is Meth a Plague, a Wildfire, or the Next Katrina?" *Reason,* September 2, 2005.

———. "Meth Myths." *Reason,* July 29, 2005.

———. "Speed Tracers." *Reason,* January 2005.

Suo, Steve. "Lobbyists and Loopholes." *The Oregonian,* October 4, 2004.

———. "The Mexican Connection." *The Oregonian,* June 5, 2005.

———. "Shelved Solutions." *The Oregonian,* October 6, 2004.

———. "Token Deterrent." *The Oregonian,* October 5, 2004.

———. "Unnecessary Epidemic." *The Oregonian,* October 3, 2004.

Swetlow, Karen. "Children at Clandestine Methamphetamine Labs: Helping Meth's Youngest Victims." Office for Victims of Crime (OVC), June 2003.

Szalavitz, Maia. "Anti-Meth Campaign a Wash." STATS (stats.org), May 5, 2006.

———. "Congressional Fury over Meth Strategy." STATS (stats.org), October 3, 2005.

———. "The Demon Seed That Wasn't." *City Limits,* March 2004.

———. "Is Meth America's #1 Drug Problem?" STATS (stats.org), July 19, 2006.

———. "The Media Go into Crack Baby Mode over Meth." STATS (stats.org), August 10, 2005.

———. "The Media's Meth Mania." STATS (stats.org), August 4, 2005.

Taylor, Guy. "Meth 'Moonshiners' on Rise." *The Washington Times,* July 10, 2005.

———. "Meth's Infection." *The Washington Times,* July 11, 2005.

Tendler, Stewart, and David May. *The Brotherhood of Eternal Love.* Bangalore, India: Panther Publishers, 1984.

Tierney, John. "Debunking the Drug War." *The New York Times,* August 9, 2005.

Topolski, James M., and Karen Kadela. "Methamphetamine in Missouri." Missouri Institute of Mental Health, 1997.

Treatment Episode Data Set (TEDS): 1994–2004. Substance Abuse and Mental Health Services Administration.

"Trial and Error." *Time* magazine, September 14, 1936.

2000 Arrestee Drug Abuse Monitoring (ADAM), National Institute of Justice, April 2003.

Ulrich, Andreas. "Hitler's Drugged Soldiers," *Spiegel,* May 6, 2005.

Uncle Fester. *Advanced Techniques of Clandestine Psychedelic and Amphetamine Manufacture.* Port Townsend, Washington: Loompanics Unlimited, 1998.

———. *Secrets of Methamphetamine Manufacture.* Green Bay, Wisconsin: Festering Publications, 2005.

———. *Silent Death.* Green Bay, Wisconsin: Festering Publications, 1997.

"United Nations Convention Against Illicit Traffic in Narcotic Drugs and Psychotropic Substances." United Nations, 1988.

United States General Accounting Office. "Stronger Crackdown Needed on Clandestine Laboratories Manufacturing Dangerous Drugs." Report to the Congress, November 6, 1981.

"Unsafe at Any Speed." *Time* magazine, October 27, 1967.

U.S. Department of Health and Human Services. "Amphetamine and Methamphetamine Emergency Room Visits, 1995–2002." *The Dawn Report*, July 2004.

———. "Drug Abuse Warning Network, 2004: National Estimates of Drug-Related Emergency Department Visits." *The Dawn Report*, July 2004.

Valdez, Angela. "Meth Madness: How the Oregonian Manufactured an Epidemic, Politicians Bought It, and You're Paying." *Willamette Week*, March 22, 2006.

Wagner, Matt. "Trial Ends in Conviction, Mistrial." *The Springfield News-Leader*, May 7, 2005.

———. "Trial: Did Seller Know Pills Were for Meth?" *The Springfield News-Leader*, April 26, 2005.

——— and James Goodwin. "State Works to Emulate Oklahoma's Meth Law." *The Springfield News-Leader*, January 31, 2005.

Weintraub, Daniel M. "Lobbyist Helped Drug Dealer Win Delay on Controls." *Los Angeles Times*, March 20, 1987.

Weissert, Will. "Mexican Limiting Access to Meth Ingredients," Associated Press, November 24, 2005.

Wells, Mathew. "Fighting the Meth Epidemic in Rural U.S., BBC News, October 31, 2005.

White, William L. and David Whiter. "Faith-Based Recovery: Its Historical Roots." *Counselor*, October 2005.

Young, Nancy K., et al. "Methamphetamine and Child Welfare: Trends, Lessons and Practice Implications." CWLA National Conference, March 1, 2006.

Zernike, Kate. "A Drug Scourge Creates Its Own Form of Orphan," *The New York Times*, July 11, 2005.

———. "Potent Mexican Meth Floods In as States Curb Domestic Variety." *The New York Times*, January 23, 2006.